HOMOEROTICISM IN THE BIBLICAL WORLD

A HISTORICAL PERSPECTIVE

MARTTI NISSINEN

Translated by Kirsi Stjerna

FORTRESS PRESS
MINNEAPOLIS

For Leena

The Library of Congress has catalogued the hardcover edition of this book as follows:
Nissinen, Martti.
    [Homoerotiikka Raamatun maailmassa. English]
    Homoeroticism in the biblical world : a historical perspective / Martti
Nissinen ; translated by Kirsi Stjerna.
    vii, 208 p. : ill. ; 24 cm.
    Includes bibliographical references (p. 183–198) and index.
    ISBN 080062985X (alk. paper)
    1. Homosexuality in the Bible. 2. Homosexuality—Biblical teaching.
3. Homosexuality—History—To 1500. I. Title.
BS680.H67 N5713 1998
220.8/306766 21   98047793

CONTENTS

ᗕᔓᕫ

PREFACE

∽◦◦◦

This book would not exist if a casual gathering of an American-Finnish group of junior colleagues had not taken place during the 1994 Annual Meeting of the Society of Biblical Literature in Chicago. I think it was Kristin Swenson, then a student at Boston University, who put forward the idea of translating my newly published Finnish book *Homoerotiikka Raamatun maailmassa* (Homoeroticism in the Biblical World, 1994) into English. Kirsi Stjerna, with a fresh Ph.D., likewise from Boston University, immediately volunteered to do the translation work, and so the deal was made and witnessed by Antti, Ismo, Kari, Matti, Petri, Raimo and Risto.

Easier said than done. It soon became apparent to me that the book, designed for a Finnish readership, needed to be completely rewritten. Already when preparing the Finnish manuscript I had become painfully aware that the task I had imposed for myself—a study on "the Bible and Homosexuality"—was virtually impossible to work out. In current usage, "homosexuality" means an individual disposition that is shared by a distinct group of people sexually attracted by persons of the same sex. This concept, one hundred years old, presupposes that human beings can be classified as heterosexual, bisexual, or homosexual on the basis of their sexual preference. Thanks to the multidisciplinary scientific studies and everyday experience influenced by these studies, this classification has become part of the consciousness of modern Westerners. Today, "homosexuality" is a fact; gays and lesbians indisputably exist. This fact, together with the various (often negative) ways to react to its existence with the Bible in hand, was the starting point of my study.

To the modern consciousness belongs also the idea of "sexuality" as a biological and psychological phenomenon. Concrete sexual acts and erotic manifestations are seen as expressions of "sexuality" that develops individually in each body and mind, substantially influencing other areas of personality and behavior.

As a representative and a product of modern Western thinking, I soon had to face the problem that sources that go back two or three millennia do not fit modern categories. Whether the texts I studied were biblical or

Jewish, Assyrian, Greek, or Roman, the term "homosexuality" was absent from them and the concept alien. When the ancient sources describe or evaluate erotic encounters between people of the same sex, they refer to various acts and practices without attributing them to individual sexual orientations—to say nothing of a "sexuality" that would govern a person's acts and desires. What they knew was *gender*—desires and tensions associated with gender difference, justified and nonjustified roles, practices and self-presentations within a gendered society, all of which involved love and hate, pain and pleasure. Same-sex interaction was but one aspect of a larger system of interpretation of gender.

I had reflected on such issues from time to time, but, after finishing the Finnish manuscript, I started to doubt whether it made any sense at all to gather ancient sources dealing with same-sex contacts and study them as a separate corpus. I became convinced that the analysis of biblical passages traditionally associated with homosexuality and of their cultural setting in ancient Near Eastern and classical sources arose from our own needs and the distinctions created by modern discourse. The heuristic historical task became more and more hermeneutically motivated. I realized that we all are responsible participants in the gender culture around us and that the interpretation of the origin of this culture is one means of taking this responsibility. It was no longer a matter of individual traits of a distinct group of people out there somewhere, but a matter of interpretation of the Bible, culture, and the individual life of each of us as gendered human beings. Ultimately, it all turned out to be about loving one's neighbor as oneself. No matter how sanctimonious this may sound, that is how I still feel.

It is my pleasant duty to express my deep gratitude to scholars wiser than I who devoted their time to criticizing my ideas and correcting my mistakes, among them Professors at the University of Helsinki: Simo Parpola (Assyriology), Saara Lilja and Maarit Kaimio (Classical Studies), as well as Dr. Sara Heinämaa (Gender Studies). If my text has not been improved by their professional insight, I have only myself to blame. I am also grateful to Professor Phyllis A. Bird, who kindly provided me with a manuscript, then yet unpublished, of an important article of hers.

I also owe a great debt to many friends and colleagues for criticism, encouragement, and "suffering together" (in Greek, *sympathein*). Especially my good friend Dr. Matti Myllykoski has been irreplaceable. Without categorizing my neighbors according to their sexual orientation or any other personal characteristics, I confess that without my gay and lesbian friends I would not understand the matter even to the extent that I do now.

During the process of publishing, the Directors of Publishing, Sirkka Stolt of Helsinki University Press and Marshall D. Johnson of Fortress Press and Senior Editor Michael West of Fortress Press, with their respective staffs, have facilitated matters for me at each stage. Special thanks are due to my friend Dr. Kirsi Stjerna, who, while giving birth to her firstborn daughter and preparing the manuscript of her own work, has translated and corrected my text patiently and skillfully over and over again. I think the contribution of her husband, Rob, in making many things (computers) work out has not been a minor one.

Finally, I am grateful to the folks I love and live with: my wife, Leena, and my big girls, Elina and Kaisa! Thanking them is daily routine; I wish it could be more. It is largely due to Leena's expertise as a pioneer in the counseling of prostitutes in Finland that I have become aware of different manifestations of sex and gender in my own environment. More than that, our common experience, sexual and other, for better or worse, has been a true adventure. This book is therefore dedicated to her, with much love.

1

INTRODUCTION

SOCIETY, CHURCH, AND HOMOSEXUALITY

Throughout human history, as both historical and anthropological sources reveal, different cultures have known same-sex erotic-sexual interaction. Response to this behavior, which, since the late nineteenth century, has been called "homosexuality," has varied in different cultures, ranging from absolute prohibition of same-sex relations to their approval in certain social circles and within accepted confines.

Perhaps no culture would regard same-sex interaction as unconditionally and unrestrictedly equal to or superior to relations between persons of the opposite sex.[1] In Judaism, Christianity, and Islam, for example, same-sex erotic relationships have been banned, secretive, and shameful, but the existence of such has nevertheless always required some acknowledgment. In practice this has often meant suppression or coercion of those involved in homosexual behavior and discrimination against them. Ever since "homosexuality" became defined and classified as a category of human sexuality—and especially after the Second World War—it has gained new attention and interest. This is evidenced in the increase of public discussion as well as in recent scholarly research. Also, the "coming out" of gays and lesbians (as homosexual men and women are commonly called) themselves as a minority group has occurred in the United States as well as in Western Europe.

As a result of research, discussion, and the efforts of homosexuals themselves, perceptions about homosexuality have begun to change toward increasingly less negative attitudes. This has influenced legislation in many countries. In some places the criminalization of homosexuality has been overruled; in others legislation has been modified.[2] General acceptance of homosexuality, however, has been debated in many countries—rarely without religious and, where appropriate, biblical arguments. This has been the case, for instance, in Finland, which serves here as a case study.

Since gaining its independence from Russia in 1917, the Republic of Finland, a member of the European Union since 1995, has been governed as a democracy with a parliamentary, multiparty system. As in the other Nordic countries (Sweden, Norway, Denmark, Iceland), the standards of living and education are high. There is relatively small disparity of income, social security is well developed, and the equality of men and women is renowned compared to any other country in the world. Finland was one of the first countries in the world to grant women universal suffrage—in 1906. Another characteristic of Finland is its unusual cultural uniformity. Only a small part of the population, 1–2% of 5.1 million people, has non-Finnish roots.

The Evangelical Lutheran Church of Finland has been the national church from the time of the sixteenth-century Reformation; 85.8% of Finns belong to it. In everyday language "the church," therefore, usually means the Lutheran church. The Greek Orthodox Church, however, which involves 1.1% of the population, also enjoys the status of an official national church. About 2% of the population belongs to other Protestant denominations (for example, Pentecostal, Baptist, and Methodist communities). There are only about six thousand Roman Catholics in Finland.[3]

Sexual attitudes of Finns are liberal, and the interaction between the two sexes is relatively unrestrained. Generally speaking, attitudes toward gays and lesbians have warmed remarkably in the last twenty years.[4] Despite this, initiatives to recognize homosexual relationships in public have met with stern resistance or silence. Finns are more willing to let people have their freedom and privacy and to mind their own business than to grant sexual difference a publicly recognized status.

The Finnish Criminal Law (RL), since 1971, no longer judges homosexuality a punishable crime, although the law still forbids public exhortation to homosexual sexual contact (RL 20:9.2). Also the age of consent is higher in a homosexual relationship (18/21 years; RL 20:5.2) than in a heterosexual relationship (16/18 years). The ongoing revision of the criminal law will probably make consistent the articles on the age of consent and also annul the exhortation ban.[5] Discrimination based on sexual orientation was criminalized in the Criminal Law in 1995 (RL 11:9).

Other initiatives have been made in an attempt to improve the status of homosexual people. The right of same-sex couples to register officially has been granted or is at the preparatory stage in several countries.[6] In Finland, a committee appointed by the Ministry of Justice proposed that homosexual relationships should be registered and considered equal to marriage. New legislation that allows homosexual couples to be registered as official unions was discussed in the Finnish House of Representatives in 1993. A new proposal to formalize same-sex relationships was presented to the House of Representatives in May 1996. This bill includes the recognition of homosexual partners as each other's most immediate relatives, for instance, in inheritance situations, but does not include the right to adopt a child or have a church wedding. By the end of 1997, the case has made no further progress, mainly because the Minister of Justice refused to forward the bill.

The Lutheran Church of Finland, according to the statement of the bishops from 1984, acknowledges homosexual orientation but does not approve its practice.[7] Homosexuality was discussed extensively within the church in 1993,[8] in response to journal articles about homosexuality as an unalterable personal condition. When Finnish archbishop John Vikström was asked in an interview about the church's reaction to gays and lesbians living together, he answered that it was not for the church to judge the people's decisions of conscience, even if their lifestyle would not conform to the ideals of the church. It was not good for a person to live alone, said Vikström, and therefore the church should encounter homosexuals with love and empathy and leave their admittance to heaven in God's hands. Upon the interview, a group of conservative theologians addressed an open letter to the archbishop, referring to the "utterly clear teaching of the Bible" about homosexuality, according to which, in their interpretation, nobody who practices a homosexual relationship can be saved. At the request of a layman akin to this group, Vikström was investigated by ecclesiastical and legal authorities whether he had violated the exhortation ban in the Criminal Law. This did not lead to any legal actions, but the issue emerged even in the presidential elections of 1994.

Finland is perceived as one of the most secularized countries in the world, at least according to those statistics that measure people's activity in the Lutheran church. The numbers fail to tell the whole truth, however. In the course of centuries, Lutheran Christianity has become such an essential part of the Finnish identity. In spite of their passive participation in the church, few Finns are ready to separate from their church. Even though Finns increasingly emphasize individualism and independence of mind, and many of them do not find themselves in a doctrinal agreement with the teaching of the church, a clear majority of the population believes in God and uses the services of the church.[9] The church, therefore, is not an insignificant institution to Finns.

Finland is only one example of how in Christian cultures the inner control of the society functions through the church, especially so in moral issues, among which homosexuality is often classified. I take Finland as an example mainly because of my nationality; equally illustrative examples can be found around the world, including the United States. The moral norms of society always interact with statements of the churches and religious communities, especially if these are constitutive of people's identity. In a culture historically influenced by the Christian church and faith, norms and values interpreted from the Bible belong to the whole community of people, not only to the church. Thus the interpretation of the Bible, often unconsciously, serves in both the secular and ecclesiastical exercise of power. This makes it relevant to ponder the relationship of homosexuality and biblical texts, not only from the perspective of theology and religious denominations, but from the perspective of the society as a whole.

What, then, have been the biblical grounds for disapproving of homosexuality? Texts that can be perceived as speaking about homosexuality have been adduced. The list is not very long: references have usually been made to the story of the destruction of the city of Sodom (Gen. 19:1–11), certain prohibitions in the Torah (Lev. 18:22; 20:13), and some statements of the Apostle Paul's (Rom. 1:26–27; 1 Cor. 6:9).

Typically these texts have been regarded as a sufficient evidence that homosexuality or at least homosexual behavior is prohibited by the Bible and therefore is to be repudiated categorically, regardless of time and place. Significant hermeneutical questions about the justification of this traditional concept, however, emerge from the challenges of today's world as well as from modern biblical scholarship. Biblical texts originated in quite a different climate compared to the modern world in terms of values, norms, and traditions. Applying the biblical texts to our time, therefore, is always a hermeneutical event, in which the differences between the biblical and contemporary worlds are in some way smoothed out. In practice, the tradition of biblical interpretation, several thousand years old, serves as the bridge, whether this is acknowledged or not. Internalized reading guided by this tradition is often unconscious to the point that the readers of the Bible do not even notice that they are constantly interpreting what they are reading.

The purpose of this book is to read the sparse biblical texts that address or pertain to same-sex eroticism, to examine them in their historical contexts, and to determine precisely what they are arguing about, their interpretation of sex and gender, and how they understand erotic same-sex interaction. The scarcity of the biblical material has made it necessary to expand the scope of inquiry to the cultural environment of the biblical writings—to Mesopotamia, Judaism, and classical antiquity.

The essential question is how ancient texts, whether biblical or other, pertain to today's understandings of same-sex interaction. Mechanical paralleling of the modern and ancient worlds often results in distorted perspectives in which modern questions are carelessly put into the mouths of ancient speakers. Not only are the ancient sources culture-bound, reflecting the values of their own environment, but so also are modern readers. To achieve a meaningful comparison and to avoid anachronism and ethnocentricity, it is necessary first to outline modern questions and then to see how these questions correlate with the old texts and their particular issues.

EXPLAINING "HOMOSEXUALITY"

It is an indisputable fact that a part of the humankind is primarily or exclusively "homosexual," that is, oriented sexually toward persons of the same sex. According to the famous Kinsey report, conducted after the Second World War, as many as 37% of white Americans had had at least one homosexual experience and 18% had had as many homosexual as heterosexual experiences. Of the people studied in this report, 4% had active homosexual sex lives.[10] For women the statistics were 10–39%, 3–28% and 0–3%, depending on the gauge.[11] Kinsey used a seven-step scale, with exclusive homosexuality and exclusive heterosexuality as the extremes and bisexuality in various degrees and either homosexual or heterosexual tendencies in between. This scale is still in active use, because it discloses the different nuances of sexual orientation better than would a strict distinction between homosexuality and heterosexuality. Kinsey's percentages for homosexuality, however, are believed by some researchers to be too high.

Newer studies, both in the United States and Finland, report smaller numbers than did Kinsey's report. According to a conclusion based on five interview studies from 1970 to 1990, 5–7% of all American men reported having had a sexual relationship with another man in the past, and 1–2% had had that experience during the previous 12 months.[12] According to the most recent Finnish study, based on a random sampling,[13] 6–7% of the Finnish men and women report that they are either exclusively or at least to some extent oriented sexually to people of their own sex. This inquiry found about 1% of men and 1/2% of women to be completely or predominantly same-sex orientated.[14] On a practical level, about 5% of Finns said that they had experienced at least exciting homosexual caresses. One and one-third percent of those interviewed had had sexual contact with a person of the same sex during the recent year, and about 2% had at some point in their life experienced orgasm in a homosexual relationship.[15]

Interview studies always involve the danger of under-reporting, because feelings of guilt and shame may have an influence on answers on a sensitive topic like this. The interviewed may also have found it perplexing to distinguish between sexual orientation and behavior, even if they had been asked specifically to do so. Statistics, therefore, never tell the full story, but they can provide an enlightened estimate about the numbers of people who are oriented toward their own sex or who have had sexual experiences with persons of their own sex. The percentages of homosexual orientation derived from interviews are probably somewhat smaller than the real numbers.

Today it is universally acknowledged that a part of humanity is, to use a modern term, homosexual. There is no agreement, however, on why this is the case. While it is not relevant or even possible in this work to examine all the explanation models for homosexuality (consult the literature mentioned in the notes), a brief survey of the most recent and influential explanation models is in order. The different views are here listed rather than analyzed; the goal is not an exhaustive history of research but to grasp the various facets of the modern scholarly understanding, whether we are dealing with ancient or modern, empirical or historical materials. A related goal is to illustrate the differences between modern and ancient approaches, to separate the problems that arise from ancient texts from the questions affected by modern disciplines and ideologies.

Modern interpretations of the reasons for and manifestations of what is called homosexuality are quite scattered; explanations offered by various studies correspond with the formulations of problems and the methods of particular disciplines. The approach and questions of a psychiatrist, a genetic specialist, and a sociologist differ considerably from one another, and the weight of each scientific explanation of homosexuality can be evaluated primarily within the boundaries of its particular model of interpretation. Further complications are caused by the fact that existing attitudes and passions often determine the ways questions are posed and tend to serve the ends of various sexual or gender politics. At least this is what scholars from different fields accuse each other of, and the question arises whether a value-free approach can ever be possible.[16]

"Medicalized" in the second half of the nineteenth century, homosexuality in most countries is no longer officially considered an illness. In the United States it was removed from the Diagnostic and Statistical Manual (DSM) of the American Psychiatric Association in 1973; similar action was taken in Finland only in 1981. It is still often considered a disorder or, more neutrally expressed, the result of abnormal psychosocial, genetic, or hormonal development.

In sciences related to psychology and psychiatry, homosexuality is generally regarded as a result of abnormal psychosexual development. Roots of this idea lie in the theory of Sigmund Freud, according to whom a male in early childhood goes through an Oedipal stage, in which he clings to his mother—a development that normally leads to a heterosexual sex life but in which a homosexual becomes fixated.[17] Research on this matter has developed in many directions since Freud. For instance, according to Irwing Bieber's (1962) popular theory, homosexuality is a result of a developmental disturbance originating in childhood with either an absent or hostile father and an over-caring and intrusive mother.[18]

Behavioral and social scientists and anthropologists have especially stressed learning factors. Some have pointed to childhood experiences of homosexual seduction or the condoning of girlishness as a factor leading to homosexuality.[19] Others have seen the lack of company of the opposite sex and in some cases—often related—homoerotic manners and rituals of the dominant culture as promoting homosexuality.[20]

Conversely, other scholars have tried to explain homosexuality biologically as related to hormones, genes, and the brain.[21] Research on the relative amount of androgens and estrogens (male and female hormones) in homosexuals and heterosexuals has produced contradictory results.[22] In spite of efforts to find a genetic origin of sexuality—for instance, with twin studies[23]— scholars have not yet been able to find a gene that would explain homosexuality as a purely hereditary phenomenon. The study by Dean H. Hamer et al. (1993), however, indicates that the sexual orientation of at least some male homosexuals might be determined by their chromosomes.

Possible structural differences between the brains of homosexual and heterosexual men have been examined. Dick Swaab (1990) discovered that the suprachiasmatic nucleus was essentially larger in homosexual men than in heterosexual men. Simon LeVay (1991) suggested that a certain group of nuclei in the anterior portion of the hypothalamus was one-half smaller in homosexual men compared to heterosexual men and the same as that of women.

For different reasons, no explanation of homosexuality has thus far found a consensus; each proposal has been rejected as inadequate. Various uncontrolled factors have been identified, for instance, the selection of research material, the relevance of animal studies, the difficulty of replicating results and feasibility of generalizations, and the question of the pre-existing attitudes of the researcher. Moreover, the overwhelming majority of studies have focused solely on homosexual men, and the results are not always applicable to homosexual women at all.

Not all the studies have attempted to explain the causes of homosexuality. "Gay and lesbian studies," developed predominantly in Western cultures, focuses on issues like the way homosexual men and women live, the social structure of a homosexual population, and the hallmarks of their own culture.[24] Expressions of same-sex relations have been studied also in non-Western cultures and societies, either cross-culturally or in a particular society. Greenberg (1988), for example, compiled a comprehensive cross-cultural study of same-sex relations in different parts of the world in different times, and classified the types of socially sanctioned homosexual relations in different cultures in four categories: (1) transgenerational homosexuality, involving an older and a younger (male) partner; (2) transgenderal homosexuality, which requires a cross-gender role (that is, a gender role opposite to a person's biological sex) on the part of one of the partners; (3) egalitarian same-sex relationships and (4) class-distinguished homosexuality.

In postmodern discourse, the discussion about homosexuality has been affected by the polarization of the so-called essentialists and constructionists. Essentialists hold that the basic structures of sexuality and gender are independent of their social context, that people are born with their sexual orientation. Support for this view is sought (albeit not exclusively) from biological and genetic studies. The influence of environmental factors is not necessarily denied, but their role is seen as secondary. In historical scholarship, the late John Boswell's *Christianity, Social Tolerance, and Homosexuality* (1980) is a classic essentialist work. The "essentialism" of this work is represented in the idea that, regardless of the era, there were and are "gay people," who have in common their orientation to their own sex.[25]

Constructionists see sexuality and its manifestations as social constructions. According to this view, gender is not a biologically determined and immutable fact but a product of social relations. Some of the constructionists actually come close to the views of social scientists and anthropologists. Since the late Michel Foucault's *History of Sexuality* (*Histoire de la sexualité,* vols. 1–3:1976–1984), in which "sexuality" is likewise strictly divorced from "nature" and is interpreted as a cultural product, the constructionist view has been applied also to interpret the homoerotic aspect in ancient cultures.[26] Constructionists do not see "sexuality" as an autonomous domain within the human mind that determines human lives from the cradle to the grave but rather as a late concept that attempts to categorize erotic experience, a cultural construction rather than an intrinsic condition. As derivatives of "sexuality," "homosexuality" and "heterosexuality" are also treated as modern categories that, according to Foucault, have penetrated Western thinking as a product of *scientia sexualis*, which, in the nineteenth century, replaced *ars erotica* as the interpretation of human erotic experience.[27]

Contemporary scientific explanations of homosexuality are rooted precisely in this *scientia sexualis*, which took as its task to map and categorize the observed forms of sex life, especially those that were considered abnormal or dysfunctional compared with the predominant lifestyle. In fact, "normal" sexuality was defined by the exclusion of various "perversions." The concept "homosexuality," as also the notion of the class of people sharing this anomaly, was born only as a result of this abnormalization and medicalization.[28] This approach is not an entirely modern phenomenon but has its roots already in the Roman and Byzantine periods; for example Soranos, a second century C.E. physician, diagnosed the *mollis* and the *tribades*, men and women who habitually engaged in same-sex interaction, as mentally ill.[29] Also the astrological literature of the Roman period made classifications of different erotic orientations.[30] Ancient authors did not create the binary categories of homosexuality and heterosexuality but rather made observations about same-sex preference, among other deviations of conventional sexual practice. Nevertheless, they can be seen as forerunners of the modern pathologization of "homosexuality."

Paradoxically, this medicalization and the resulting marginalization set the foundation for modern gay and lesbian identities, which scarcely would have been possible before the creation of a distinct group that was pushed to the margins of the society. "Otherness" was and still is a central motive in the existence of gay and lesbian movements, although those involved no longer are satisfied with the definitions coming from outside and want instead to define their identities themselves. Some groups, making a virtue of necessity, "marginalize" themselves in the form of an exclusive subculture. By contrast, in feminist discussions a lesbian identity and ethics has been created, based more on the abandoning of patriarchal tradition rather than on sexual orientation.[31]

In general, research on same-sex orientation and sexual relations has been characterized by the traditional distinction between "nature" and "nurture," a sophisticated outcome of which can be seen in the differentiation between biological "sex" and sociocultural "gender." Recent approaches in gender studies have challenged this once-influential dichotomy, which has both its advantages and difficulties. On the one hand, using this dichotomy has meant liberation from fixed roles of the sexist straitjacket; on the other hand, "sex" has easily been associated with the essential, "actual" sex, whereas "gender" as an outcome of environmental factors has been understood as a mask for the "real" sex. In the most recent discussion precisely the opposite has been argued: "sex" is "gendered," which means that gender is prior to biological sex, which as such is more ambiguous than has often been thought.[32]

Feminist scholars, especially, have found androcentrism behind the traditional concept of biological determinism and have questioned the role of "biology" and "nature" in the formation of gender as self-evident, self-directing factors that define social processes. Also plain constructionism has been challenged, because it can be seen as leading to new social categorialism, which neglects the reality and importance of the body. This does not mean a return to biological determinism, because the body is not understood as a fixed and foundational constituent of gender but rather as the location where eroticism, reproduction, illness, health, asceticism, religion, and so forth take place and through which social relations and power structures are formed.[33] Modern feminism challenges such fundamental distinctions as sex/gender and nature/culture altogether.[34]

The perspectives of gender studies are significant to our topic, because they bring discussion about "homosexuality" into a larger context. Same-sex or both-sex eroticism is no longer simply a matter of sexual preference and its sociobiological preconditions; it must be examined in the wider framework of gender, body, and society.

INTERPRETATION OF GENDER

All the sources examined in this study derive from the time "before sexuality," that is, before "sexuality" and its derivatives were conceptualized through the *scientia sexualis* in the nineteenth century C.E.[35] Without holding any particular brief for constructionism, the study of the sources written "before sexuality" has compelled me to recognize the limitations of modern concepts and distinctions like "homosexuality"—and I mean conceptualized homosexuality with all its modern implications.[36] I have become convinced that same-sex interaction cannot be simply equated with "homosexuality" but must be viewed within the broader framework of gender identity, which in each culture and in each individual involves different interpretations.

Depending on current trends, it might or might not be fashionable to talk about personal "identity." In any case, this concept has proved to be helpful to my work, and I would define it as the way in which each individual interprets her or his existence and experience in his or her specific environment and social relations. Considered from this perspective, identity is equivalent to the interpretation of the self.

Identity should not be confused with "nature," "essence," or similar concepts that suggest something given, inborn, or unalterable. The concept of identity includes both variability and constancy. Identity can exist only within a social setting, the changes of which it reflects. There are many aspects of identity: ethnic, national, professional, religious, sexual, and so on. Some aspects are conscious, actively constructed, developed, and practiced (for example, professional identity), whereas others are more or less subconscious and governed by the culture (for example, ethnicity). Active aspects of identity do not necessarily conform to the norms of society, which may even be contradictory to the subconscious aspects of identity. Different aspects of identity in one and the same person, therefore, do not necessarily constitute a well-organized and harmonious whole.

The ancient sources examined in subsequent chapters do not utilize— or even know—the concept of gender identity, which did not exist in the time "before sexuality." This does not mean, however, that people would not have had identities before these were invented by modern scholars. Even if the concept of sexuality was nonexistent before the nineteenth and twentieth centuries C.E., gender or, if we prefer, sexual difference always did exist as a factor of human biology, erotic experience, social life, and individual consciousness.

It might well be true that gender identity—like "sexuality"—is nothing but "one of those cultural fictions which in every society give human beings access to themselves as meaningful actors in their world, and which are thereby objectivated."[37] Surely the people who lived in ancient cultures—the subject of this study—did not interpret their existence in terms of modern classifications. Modern concepts like "sexuality" or "gender identity" are therefore inevitably anachronistic, all the more because they are used not just to describe but also to constitute reality. (Whether or not this anachronism is acceptable is another matter.) It is also true that "sexuality" or "gender identity," even as objectivized fictions, are not false categories without any real basis.[38] Because objectivizing causes realization, these concepts are meaningful in the modern discussion. The real issue is the degree to which the reality described or connoted by this terminology is comparable with the reality reflected in ancient sources. This question cannot really be solved, because modern knowledge is restricted to information obtainable from the limited set of sources. It is possible only to test certain terms, bearing in mind that they are not the vocabulary of ancient sources.

Many phenomena have existed before they have been labeled. Humankind, for example, has always had a variety of religions that can be studied, in spite of the fact that there is still no agreement about the meaning of the word "religion." Whether or not "sexuality" also is this kind of term deserves serious consideration. Much depends on the definition. If I use the word "sexuality" mainly with its Foucauldian connotations, I am aware that the word does not necessarily have to be so interpreted. In fact, it is only after Foucault that the term "sexuality" could move semantically from its more or less unconscious ideological function toward something more neutral. As a matter of fact, the semantic field of the word "sexuality" in colloquial use often corresponds with that of "the construction of erotic experience," an expression preferred by constructionists.

In the following I sketch an outline of the construction of gender identity—not as an image of "objective truth" but rather as a working hypothesis that I hope proves helpful in the study of ancient sources. As components of gender identity, the following aspects are taken into account: (1) sexual orientation, (2) gender identification, (3) gender roles, and (4) sexual practice. I use these modern concepts with the awareness that they are understood in a variety of ways and on the basis of different presuppositions. For this reason, they must be defined before they can be accurately used.[39]

Sexual Orientation

Sexual orientation refers to the sexual preference of an individual toward the same, the opposite, or even both sexes. It can thus be heterosexual, bisexual, or homosexual. A person has a homosexual orientation when there is awareness of sexual interest in a person of his or her own sex and when there are no similar feelings toward persons of the opposite sex. The opposite is the case with a heterosexual person, while a bisexual person feels interest in both sexes. Sexual orientation is a part of a person's unique experience and self-interpretation, mind and body and, as such, is a part of a person's sexual and gender identity.

These categories of sexual orientation represent a modern classification and cannot be found in ancient sources. The demarcation of homosexuality and heterosexuality presupposes a conceptualization of "sexuality."[40] It corresponds with modern Western thinking but may be less useful in the study of ancient cultures. This does not mean that various individual sexual orientations would not have existed among ancient people. Persons with such preferences do appear in ancient sources, and their existence was noted and commented on by their contemporaries.[41]

Gender Identification

Sexual orientation should not be confused with gender identification, that is, whether a person perceives himself or herself as a man or a woman. Contrary to a common misconception, having a homosexual orientation does not mean having the self-identity of the opposite sex. When a person's gender identification is different from his or her biological sex (a biologically man who feels himself to be a woman, or the converse), it is a matter of transsexuality.[42] A transsexual (or transgender) person is "someone whose physiological sexual identity is at odds with his or her psycho-social sexual identity (preoperative) or someone who has undergone surgery to bring these into closer conformity (postoperative). This person's erotic needs in either case make him or her heterosexual, bisexual, or homosexual."[43]

In most cultures, including modern Western culture, gender identity is thought of as either masculine or feminine. There exist, however, gender systems that tolerate an intermediate, "third" gender, neither masculine nor feminine.[44] Moreover, even biological sexual identity is not always clearly defined. Persons with indefinite sex (hermaphrodites) were born in ancient times as they are today, even if modern technology makes it possible to "hide" or even eliminate this "anomaly."[45] Nonetheless, the fact that human sex is not a strictly binary category even today is involved in the construction of gender identity.

Gender Roles

Gender roles are derived from the conceptions of masculine and feminine in a gendered society. The roles are explicitly social and culture-bound, and they can vary even in the case of one individual, depending on the person's activity. Male and female roles sanctioned by society affect the ways sexuality is realized and expressed; thus roles and practices are closely connected. Roles and orientation, however, do not necessarily require one another, although there is a strong social pressure for their correlation. For instance, a man's feminine role does not necessarily have anything to do with homosexuality, and a man's homosexual orientation itself does not generate feminine appearance or behavior.

A particular form of role identification is transvestism (cross-dressing), a need to dress in a fashion characteristic of the opposite sex. Transvestism does not require a homosexual identity; the majority of transvestites, in fact, are heterosexual men.[46]

Sexual Practice

Sexual practice involves much more than sexual intercourse or other physical expressions of sexuality. It includes both public and private eroticism, and, broadly conceived, also autoeroticism and sex fantasies. Sexual practice is definitely bound to gender roles. It does not always correlate with orientation, and it does not necessarily coincide with the different aspects of a person's identity. Customs and norms of a society, more than a person's identity or identities, often determine the forms for the expression of one's sexuality. It is therefore possible for a person to behave in a homosexual or heterosexual manner without having a corresponding orientation. Even sexual fantasies may have an occasional homosexual or heterosexual component regardless of one's sexual orientation.

On the basis of the preceding definitions, the construction of gender identity can be outlined by the following quadripartite figure.

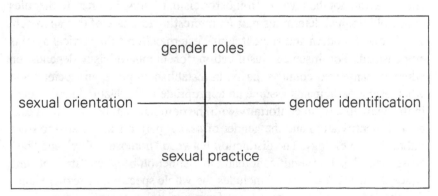

The horizontal line runs between sexual orientation and gender identification (the bipolarity of being a man or a woman). The vertical line between gender roles and sexual practice is dominated by the definition of male and female. It is a common expectation that the heads of the axials correlate, so that gender identification determines sexual orientation and sexual practice corresponds with accepted gender roles. Furthermore, it is expected that a man is male and a woman is female, which connects the roles and behavior with orientation and gender identification. General expectations, however, rarely materialize, and the deviations are interesting because they show which areas are considered most important.

One might think that the horizontal line represents the primary, inborn "sex" dictated by anatomy and that the vertical line depicts the secondary "gender" formed by culture. The figure, however, is not based on nature/culture or sex/gender distinctions nor on the separation of "biological" from "environmental" factors. More important is the gender differentiation implied in every component of this figure. Biology, social environment, individual consciousness, and bodily experience are intertwined and interacting factors of every component of this figure without any of them taking precedence in causation.[47] The figure must not be interpreted as fixed and unchanging, neither individually nor socially, but rather as subject to historical and individual processes, so that the components will have different emphases in different times, individuals, and cultures.

Societies usually have quite clear expectations for the emphasis in different areas. Modern Western sociobiological determinism emphasizes that the horizontal axial, based on biologically and psychologically understood manhood and womanhood, determines—or should determine—other aspects of life. "Naturalness" and acceptability derive from this perspective. With regard to homosexuality, for example, the discussion concentrates on its biological or psychological existence, and its justification is argued from there. Orientation and identification should designate roles and behavior, not the reverse. Homoeroticism, running contrary to the rules of sociobiological determinism, is an interesting test case of this approach.

In many modern and ancient non-Western cultures the vertical axial is emphasized. For instance, justification for homoeroticism depends on whether same-sex contacts have an established place in society and whether the participants assume an appropriate role. "Naturalness" means in this view first of all conformity with the dominant culture, in which case gender identification and the gender of sexual partners are related to roles rather than to biology. The distinction between "homosexuality" and "heterosexuality" is less significant than the distinction between "straight" and "queer"—when "queerness" includes the whole spectrum of sexual identities that are regarded as deviations from societal standards and as something that might be called "unnatural." (This attitude can be found also behind Western quasi-scientific discussion.)

Ancient sources also clearly reflect an understanding of sexual life from the genital and procreative perspectives, which not infrequently makes "queer" aspects appear as something that must be condemned, defended, or explained. Ancient approaches differ from modern in that ancient people, unaware of the biological processes that we know (or at least believe) produce gender differences, categorized maleness and femaleness as roles and functions in society—which indeed was gendered. Differences between the bodies of women and men were obvious, to mention only the appearance and reproductive function of the genitals as well as physical strength. These differences doubtless also had an important part in the construction of social roles. However, "manliness" and "effeminacy" were socially determined concepts not strictly bound to anatomical sex, and anatomical features were but one component of the "body language" that members of society had to learn to speak.[48] A good example of how human self-presentation was gendered is provided by Polemo the sophist, a second century C.E. Roman physiognomist:[49]

> You may obtain physiognomic indications of masculinity and femi-
> ninity from your subject's glance, movement, and voice, and then,
> from among these signs, compare one with another until you deter-
> mine to your satisfaction which of these two sexes prevails. For in the
> masculine there is something feminine to be found, and in the femi-
> nine something masculine, but the name *masculine* or *feminine* is
> assigned according to which of the two prevails.

This suggests that gender categories, at least in Roman antiquity, did not constitute a strict binary system based on biology. Whether this was true of ancient Near Eastern societies will be observed later.

Even if the interpretation of the human body began to change already with Aristotle (384–322 B.C.E.),[50] with the development of the concept of woman as a physiologically inferior and deficient being, the understanding of gender was still undeniably role-centered and far removed from our psychobiologically oriented concept of "sexuality." To take just one example, the Greeks had long pondered whether the child was born only from its father or also from its mother. Some, for example, the physician Hippocrates (*c.* 460–377 B.C.E.),[51] spoke for the second alternative, but the majority of scholars, including the Stoics, as well as public opinion generally thought that the child was born only from his father. This was also the opinion of Aristotle, whose theory was to have paramount importance in Western thought.[52] According to Aristotle, menstrual blood cooperates with male sperm to form the embryo: "The menstrual fluid is semen, not indeed semen in the pure condition, but needing still to be acted upon."[53] Nonetheless, because menstrual fluid cannot accomplish the final transformation, it is the male seed that plays the active role in creating new life: "The male provides the 'form' and the 'principle of movement,' the female provides the body, in other words, the material."[54] The subordination of women thus became justified quite early also on "biological" grounds, the interpretation of which was influenced by the societal interpretation of gender.

There is no reason to deny or even minimize the role of the physical (genetic, hormonal, etc.) and psychological processes in the construction of the human body and mind, ancient or modern. Bodies have always existed as living organs and points of individual experience, not just as neutral frameworks of a disembodied person or mind. But these processes in antiquity were for the most part unknown and therefore could not be such a dominant and conscious factor in the construction of personal and social identity as they are in modern times.

HOMOSEXUALITY, HOMOEROTICISM, HOMOSOCIABILITY

Finally, some central concepts used in this study need to be defined, especially because there is yet no agreement about their meanings. The term "homosexuality" is used quite incoherently, despite its apparently unambiguous nature. The term has with good reason been criticized in many quarters, for instance, for its peculiar etymology: The word is a Greek-Latin hybrid (Greek *homoios*, "same," plus Latin *sexus*, "sex"). A more serious weakness of the term is that it overemphasizes the sexual aspect of a phenomenon that actually includes much more. It therefore bolsters prevalent prejudices. Perhaps the biggest difficulty with the term, however, is its link with the modern concept of sexuality and its associated classifications. This makes the term anachronistic when applied to the ancient world.

In spite of its inadequacies, the term has prevailed, and attempts to replace it have failed. More neutral terms like "homophilia" (same-sex love) and "homotropia" (same-sex orientation) have never gained common use. Therefore, I use the old term with its deficiencies, but want to explain how I understand it.

I use the adjective *homosexual* in its neutral meaning, "between the same sex" or "related to the same sex." But the noun *homosexuality* will be used in a more restricted sense to denote homosexual orientation. Consequently, *homosexual* as a noun signifies a person "who has most or all of his or her erotic needs met in interactions with persons of the same sex"[55] (whether "by nature" or "by nurture" is beside the point here). Unless mentioned otherwise, this terms applies to both men and women, but homosexual women may be referred to also with the generalized word "lesbian." Because the terms "homosexual," "gay," and "lesbian," however, are easily understood as labels of distinct classes of people in the modern sense of "sexuality," I minimize their use in connection with ancient sources, in which this classification is not relevant.

I have chosen not to use the term *homosexualism* (or homosexualist) at all. This term could betoken a "gay ideology" and its representatives, but it is not proper in describing sexual orientation or identity.

In practice I find it necessary to use another term along with "homosexuality," a term that has a broader meaning, is less tied to modern concepts of sexuality, and describes men's and women's mutual erotic interaction also on the level of roles and practices, even without a thought of homosexual orientation: For such functions I use the term *homoeroticism*. By this term I mean all erotic-sexual encounters and experiences of people with persons of the same sex, whether the person is regarded as homosexual or not. This concept encompasses also bisexual behavior as long as it occurs in an erotic contact with a person of the same sex. Because it has proved quite problematic to identify sexual orientations in ancient sources, I have to use this term rather often. For that reason, this term appears in the title of the book instead of the more restrictive term "homosexuality."

Because "homoeroticism" has an erotic-sexual connotation, it is necessary to use a different term to describe such interaction between persons of the same sex where the erotic-sexual aspect is less emphasized. For this purpose I will use the term *homosociability*, a term that, according to the definition of David Morgan, "is a collective name for an important set of relationships, referring not simply to the preference of men for each other's company, but for the location of these relationships in public or semipublic regions . . . and for the particular set of exchanges and interdependencies that grow between men."[56] Erotic expressions of sexuality may or may not be included in homosociability, which encompasses also different sexual identities.

2

MESOPOTAMIA

Ancient Near Eastern sources document same-sex erotic interaction meagerly and ambiguously. The available material comes mostly from Mesopotamia. With regard to other significant cultures of that area, those of Egypt and Ugarit, for instance, we are left almost entirely in the dark.

Of the vast amount of extant material from ancient Egypt, only a couple of texts give any attention to same-sex conduct. The Egyptian *Book of the Dead*, in which the dead account their affairs during their earthly lives, is a good reflection of the morality of the time from which it derives (the fifteenth century B.C.E.). Its confessional part twice includes the statement, "I have not had sexual relations with a boy."[1] This confession gives reason to believe that the Egyptians viewed sexual relations between men as morally dubious. The sources do not make it clear whether it was also a punishable act and whether some other type of same-sex interaction would have been more acceptable.[2]

The most significant Egyptian text in our context is the myth about the power struggle between two gods, Horus and Seth.[3] Horus, son of the late Osiris, contends with Seth, brother and murderer of Osiris, for supremacy among the gods. In one of the episodes of this story (11:1–12:2), Seth summons his nephew with gestures of reconciliation. However, his ulterior motive is to neutralize the status of the legal heir to be king of the gods. For this reason Seth abuses Horus sexually, by anal intercourse, while the latter is asleep. Seth's purpose is to show his superiority by forcing Horus into the position of a defeated and raped enemy, thus making him unfit for the status of king. Seth, however, fails, because Horus manages to get Seth's sperm in his hand. On the advice of his mother, Isis, Horus secretly mixes the sperm with Seth's food and gives him a dose of his own medicine. This story obviously deals not with same-sex desire but with sexual aggression used in exercising power. In this particular sense, however, it has parallels in ancient Near Eastern and biblical sources (the *Middle Assyrian Laws* and Gen. 9:20–24; 19:1–11) which will be discussed later in this book.

Texts from Ugarit make no single clear reference to homoeroticism.[4] Some Hittite laws resemble the literary context of the biblical prohibitions of sexual conduct between two men (Lev. 18:22; 20:13). They forbid various forms of incest, including sexual relations with one's own son (and with animals), but mention no other types of same-sex acts.[5]

More information is available from the cultures of Mesopotamia. Some literary works, myths, omens, and law codes offer crumbs of information about different types of sex life and gender roles—occasionally also in terms of same-sex encounters. To grasp the whole picture is difficult, because the information consists of fragments from masses of material. Individual sources derive from different times and places, dating anywhere in a period of two or three millennia. Moreover, the extent to which the sources actually speak about "homosexuality" in the modern sense of the word can only be inferred.

THE EPIC OF GILGAMEŠ

The *Epic of Gilgameš,* with its central theme of love between two men, Gilgameš and Enkidu, is sometimes considered the most important ancient Near Eastern depiction of homoeroticism.[6] Gilgameš is the king of Uruk who built the famous walls of that city as well as the temple of Anu and Ištar, called Eanna. Gilgameš is described as a giant who is "two-thirds god and one-third human being." His eagerness to build is endless and so is his sexual energy. Gilgameš is said to rend young men from their fathers and young women from their husbands and rage day and night uncontrollably. His insatiety drains the people of Uruk to the point that they turn to their gods and plead the creator goddess, Aruru, to create him a suitable partner on whom he could spend his energy. And so Aruru creates Enkidu, a primitive, hairy man who lives among animals. His size is massive, his physique awe-inspiring, and he is "furnished with tresses like a woman:"[7]

> "You, Aruru, you created [mankind(?)]!
> Now create someone *(zikru)* for him, to match (?) the ardor (?) of his
>   energies!
> Let them be regular rivals, and let Uruk be allowed peace!"
> When Aruru heard this, she created inside herself the word (?) *(zikru)*
>   of Anu.
> Aruru washed her hands, pinched off a peace of clay, cast it out into
>   open country.
> She created a [primitive man], Enkidu the warrior: offspring of
>   silence (?), sky-bolt *(kiṣru)* of Ninurta.

His whole body was shaggy with hair, he was furnished with tresses
   like a woman,
His locks of hair grew luxuriant like grain.
He knew neither people nor country; he was dressed as cattle are.
With gazelles he eats vegetation,
With cattle he quenches his thirst at the watering place.

A hunter, terrified to see Enkidu at the animals' watering place, tells
Gilgameš about him. Gilgameš orders Šamhat,[8] a harlot, to be brought to
the wild man so that he would fall in love with her and leave his bestial life.
This happens: The harlot goes to Enkidu, takes off her clothes, spreads her
legs, and Enkidu copulates with her. For six days and seven nights these
two make love. Then Šamhat urges Enkidu to give up his primitive life and
join the world of human beings. Enkidu wants to go to Gilgameš and challenge him to a duel. But Šamhat describes Gilgameš as a beautiful, strong,
and seductive man and advises Enkidu to abandon his intentions to fight:[9]

Let me show you Gilgameš, a man of joy and woe!
Look at him, observe his face:
He is beautiful in manhood, dignified,
His whole body is charged with seductive charm.
He is more powerful in strength of arms than you!
He does not sleep by day or night.
O Enkidu, change your plan for punishing him!

Meanwhile, Gilgameš tells his mother about his dreams:[10]

Mother, I saw a dream in the night.
There were stars in the sky for me.
And (something) like a sky-bolt of Anu kept falling upon me!
I tried to lift it up, but it was too heavy for me.
I tried to turn it over, but I couldn't budge it...
I loved it as a wife, doted on it.
[I carried it], laid it at your feet,
You treated it as equal to me.
- - - - - -
Mother, I saw a second dream:
An axe *(ḫaṣṣinnu)* was thrown down in the street (?) of Uruk...
[I carried it], laid it at your feet.
I loved it as a wife, doted on it.
and you treated it as equal to me.

Ninsun, the wise mother of Gilgameš, interprets his dreams:[11] Gilgameš
will find a friend—a gigantic, muscular man, whom he will love as ten-
derly as he loves his wife, and who will save his life.

The two men meet for the first time on the street of Uruk, as Gilgameš is on his way to a certain bride's bedroom to act on his right as a king to sleep with the bride on the wedding night before the groom does (the so-called *ius primae noctis*). Enkidu blocks his way, and this leads to a fiery fight that ultimately ends in their embrace and friendship.[12] The story moves along to narrate at length a victorious battle Gilgameš and Enkidu fight in a cedar wood against the demon Humbaba. Afterwards, as Gilgameš bathes himself, dresses, and shows himself in all his comeliness, Ištar, the goddess of love and war, tries to seduce him to become her spouse. Ištar assumes a very active, if not a "phallic" role. She proposes to Gilgameš and makes the first move, and her speech is "an odd mixture of a harlot's proposition and an actual marriage proposal."[13]

Gilgameš, however, refuses the goddess' advances and avers that his fate would be as sad as that of the lovers of Ištar, all of whom had ended up dead. Ištar's proposal is that of death; to accept it would mean a descent to the underworld.[14] Gilgameš's response enrages Ištar, who requires her father, Anu, to send the Bull of Heaven to destroy Gilgameš. The Bull dashes to Uruk, knocking over hundreds of men in a splatter, but Gilgameš manages to kill it. Enkidu throws the bull's "shoulder"—its penis or testicles—at Ištar's face, upon which she assembles her devotees and arranges lamentation for the bull's "shoulder." Gilgameš donates the bull's horns to Lugalbanda, his father and god, and celebrates in his palace.

In the night, Enkidu dreams an omen of his imminent death. In his deep sorrow Enkidu curses Šamhat, who lured him away from his previous life. The sun-god Šamaš, however, reminds Enkidu of the moments of happiness he had shared with Gilgameš and promises that even in his grave he would have a change to rest next to him.

Enkidu withdraws his curse but is overwhelmed by new horrors and, after twelve days of illness, he dies. Gilgameš bursts into a heartbreaking lament for Enkidu's death:[15]

> Listen to me, young men, listen to me!
> Listen to me, elders of Uruk, listen to me!
> I myself must weep for Enkidu, my friend,
> Mourn bitterly, like a wailing woman.
> As for the axe *(ḫaṣṣinnu)* at my side, spur to my arm,
> The sword in my belt, the shield for my front,
> My festival clothes, my manly sash:
> Evil (Fate (?)] rose up and robbed me of them.
> My friend was the hunted mule, wild ass of the mountains,
>   leopard of the open country. . . .
> We who met, and scaled in the mountain,
> Seized the Bull of Heaven and slew it,

Demolished Humbaba the mighty one of the Pine Forest,
Now, what is the sleep that has taken hold of you?
Turn to me, you! You aren't listening to me!
But he cannot lift his head.
I touch his heart, but it does not beat at all.
My friend has covered his face like a bride.[16]

- - - - - -

Enkidu, my friend whom I love so much, who
      experienced every hardship with me—
The fate of mortals conquered him!
For six days and seven nights I wept over him,
I did not allow him to be buried
Until a worm fell out of his nose.

After having lamented six days and seven nights, Gilgameš buries his friend. The last part of the epic narrates Gilgameš's travels to find a means to overcome death, and how on this journey he passes the Stream of Death and finds himself with his forefather Utnapištim. After numerous episodes and pleas, Utnapištim provides Gilgameš with a herb that grants eternal life. A snake, however, snatches the herb from Gilgameš. The last tablet (XII)[17] tells how Enkidu is able once more to pass the border between the living and the dead, and thus Gilgameš finally has the occasion to meet Enkidu's ghost and converse with him.[18]

Homoeroticism is certainly not a central theme in the *Epic of Gilgameš*. Nevertheless, the relationship between Gilgameš and Enkidu is described as most intimate, and the text suggests several erotic associations. Gilgameš, who is famous for his outrageous sexual activity, leaving neither women nor men in peace, loves Enkidu "like a wife," covers his body "like that of a bride," and even declines Ištar's proposal. His friendship with Enkidu is more important for him than anything else, and his feelings express deep love. Certain insinuations regarding Enkidu are hidden by play on words (*zikru, kisru, hassinnu*); these will be discussed later.

Ištar's proposal, one of the crucial episodes in the epic, appears as an alternative to Gilgameš's relationship with Enkidu. Gilgameš does not refuse this honor because of his sexual orientation; it is not a matter of homosexuality or heterosexuality. The issues lie deeper in the ideological structure of the epic. Ištar represents the world Gilgameš is leaving behind—the lavish and sex-hungry city culture, the world fostered by his own excessive life. Enkidu, coming from a different, wild and ascetic world, becomes the real Other of Gilgameš. Enkidu induces him a change that manifests itself in Gilgameš's renouncing of his old life and that leads him after Enkidu's death to search for his own world in the desert. Sex he leaves behind to his former life; relationships with women and women's world are now replaced by an accentuated masculine asceticism.[19]

At most, the *Epic of Gilgameš* can be described as a characterization of love between two men, with a homoerotic aspect that expresses their deep friendship. Nevertheless, the epic neither emphasizes nor idealizes the sexual aspect of the relationship. At the beginning, there is plenty of sex in the lives of Gilgameš and Enkidu, but this lifestyle is presented as primitive and reckless. Already the dream of Gilgameš brings a new, formerly unknown tone to his sexual fantasies: loving tenderness. As the story proceeds, the relationship between Gilgameš and Enkidu deepens and, simultaneously, the sexual passions seem to subside to the point that one can speak of a "spiritual" love between the two men.[20] The erotic tension between Gilgameš and Enkidu is not lost, but it is transformed in the way that the same-sex interaction of the two men finally is characterized by love, with little if any sexual activity. Eroticism is important first and foremost as the impetus to the transformation which leads first from savage sexual behavior to mutual love, and finally away from physical sex.[21]

Especially noteworthy is the equal relationship between the men, with no clear social or sexual role division. That Gilgameš finds Enkidu his equal counterpart is the basis of their love. These men are united and become one on a level that was exceptional for a man and a woman under the normal conditions of the surrounding culture. They experience unity and share each other's worlds—unlike a man and a woman, who lived in separate worlds.[22] This exemplifies less a homoerotic than a homosocial type of bonding, which is often strong in societies in which men's and women's worlds are segregated. Ancient literature knows also other examples of men's relationships of equality, intimate affection, and companionship, for example that of Achilles and Patroclus in Homer's *Iliad*[23] or David and Jonathan in the Hebrew Bible.[24] Achilles' lament over the death of Patroclus (*Iliad* 24) is reminiscent of Gilgameš's lament over the body of Enkidu, as is David's lament over Jonathan (2 Samuel 1:19-27). These stories, however, do not share the sexual pessimism and masculine asceticism of the *Epic of Gilgameš*.

Because the *Epic of Gilgameš* does not provide us with glimpses of everyday life, it does not indicate how Mesopotamian societies reacted to homoeroticism. There are, however, other cuneiform sources that approach same-sex erotic interaction from quite a different perspective.

LAWS AND OMENS

Two men involved in a sexual act is undoubtedly the subject in articles A §§19 and 20[25] of the *Middle Assyrian Laws*[26]:

§18 If a man says to his comrade, either in private or in a public quarrel: "Everyone has sex *(ittinikkū)* with your wife, I can prove the charges," but he is unable to prove the charges and does not prove the charges, they shall strike him 40 blows with rods; he shall perform the king's service one full month; they shall cut off (his hair?) *(igaddimūš)*[27] and he shall pay one talent of lead.

§19 If a man furtively spreads rumors about his comrade, saying: "Everyone has sex with him *(ittinikkūš),*" or in a quarrel in public says to him: "Everyone has sex with you *(ittinikkūka),* I can prove the charges," but he is unable to prove the charges and does not prove the charges, they shall strike him 50 blows with rods; he shall perform the king's service one full month; they shall cut off (his hair?) *(igaddimūš)* and he shall pay one talent of lead.

§20 If a man has sex with his comrade *(tappāšu inīk)* and they prove the charges against him and find him guilty, they shall have sex with him and they shall turn him into a eunuch *(inikkūš ana ša rēšēn utarrūš).*

Regulations regarding sexual acts between men follow laws regarding adultery (§§12–18). The above quoted §§18 and 19, with a similar structure, address cases in which a person is falsely accused of prostitution—first the wife of another man, then another man; the accusers are meted almost the same punishment.[28] From that point the law moves to deal with homosexual acts between males (§20).

The punishments are severe and unconditional: spreading false rumors has severe physical and economical consequences in itself; the suspect caught in the act has to part with his genitals. Having sex with another man, however, does not seem to be as severe a crime as sexual relations with another man's wife. Punishment for adultery could be as harsh as death (§§12–13), but in some cases involved castration or marring one's appearance (§15).[29]

The punishments have various aspects. On the one hand, the laws apply the principle of talion, that is, analogous punishment ("they shall have sex with him").[30] On the other hand, the intent is to prevent the malefactor from repeating the crime (by castration). Also, the punishments essentially include disgracing the offender; castration was a permanent change in his gender role.

Sections regarding adultery distinguish rape from consensual sex; in the case of rape, a woman avoids punishment (§12). When a man forces sex on another man, the perpetrator is punished while the other man is not. This law seems to indicate a case in which a man is sexually subjected to another man; it can also mean a rape. The verb for coercing somebody to have sex, *niāku*, does not in itself express force or violence on the part of the one who commits the crime. Yet its subject is the active and dominant partner of the sexual contact,[31] and §19 refers to the shame of consenting to homosexual acts as the passive partner, at least if this happens repeatedly and voluntarily.

Thus it cannot be said that *Middle Assyrian Laws* would take into consideration a case in which two men were involved as equals in a voluntary homoerotic relationship and for mutual satisfaction. The reason for the silence about this kind of relationship is scarcely that erotic interaction of this kind would have been common and approved but rather the fact that neither homosexual acts nor heterosexual acts were considered as being done by two equals. The *Middle Assyrian Laws* assume that one partner actively lies on top of the other. This becomes criminal in the case when the object is a *tappā'u*, a man of equal social status, or a man who was otherwise socially involved with the perpetrator, like a neighbor or a business partner.[32] The *Laws* do not specify a case of penetrating a male who is not a *tappā'u*, for instance, a defeated enemy or someone of lower status who does not belong to the social circles of the perpetrator. Presumably the *Laws* do not apply to the *assinnu* and other devotees of Ištar whose gender role is blurred and who, for this reason, hardly were definable as a *tappā'u* (see below).

Penetrating a *tappā'u* was tantamount to rape and deliberate disgrace, because the penetrating partner effects a change in the other partner's role from active (male) to passive (female). Castration as a punishment was obviously intended not only to prevent the crime from happening again but also to alter permanently the role of the man who committed it. Many other texts take the raping of a man as an ultimate act of disgrace, which illuminates the role-division presumed in the *Laws*. The following example of an extremely scurrilous malediction of another male person is from Neo-Assyrian times:[33]

> Bel-eṭir, raped captive, doubly so, runny-eyed one, doubly so, squint-eyed man, doubly so, son of Ibâ . . . lowly family, servant of a dead god, house whose star has disappeared from the heavens, slave girl, woman, slave of the woman Baliḫitu, 'beard' of raped girls. . . . He swore by Bel: "I will not let go until I have fornicated *(niāku)* with him!"

This sort of curse could be included even in treaties between the Assyrian king and minor kings. The following example comes from the treaty between Aššur-nerari V, the king of Assyria, and Mati'-ilu, the king of Arpad:[34]

> If Mati'-ilu sins against this treaty with Aššur-nerari, king of Assyria, may Mati'-ilu become a prostitute *(ḫarimtu)*, his soldiers women,

may they receive [a gift] in the square of their cities like any prostitutes, may one country push them to the next; may Matiʾ-ilu's (sex) life be that of a mule, his wives extremely old; may Ištar, the goddess of men, the lady of women, take away their bow, bring them to shame, and make them bitterly weep: "Woe, we have sinned against the treaty of Aššur-nerari, king of Assyria."

This paragraph belongs to the curses that would fall on Matiʾ-ilu if he should break the stipulations of the treaty. Notably, the one who puts it into effect is Ištar, the goddess of love and war; it is in her power even to change a person's gender (see below). The curses of the treaty do not mention rape but threaten to make a man a prostitute, which amounts to the same effect. To become sexually subject to another man meant to be forced into the role of a prostitute. Rape to a rapist demonstrates power and superiority and is motivated by something other than sexual lust: sexual subjection involves surrender and loss of power.

The above examples show that the Assyrians distinguished between active and passive roles in sexual acts. The passive role generally belonged to the woman, as indicated in the juxtaposing of §§18 and 19 in the *Middle Assyrian Laws*. If a man assumed the passive role, he was acting as a woman and his whole masculinity became questionable.[35] The one who perpetrated sex with a man was to be brought to the same position and given the same permanent shame, according to §20.

A sexual act between two males is occasionally mentioned also in omen texts, perhaps more as a theoretical possibility than as a concrete act. Interpretation of omens had developed in ancient Mesopotamia as a discipline that aimed to understand the prevailing reality (and even the future) not only from the stars of the sky and the entrails of the sacrificial animals but also from dreams and unusual occurrences. Among the dream omens, there are some erotically interpreted dreams in which a man dreams of a male sexual partner.[36] Some more apparent hints come from the omen series *Šumma ālu*, which includes a series of thirty-eight omens that deal with various aspects of sexual life.[37] Four of them involve a male-to-male act:[38]

If a man copulates (*iṭeḫḫe*) with his equal (*meḫrīšu*) from
   the rear, he becomes the leader among his peers and brothers.
If a man copulates with an assinnu, a hard destiny will leave him (?).[39]
If a man copulates with a *gerseqqû*, terrors will possess him for a
   whole year but then they will leave him.
If a man copulates with a house-born slave (*dušmu*), a hard destiny
   will befall on him.

These omens display no moral reservations regarding a male-to-male homosexual act that is explicitly defined as anal intercourse. And yet, there is here not a particularly positive attitude either; in general, omens are not moral codes. Note that the first omen is as unambiguously positive as the last two are negative, the criterion being the social position of the passive party. Because the phenomena listed in the omens are exceptional rather than widespread, sexual contacts between men cannot have been considered common, even if there are a few random texts that suggest that men could sometimes find amusement in taking the role of the opposite sex.[40]

The omens classify four different cases according to the social position of the man who is the object of "approaching" (*teḫû*), that is, anal intercourse. In the first incident, the man is described as a *meḫru*, as equal to the one who acts. This omen—recalling the *Interpretation of Dreams*, written centuries later by Artemidorus[41]—appears in a positive light, as it promises the penetrating partner power over his peers. This is at odds with the *Middle Assyrian Law*'s decree for a severe punishment for the same action. However, both texts assume the thought recognized already in the struggle between Horus and Seth: to become subjected to (anal) intercourse by another man involves shame and suppression; to do the same to another brings superiority and power. The law obviously was designed to prevent this power from being executed in concrete terms.

In bad omens the partners of the sexual contact are less equal, yet they belong to the same social environment. A slave born at home (*dušmu*) is comparable to a family member. The term *gerseqqû* usually translates as "courtier,"[42] and, in the present context possibly meaning the assistant or the "right hand" of the one who acts.[43] Whether the omen related to *assinnu* is positive or negative is linguistically unclear. Nonetheless, *assinnu* is without doubt the most important character in the omen list related to this study.

DEVOTEES OF IŠTAR: *ASSINNU, KURGARRÛ, KULU'U*

Mesopotamian sources from Sumerian times down to the Neo-Assyrian period know *assinnu* as belonging to the worship of Ištar.[44] Characteristic of the people under this designation is their wavering gender; the corresponding cuneiform sign is UR.SAL which means a "man-woman."[45] A similar role and duty in the worship of Ištar belongs also to the people called *kurgarrû* (KUR.GAR.RA) and *kulu'u*. The androgynous gender role is denoted by the word *sinnišānu*, "man-woman," and this role also belongs to the lamentation priests called *kalû*.[46]

The duty of these cult functionaries had a mythological foundation in the myth about *Inanna's* (in Assyrian, *Ištar's*) *Descent to the Underworld*, which is known in a longer Sumerian and a shorter Assyrian version.[47] In both versions, the Lady has to thank an *assinnu* or a *kurgarrû* for her rescue from the underworld. According to the myth, she wants to have dominion over the kingdom of the dead and for that reason descends to the "Great Below" which is ruled by her sister Ereškigal. She gets there but is condemned to death by the infuriated Ereškigal. When the body of Inanna has hung on a nail in the wall three days and three nights, her female Grand Vizier, Ninšubur, (Ass. Papsukkal) sets up laments for her death and looks for help from the god Enki (Ass. Ea) to get her Lady out from the underworld.

According to the Sumerian version, Enki creates from the "dirt under his fingernails" a *kurgarrû* and a *kalaturru*[48] and furnishes them with the plant and water of life, sending them into the Underworld to revive Inanna and to bring her back.[49] The *kurgarrû* and *kalaturru* meet Ereškigal when she is in pain and show her sympathy which makes her grateful enough to offer them impressive gifts, but all they want is the body of Inanna which they then receive. They revive Inanna by sprinkling her with the water and plant of life and finally escort her back to the world of the living.

In the Assyrian version Ea creates an *assinnu* called Aṣûšu-namir:[50]

Ea, in the wisdom of his heart, created a person *(zikru)*.
He created Aṣûšu-namir, the *assinnu*.
"Come, Aṣûšu-namir, set your face towards the gate of the
    Underworld.
The seven gates of the Underworld shall be opened before you.
Ereškigal shall look at you and be glad to see you.
When she is relaxed, her mood will lighten.
Get her to swear the oath by the great gods.
Raise your head, pay attention to the waterskin,[51]
Saying: "Hey, my lady, let them give me the waterskin, that I may
    drink water from it."

In other words, the *assinnu* effects an infatuation in Ereškigal, and their encounter is erotically loaded. Ereškigal can do nothing but agree to awaken Ištar and let her leave the underworld, although she finally curses bitterly the *assinnu* who made her do this.

Ištar's/Inanna's Descent to the Underworld demonstrates how closely the *assinnu* and the *kurgarrû* are connected with this goddess and her cult. The myth was the *hieros logos*, the mythological justification of their existence and activity. They constituted a connecting link between myth and everyday life which provided them with a divine power, effective in curing diseases, for example. Interpreted against the background of the myth, falling ill meant that Ištar, after being released from the underworld, was looking for someone to replace her as a victim of the demons of the world of the dead. Since *assinnu* had freed Ištar from there, his presence could also release the sick person from the power of the demons:[52]

> Let the *assinnu* stand by and take my sickness away. Let him make
> the sickness that seized me to disappear through the window.

The *assinnu*s and his colleagues were specially trained for their role[53]
which was a permanent one, as demonstrated in the words *assinnūtu*, *kurgarrûtu* and *kuluʾūtu*, all of which indicate a status or condition. Their
duties consisted of ecstatic dance, music, and plays.[54] They dressed up and
wore make-up like a woman,[55] and they carried masks and weapons,
which they used in their dances and plays.[56] According to the Neo-
Sumerian *Hymn of Iddin-Dagan to Inanna*, they played an important role
in the New Year's festival in which they proceeded before Inanna dressed
as androgynes.[57] Their most typical gear was a spindle (*pilaqqu*)—a feminine symbol—but they also bore swords and other cutting weapons.[58] In
addition to the battle dances, these may also have been used for a ritual
self-torture, the purpose of which was to participate in the dolor of their
Lady.[59]

In addition to—rather, as a part of—their cultic function, the role of
the *assinnu*s also had a sexual aspect which was connected with their
ambiguous gender. Ištar desires them as her sex partners.[60] They are often
mentioned in the same context as Ištar's female devotees, whose role also
was sexually colored (*ḥarimtu, kezertu, sekretu, šamḥatu*, etc.),[61] and they
have duties in rituals concerning sex-related matters.[62] The *assinnu, kurgarrû*, and *kuluʾu* were men (or, eventually, hermaphrodites) by birth as
regards their physiology, but their appearance either was feminine or had
both male and female characteristics. This was due to their devotion to Ištar
who herself had "transformed their masculinity into femininity."[63]

> Uruk is the dwelling of Anu and Ištar, a city of *kezertu*s, *šamḥatu*s and
> *ḥarimtu*s whom Ištar deprived of husbands and kept in her power . . .
>
> (a city of) *kurgarrû*s and *assinnu*s whose masculinity Ištar changed
> into femininity to strike horror into the people—the bearers of dag-
> gers, razors, pruning-knives and flint blades who frequently do abom-
> inable acts[64] to please the heart of Ištar.

Transgressing conventional gender boundaries was typical of Ištar herself
whose astronomical manifestation was Venus, which is masculine as a
morning star but feminine as an evening star.[65] Accordingly, Ištar was worshipped not only as a charming, erotic woman—harlot or virgin—but also
as a bearded soldier.[66] As the goddess of war and love, she assumed both
male and female roles; these were represented in a ritual in which men
played the role of a woman and women the role of a man.[67] It was within
Ištar's power to cause the same effect on people, a result of which was a
human being like an *assinnu*—a person whose gender role the goddess had

changed permanently. These people symbolized the androgynous aspect of the goddess not only occasionally in rituals but in their whole life, action, and self-presentation, and thus separated them from conventional gender identity and lifestyle. Ištar did this in order to "keep people in fear," which meant not only religious veneration[68] but also real fear of her puissance, as the following curse reveals:[69]

> If somebody moves this monument, removes my name from it and writes his own name instead, covers it with dust, throws it in the water, burns it with fire, or hides it in a secret place, let Ištar transform his masculinity into femininity and put him tied in front of the feet of his enemy.

The exact way of transforming masculinity into femininity is not known, and it is debated whether it was simply a matter of a transvestite role-play or whether the new gender status was enforced also physically. Depriving the masculinity and the symbolism of cutting weapons may imply that *assinnu*s were castrated,[70] even if there is no unambiguous evidence for this. Whether castrated or not, their irrevocably changed gender role and identity largely fulfilled the same function as did the life subsequent to castration. In Mesopotamia castration was a token of a lifelong devotion to the goddess, which in any case was the fate of an *assinnu*. Mesopotamian society included a considerable number of eunuchs (*ša-rēši*) who frequently rose to high civil and military offices.[71] Even if their duties were not limited to the cultic sphere, the eunuchs had a special relationship with Ištar. This is revealed, for example, in seals of eunuchs, which typically portray their bearers worshipping the goddess or her symbol.[72]

Relevant comparison material comes from later documents from Syria and Asia Minor, and subsequently also from Rome, where the emasculated priests, called *galli*,[73] had a significant role in the worship of the Syrian goddess Atargatis as well as in that of Cybele—the Mediterranean Great Mother (*mētēr megalē, magna mater*), assimilated with Atargatis and analogous to Ištar—and her consort, Attis.[74] Lucian (third century C.E.), for example, relates that these people were called "holy." The *galli* had castrated themselves to dedicate themselves to the Syrian goddess for the rest of their lives; by doing this they shared the fate of Attis, who died of self-emasculation and subsequently rose from the dead. According to Lucian, the self-castration of the *galli* took place in a fervid trance in the middle of the crowd; a young man in an ecstatic state grabbed a sword, slashed with it his testicles and walked from house to house holding them in his hand and receiving women's clothes and accessories from the people.[75] The result was a "third gender," which separated the *galli* irrevocably from ordinary people's lifestyle and, later on, became the target of the promoters of the Christian faith, who saw in them the most outrageous example of the corruptness of the pagan world.[76]

The *galli* not only had in common with the *assinnu*s and *kurgarrû*s a feminine character and dedication to their goddess, but their duties also were similar: ritual shout, song, dance, and self-mutilation.[77] Because of their emasculation they could never return to the past but had to live the rest of their lives in a permanently changed social and gender role: "*Galli* are made of men but never men from *galli*."[78] A historical connection between the Mesopotamian *assinnu* and the Syrian *galli* is easily imaginable, in spite of a chronological gap of a few centuries. Because this has not yet been the subject of serious investigation, however, it is difficult to say much about the cultural continuum between these two phenomena. In any case, as demonstrated by Will Roscoe,[79] the similarities are manifold and profound. The parallels suggest more than a mere coincidence, as do the cultural and geographical factors.[80]

The unusual gender role of the *assinnu* and his peers was not everybody's cup of tea but reserved to few chosen ones. Their role was institutionalized and socially approved, because it was divinely decreed and they lived under the aegis of Ištar. They, like the female devotees of Ištar, did things on her behalf that exceeded social conventions and were forbidden to ordinary people, and their activities were a part of the divinely sanctioned world order.[81] As human beings, however, they seem to have engendered demonic abhorrence in others; few would have envied their lot. The fearful respect they provoked is to be sought in their otherness, their position between myth and reality, and their divine-demonic ability to transgress boundaries.[82]

That the *kurgarrû* is said to have been created from the dirt under Enki's nails indicates that his social position was marginal. One of the *Šumma ālu* omens considers it a threat if the *kurgarrû*s become numerous.[83] Moreover, Ereškigal's curse on the *assinnu* who forced her to release Ištar's body is hardly flattering:[84]

Come, Aṣûšu-namir, I shall curse you with a great curse.
I shall decree for you a fate that shall never be forgotten.
Bread from the city's ploughs shall be your food,
The city drains shall be your only drinking place,
The shade of the city wall your only standing place,
The drunkard and the thirsty shall slap your cheek.

This curse, similar to that of Enkidu against the harlot Šamhat,[85] may reflect the general station of *assinnu* and *kurgarrû*. Although their role in the cult of Ištar was indisputable, they were strange and despised among "ordinary" people. Already the cuneiform sign UR.SAL ("dog/man-woman") is demeaning. The *kurgarrû* is connected with a broken jar,[86] which may allude to his eventual castration and highlight his "brokenness" in people's eyes. A man could be ridiculed by saying, "He is a *kulu'u* and not a man."[87] The same attitude is manifested in some less friendly sayings:

> When the *kalû* wiped his anus, (he said): "I must not excite that which belongs to my lady Inanna."[88]

> When a *sinnišānu* entered the brothel (*bīt aštammi*), he raised his hands and said: "My hire goes to the promoter (*anzinnu*). You are wealth (*mešrû*), I am half (*mešlu*).[89]

The second saying raises the question whether sexual contacts with men belonged to the duties of *assinnu*, *kurgarrû*, and *kulu'u*. The text implies that they had something to do in the taverns near the temple (ÉŠ.DAM, *bīt aštammi*), which, at least since the Old Babylonian times, were associated with alcohol and sex, and where Ištar herself was said to pick up men.[90] As noted earlier, *assinnu* and his colleagues are often mentioned in connection with women associated with sex. However, there is no mention of them having intercourse with women (Ištar and Ereškigal are goddesses and thus special cases). Instead, the "plough" (*epinnu*) mentioned in Ereškigal's curse is a euphemism for penis,[91] and the "bread from the city's ploughs" thus refers to sexual contact with a man (this is assumed also in the *Šumma ālu* omen discussed above). Even though sexual contact with an *assinnu* is regarded as an omen and hence as rather exceptional, another *Šumma ālu* omen takes it for granted: the omen is that a man will have a need to have sex with another man, "like an *assinnu*."[92] An astrological omen describes the role of the *kurgarrû* as follows: "Men take into their houses *kurgarrû*s who deliver them children."[93] Even as an ironic exaggeration, this is an utmost expression of the sexual reputation of the *kurgarrû*'s duties.

All things considered, it is possible that an *assinnu* occasionally served as the passive partner in a sexual contact with a man. How often and under what circumstances this happened is difficult to determine; the *bīt aštammi* suggests itself as a convenient environment. To have this kind of sexual contact was not an expression of sexual orientation of either of the partners, nor had it anything to do with insuring fertility. It meant a connection to the goddess who had visited the underworld and had been released from there. Sexual contact with a person whose whole life was devoted to the goddess was tantamount to union with the goddess herself.[94]

To return to the *Epic of Gilgameš* and its word-plays: An alert reader may have already noticed that Enkidu, like Asûšu-namir, was called *zikru*. He also had the designations "sky-bolt" (*kiṣru*) and "ax" (*ḫaṣṣinnu*), which typified him in the dream and lament of Gilgameš.[95] These words have an immediate association with the words *sekertu*, *kezretu* and *assinnu*—all devotees of Ištar with a role that has a sexual aspect. These verbal associations are obviously deliberate in the epic, which has many parallels with *Inanna's/Ištar's Descent to the Underworld*. The roles of Enkidu and *assinnu* do not appear at first glance to be similar, but they have certain things in common: a divinely sanctioned "otherness" compared with ordinary people, the role of the guarding of life, lifelong devotion and, finally, also of their appearance demonstrating the sexual aspect of "otherness."

Enkidu's role, however, does not entail passive asexuality but rather an emphasized masculinity. If *assinnu* and his peers played the passive part in sexual contacts with men, they did it as a part of their role as mediators between myth and reality. Another question is whether, behind this role, they were homosexually oriented, and whether this can be solved in retrospect.[96] The sources from Mesopotamia do not speak of their sexual orientation but of their role and identity as devotees of Ištar. This role was characteristically asexual rather than homosexual.

In the final analysis, then, it is misleading to affiliate *assinnu* with our concept of homosexuality. After all, there is no way of knowing whether they were sexually oriented toward men—or, if emasculated, toward anybody. We can speculate, of course, that men who looked for this role already had a homosexual orientation or a transvestite need and were better able to express it in that role[97] or that they felt themselves otherwise incapable of fulfilling the requirements of the male role in a patriarchal society. Their gender identity certainly changed along with the change of gender role and after the eventual castration. Moreover, there may have been persons among them who were transsexual or born intersexed.[98] All this is beyond modern knowledge. Unknown also is whether anyone was forced to become an *assinnu*, for instance, as a mythologically justified means to control overpopulation.[99] In any case we have to do with gender-blending not as an impulse but as a role that required education and lifelong dedication, not simply an act of cross-dressing or castration.[100]

In an attempt to find a cross-cultural point of comparison in the modern world, references have been made, among others, to the Siberian and Central Asian shamans, who engage in ecstatic rituals and androgynous attire.[101] A better present-day comparison, however, are the Indian hijras, "a religious community of men who dress and act like women and whose culture centers on the worship of Bahuchara Mata, one of the many versions of the Mother Goddess worshipped throughout India."[102] The hijras function as an institutionalized "third gender" as "neither men nor women."[103] This role is explained mythologically as the work of two gods, Arjuna and Pandava,[104] and it can be traced back as far as the early first millennium C.E.[105] Thus, although their sexual appearance and behavior differ from the norms of the majority, they are accepted as divine exceptions and their character carries magical, even intimidating power. They dress like women, perform after the birth of a child, at weddings, and at temple festivals,[106] and engage in a passive sexual role as prostitutes.[107] Most of them undergo an emasculation ritual,[108] and some are even born intersexed.[109]

We may conclude that the Mesopotamian interpretation of sex and gender differed from the modern understanding. That the central characteristic of the servants of Ištar is androgynous with a feminine emphasis and a passive sexual role reflects a conception of role that is similar to what we find in the *Middle Assyrian Laws*. The distinction between active and passive partners appears to have been a central factor in sexual relationships, both in heterosexual and homosexual contacts. A person's role was connected with one's physical sex, which was not conceptualized as irrevocably fixed and strictly binary. The Mesopotamians were ready to manipulate human biology when a role so necessitated, either as a punishment or a destiny ordered by the goddess. In the light of Mesopotamian texts, then, it may be more appropriate to speak of the male roles changed into either female roles or into a "third gender" or genderless roles in which the line between masculinity and femininity vacillates or disappears altogether. Homoeroticism appears only as a side-issue within this role formation. Cross-dressing and castration—today understood as entirely independent of homosexuality—belong to the same context. In Mesopotamian society they were characteristics of the "otherness" of the persons involved, a part of the constructing of the intermediate gender role.

Finally, I turn to the sole Mesopotamian text that, at least in theory, considers also homosexual love. An almanac of incantations enumerates categories of incantations with the corresponding heavenly constellation, among them "love of a man for a woman" (Libra), "love of a woman for a man" (Pisces), and "love of a man for a man" (Scorpio).[110] What this means in concrete terms is extremely difficult to determine. The analogy of love between two males with that between man and woman suggests that something other than an intimate friendship after the model of Gilgameš and Enkidu is intended. The word "love" (*râmu*) has an emotional connotation, but the analogy to heterosexual love also implies a role differentiation inseparable from gender, which is evident also from the fact that the love of a man for a woman and that of a woman for a man are distinct categories. The text, therefore, can scarcely be interpreted as referring to mutual love between two equal and consenting male citizens.

The most noteworthy aspect of this text may be that, unlike later Roman astrological texts,[111] it does not mention the love of a woman for a woman even as a logical theoretical option. In fact, the copious source material mentions women's mutual sexual relations virtually not at all. The topic surfaces only in one omen, in which it is parallel to such a curiosity as the copulation of two male dogs.[112] The silence may be due to the connection of same-sex eroticism with the dynamics of active and passive sexual roles. Because only the passive role was attributed to females, their mutual eroticism did not presuppose the change from an active to a passive role, and the "honor" of males—which in terms of morality was the main concern—was not threatened. Lesbian practices, therefore, if there were such, may have been of little or no concern for patriarchal Mesopotamian society.[113]

All in all, the limited sources require caution in speaking about homoeroticism in the ancient Near East. The problem cannot be by-passed by simply assuming that it was either an unknown or an irrelevant matter. The sources discussed above demonstrate that same-sex erotic interaction was not unheard-of, and that moral reservations could be expressed about it.[114] Disapproved of in private life, male-to-male sexual conduct may have been permissible in specific contexts, with particular persons whose gender role was not that of an ordinary male. It is questionable, however, whether the modern concept of "homosexuality" is applicable in this context.

3

THE HEBREW BIBLE

THE HOLINESS CODE: LEVITICUS 18:22 AND 20:13

The writings of the Hebrew Bible include only two sentences of the Torah and a few narratives that relate in some way to the issue of homoeroticism. This allows us to learn little about same-sex erotic interaction in the actual lives of the ancient Israelites. To judge from the scarcity of the sources, it could be claimed that it was a rather rare phenomenon in ancient Israel, but we cannot be sure what the virtual silence of the sources really implies. The focus of this chapter, therefore, cannot be "homoeroticism in ancient Israel" but rather attitudes toward same-sex conduct reflected in each text as well as the literary, ideological, and, possibly, historical raison d'être of these attitudes.

The Torah includes two prohibitions of sexual acts between males, Lev. 18:22 and 20:13, the latter of which prescribes the death penalty for them. These verses are part of the so-called Holiness Code (Leviticus 17–26), the historical background of the present form of which is the post-exilic Jewish community.[1] The correlation between the Holiness Code and the concrete implementation of its provisions are ambiguous; in no way can the code be likened to civil or criminal law in the modern sense of the word. It might instead be compared to a catechism that teaches Israelites, especially adult males,[2] God's will and, accordingly, the rules for just behavior. To what extent its sentences were actually put into practice remains unknown. At least the death penalty cannot realistically have been implemented to the extent that the law dictates.[3]

Leviticus 18 and 20 consist of similar prohibitions and commands; chapter 20 was probably formed on the basis of chapter 18.[4] The wording in the sentences regarding sexual contact between men is analogous. Their form, however, is consistent with the respective context: chapter 18 gives direct prohibitions, whereas chapter 20 consists of circumstantial case-by-case commands with corresponding punishments. While Leviticus 18:22 seems to be directed to only one of the participants in the sexual act, Leviticus 20:13 mentions both, declaring both parties guilty of the offense and imposing the maximum punishment for both:[5]

> You shall not lie with a man as with a woman *(miškĕbê ʾiššâ)*: that is an abomination *(tôʿēbâ)*. (Lev. 18:22, NEB)

> If a man has intercourse with a man as with a woman *(miškĕbê ʾiššâ)*, they both commit an abomination *(tôʿēbâ)*. They shall be put to death; their blood shall be on their own heads. (Lev. 20:13, NEB)

Both texts belong to a long list of sexual transgressions. Male same-sex contact is listed along with incest and other forbidden sexual relations between family members (18:6–18; 20:11–14, 17, 19–21), intercourse during menstruation (18:19; 20:18), adultery (18:20; 20:10), and sex with animals (18:23; 20:15–16). In the same context, child sacrifice to Molech (18:21; 20:1–5) and the calling of ghosts and spirits (only 20:6, 27) are forbidden. Typical of the Holiness Code, both collections are framed with a didactic sermon (18:1–5, 24–30; 20:7–8, 22–26) that urges people to follow the commandments of Yahweh and to separate themselves from other nations and their practices:

> You shall not do as they do in Egypt where you once dwelt, nor shall you do as they do in the land of Canaan to which I am bringing you; you shall not conform to their institutions. . . .
> Observe my charge, therefore, and follow none of the abominable institutions customary before your time; do not make yourselves unclean with them. I am the LORD your God. (Lev. 18:3, 30, NEB)

> You shall not conform to the institutions of the nations whom I am driving out before you: they did all these things and I abhorred them. . . .
> You shall be holy to me, because I the LORD am holy. I have made a clear separation between you and the heathen, that you may belong to me. (Lev. 20:23, 26, NEB)

The Holiness Code thus presents sexual activity between two men as an example of the repulsive ways of the so-called Canaanites, which the people of Yahweh should avoid. In its present literary context these prohibitions (as the whole Holiness Code) belong to the Torah received by Moses on Mount Sinai and are thus linked with the future risks involved with the seizing of the land of Canaan. From a social-historical perspective, however, the composition belongs to the postexilic situation of the fifth century B.C.E., when the early Jewish community attempted to detach itself from outsiders and struggled with its own identity against the tradition of the neighboring cultures (which, paradoxically enough, themselves formed a part of Israel's own heritage).

"Abomination" is a translation of the Hebrew word *tôʿēbâ*. It is a general term with strongly negative connotations and which denotes a transgression of a divinely sanctioned boundary. It is often used in connection with different, usually not fully defined customs of a mostly cultic nature affiliated with worship of foreign gods.[6] This has raised the question of the kind of homoeroticism envisioned in the Holiness Code. Both the term *tôʿēbâ* as well as the sermon that frames the commands has led many commentators to think that same-sex sexual acts between men were attached to a cult that involved sexual activity and that was practiced by the neighboring people (and, implicitly, by the Israelites themselves!).[7] The surprising reference to child sacrifice in a list of sexual offenses strengthens the impression that there is a cultic background. It has been commonly assumed, therefore, that the writers of the Holiness Code associated homoerotic behavior with sex connected to cultic practices.

Scholars have often referred to "sacred prostitution" affiliated with the so-called "fertility cult,"[8] but both terms are loaded with problems. Once declared a "historiographic myth" belonging to the "Golden Bough" school of historical anthropology,[9] the idea of sacred prostitution has been invalidated also because the term reflects post-Victorian attitudes towards sexuality, represents patriarchal power of definition, and stimulates anachronistic perceptions.[10]

The term "prostitution" suggests that sexual intercourse was the main function and source of income for certain cult functionaries, which is not at all certain.[11] It is doubtful that the same term can be used for professional commercial sexual services and for "sacred" sex-related practices that may have taken place in specific, strictly controlled religious-social circumstances[12] and that fulfilled specific purposes.[13] Some scholars still talk about "prostitution" without hesitation in both cases, while others use the word in a more qualified meaning, excluding the aspect of cultic eroticism.

A connection between homoeroticism and "sacred sex" has been found in the following prohibitions of Deuteronomy (Deut. 23:18–19 [Eng. 23:17–18]):

> There shall be no *qĕdēšâ* among the daughters of Israel, nor shall there be a *qādēš* among the sons of Israel. You shall not bring a fee of a harlot *(zônâ)* or the pay of a "dog" into the house of the LORD your God in fulfillment of any vow, for both of them are abominable to the LORD your God. (my translation)

This passage not only suggests that vows were paid by means of prostitution and that the temple profited from that practice,[14] but it also makes parallel the normal Hebrew word for a female practicing illicit sex, *zônâ*, and *qĕdēšâ* and *qādēš*, the female and male equivalents of a "consecrated person." Usually this is interpreted as meaning sacred prostitutes (thus such translations as "temple-prostitute" and "sodomite") or at least cult professionals who were devoted to the deity and had sexual functions. This interpretation, however, has been challenged as derived directly from the construct of "sacred prostitution."

Every biblical occurrence of *qĕdēšâ* is in some way or another paralleled with *zônâ* (Gen. 38:21–22; Deut. 23:19; Hos. 4:14). This gives an apparent sexual connotation to the word and indicates that at least the writers of these particular texts have consciously associated *qĕdēšâ* with prostitution.[15] The male counterpart, *qādēš* (Deut. 23:18; 1 Kings 14:24; 22:47; pl. *qĕdēšîm* 1 Kings 15:12; 2 Kings 23:7; Job 36:14) is more ambiguous,[16] and the only reference that links it to prostitution or sexual behavior come from the above quoted verses of the Deuteronomy. The *qĕdēšîm* are said to have existed in Israel already at the time of Rehoboam, son of Solomon (1 Kings 14:24). His grandson Asa, however, put a stop to this activity (1 Kings 15:12), and what Asa left unfinished, his son, Jehoshaphat, completed (1 Kings 22:47). After a couple of hundreds of years the issue reemerged: the great religious reform of Josiah in the 620s B.C.E. destroyed "the houses of *qĕdēšîm* in the temple of Yahweh," where women wove vestments for the goddess Asherah (2 Kings 23:7).

These texts give no concrete historical idea of the role and activity of the *qĕdēšîm*, because they date from a considerably later period than their setting, and they almost without exception represent Deuteronomistic polemics against disapproved cultic practices.[17] Echoing the Holiness Code, these cult customs are defined as the abominable acts of other people (*tôʿēbâ* 1 Kings 14:24), without detailed specification. Because of the meager evidence, there is little if anything to learn about the actual activities of the *qĕdēšîm*, let alone of the allegedly homoerotic aspect of their role. It may be that the whole issue is literary rather than historical; Phyllis A. Bird has recently argued that the biblical *qĕdēšîm* are a literary creation rather than historical fact.[18] In any case, it deserves to be considered what the Deuteronomistic writers had in their minds when they used this particular word.

Extrabiblical evidence has often been sought for help in determining the social-religious setting of the *qĕdēšîm*. There are linguistic equivalents derived from the root *qdš*, which mean "consecrated" persons—those dedicated to serve a temple or a deity, for example, the Akkadian *qadištu*, which is a class of female devotees with a disputed sexual function,[19] and the Ugaritic *qdš*, which also belongs to cult personnel, albeit without a clearly defined role or connection to sexual acts.[20] These parallels do not shed much light on the position of the *qĕdēšîm* in concrete terms, let alone their alleged role as male cult prostitutes. It may be more important to note that the Syrian *galli* who were devoted to the Mother Goddess and who had a similar "third gender" role as the Mesopotamian *assinnu*s, were called "holy" (*hieroi*).[21]

The payment of the *qādēš* is called "dogs-money" (*mĕḥîr keleb*) in Deut. 23:19, which suggests that they were derisively called dogs. In this context scholars often refer to a Phoenician wage-list from the temple of Astarte, which also mentions the "dogs" (*klbm*). The list does not specify their duties; their alleged sexual role has been inferred mainly from the verses of Deuteronomy.[22] Less attention has been paid to the fact that the cuneiform compound UR.SAL, "dog/man-woman," signifies the devotees of Ištar, the *assinnu*s, ambiguous with respect both to gender and sex.

If the *qĕdēšîm*, whether historical or imaginary, that the Deuteronomistic historians had in their minds can be compared with *assinnu*s, *kurgarrû*s, and the Syrian *galli*, then it is possible that the *qĕdēšîm* were thought of as men who had assumed an unusual gender role and thereby expressed their lifelong dedication to a deity.[23] In practice this could have meant transvestism or castration, possibly also homosexual or heterosexual sexual acts.[24] All this speculation is based on circumstantial evidence. Also, the extent to which the Deuteronomist writers were aware of the existence of *assinnu*s and the like is not known, even though complete ignorance of them is less likely after the strong cultural impact Assyria had on Syria-Palestine during the eighth and seventh centuries B.C.E.

The conclusion that Leviticus 18:22 and 20:13 refer solely to homosexual acts related to cultic practices, therefore, leaves many things hanging in the air. In the present textual context of these prohibitions, this conclusion would easily suggest itself, but the scanty evidence for the practice of cultic homoeroticism makes it appear enigmatic at best. Therefore it is unwarranted to restrict the prohibitions to a sacred sphere, and it is also unrealistic to assume that the Holiness Code would assess other kinds of homoeroticism as more acceptable. Individual commands must be considered also apart from their framework. Even if sexual offenses in the present context are linked with foreign cult customs, the commands themselves may be older and may have originated separately from the cultic context.

Alternate explanations for the condemning of male same-sex conduct in the Holiness Code should therefore be sought. Two interacting explanations suggest themselves: ancient sociosexual taboos, on the one hand, and the identity struggle of the Israelite community, on the other. Both of these explanations are closely affiliated with the societal interpretation of gender.

Internalized taboos, originating from archaic times, had an influence on all kinds of restrictions of sexual life, much more so and earlier than the need to reject alien cults.[25] The taboos functioned to protect society and its members. Social identity in an ancient Israelite community did not proceed from the perspective of fulfillment of one's individual rights or preferences but from that of the protection of society. Things that shook the internal peace of the community and the coherence of its basic structures, interfered with the vital growth of population, or caused problems in family relationships were hazardous to a society that had to struggle constantly for its very existence. Sexual activity had to be regulated so as to strengthen the identity of society, its integrity and growth. This necessitated taboo-protected gender roles and, accordingly, rules for sexual customs, the transgression of which was perceived as fatal. It was not just procreation, important in itself, that was protected[26] (the concern about "wasted seed" is clearly of later origin)[27] but the entire gendered structure of the community, in which each and everyone was expected to conform to his or her gender role and social class.[28]

The basic ideology of the Holiness Code centers on cultic purity, guaranteed by separation from other nations. This had an influence on the later Jewish thinking of homoerotic practices as specifically pagan, a result of idolatry. The regulations of the Holiness Code portray Israel's neighbors as perverse people. Although even scholarly literature still quite carelessly includes comments on the perversions of the Canaanites, extant historical sources do not present Israel's neighboring people as any more obscene or corrupt than the Israelites themselves. Actually, other ancient Near Eastern sources display sexual ethics, taboos, and gender roles basically similar to those in the Hebrew Bible, with certain qualifications that serve the ends of the identity struggle. Linking sexual transgressions with the customs of neighboring peoples must be seen as an attempt to protect the identity of the early Jewish community, which had to maintain a distinctive profile in order to survive.[29] Their strategy was an absolute separation from other nations (*gôyîm*). This was the goal both in worship, where all customs considered foreign were abandoned, and in civil life—for instance, by demanding the annulment of marriages with people of foreign origin (Ezra 9–10; Neh. 13:23–31; Mal. 2:11–12).

In Deuteronomy there are a few gender-related commandments that can readily be seen against the background of ancient Near Eastern worship, notably those in which eunuchs are excluded from the people of Yahweh (Deut. 23:2; cf. Isa. 56:3–5!) and the prohibition of cross-dressing (Deut. 22:5). The prohibition of the mixing of gender roles, implied in the banning of cross-dressing, may have belonged to the same context as the rules of prohibited mixtures in general—whether a taboo or not[30]—that appear not only a few lines later in Deuteronomy (22:9–11) but also in the Holiness Code (Lev. 19:19).[31] In the case of cross-dressing, the motivation of prohibiting the mixture had clear socioreligious aspects. In postexilic Israel, at the latest, one of the distinctive features of the people of Yahweh that separated them from others seems to have been that there was no compromise of gender identification: a "third gender" role comparable to that of the Mesopotamian or Syrian devotees of the goddesses was an impossible option for an Israelite. Both castration and cross-dressing were signs of devotion to an alien deity, special traits of gender identification and gender roles that were associated with cultures forbidden to the Israelites.[32] Mixing gender roles was not a matter of personal preference or orientation but a cultural signifier. This doubtless was a factor in the later Jewish abhorrence of homoeroticism.

It can thus be plausibly maintained that regulations about same-sex acts and other gender-related commandments involved the linking of an ancient taboo with society's strategy to survive. The specific way of regulating sexual relationships in pursuing these life-determining goals was the result of an *interpretation of gender* as a fundamental factor of social structure and control. This, finally, leads us to the issue of gender roles and their transgression as a basis for the understanding of Leviticus 18:22 and 20:13.

The Holiness Code never mentions women's homoeroticism, nor does the Hebrew Bible anywhere. It has been suggested the male legislators lived so much apart from women's concrete lives that they were not in a position to understand this aspect of women's sexuality.[33] But there may be another explanation, one that arises from the patriarchal nature of society and helps to understand also men's same-sex sexual relations. A woman could not lose her manly honor, and it was inconceivable to think of woman in an active role in a sexual act. Neither did female same-sex activity challenge male domination.[34] Therefore, women's homoeroticism did not pose nearly as big a problem as that of men.

Ancient Near Eastern sources in general are concerned with gender roles and their corresponding sexual practices, not with expressing a particular sexual orientation. Mesopotamian sources touch upon same-sex activity whenever a man's sexual appearance, in one way or the other, becomes feminized. The *Middle Assyrian Laws* decree that a man who has raped another man be raped and castrated himself; his manly honor was to be disgraced, and he was to lose his masculinity and change his gender identity permanently. Also the Holiness Code interprets sexual contact between two men as a confusion of gender roles: "Do not lie with a man as you lie with a woman." This formulation, especially against the patriarchal societal background, already exhibits linguistically the division of masculine (active) and feminine (passive) roles, a distinction familiar already from the Mesopotamian texts. Whenever the verb *šākab* describes sexual intercourse, its subject is a man, except in two cases.[35] Sexual contact had two aspects bound to the roles: "lying of a woman" from a male point of view (*miškĕbê ʾiššâ* [only pl.] Lev. 18:22; 20:13) and "lying of a man" from a female perspective (*miškab zākār* Num. 31:17–18, 35; Judg. 21:11–12).[36] A sexual contact between two men mirrored the male and female roles: it was the former from the active partner's point of view and the latter from that of the passive partner. Since these expressions, in practical terms, hardly can indicate anything else but penetration or being penetrated, the concrete point of reference in Leviticus 18:22 and 20:13 seems to be male anal intercourse, which caused the other partner to acquiesce in a female role. Hence, the penetrated partner lost his manly honor, gender boundaries were transgressed, and gender roles mixed.[37] All this constituted a *tôʿēbâ*. Unlike the sources from classical antiquity, the Holiness Code does not even make any difference with regard to the social status of the partners; the prohibition concerns all male couplings even if the social stratification is otherwise widely recognized in its proscriptions.[38]

The societal interpretation of gender roles, combined with ancient taboos and the societal survival strategy, caused "lying with a man" to have a tremendously negative symbolic value. Like castration or cross-dressing, male anal intercourse manifested a forbidden mixture, a mixture of gender roles,[39] which, according to the theology of the Holiness Code, was considered a *tôʿēbâ*, a transgression of boundaries that constituted a threat to the purity of the land. Nevertheless, it was the act that was condemned, not same-sex desire, the existence of which is not even acknowledged.

In summary:

1. The prohibition of sexual contact between males in the Holiness Code in Leviticus 18:22 and 20:13 is done in a context of a polemic against a non-Israelite cult. Because the records of cultic homoeroticism are scanty and not unequivocal, however, historical description of this context is difficult.

2. The strategy of postexilic Israelites to maintain their distinct identity by, among other ways, separating from others strengthened the already existing taboos and social standards regarding sexual behavior and gender roles, banning, for instance, castration, cross-dressing, and male same-sex behavior; it was not simply the "objective" facts of physiology that established gender identity.[40]

3. Israel shared with its cultural environment an understanding of sexual life as an interaction between active masculine and passive feminine gender roles. This interaction was the cornerstone of gender identity, but the concept of sexual orientation was unknown. Sexual contact between two men was prohibited because the passive party assumed the role of a woman and his manly honor was thus disgraced.

SODOM: GENESIS 19:1–11

The biblical story of the destruction of Sodom begins by the terebinths of Mamre. Three men visit Abraham in his tent—God and God's two companions in human form. After Abraham has entertained his guests, they leave for Sodom to find out whether the people of Sodom had committed all the evil they were accused of. Outcry about the sinfulness of the city had reached God's ears (Gen. 18:21). When God's two companions arrive at Sodom in the evening (God is not with them), they meet Lot, who invites them to stay overnight at his house. The guests at first politely decline the offer but eventually accept Lot's invitation and enjoy with him a generous meal.

Meanwhile a group of men of Sodom gather in front of Lot's house and threateningly demand that Lot bring his guests out: "'Bring them out,' they shouted, 'so that we can have intercourse with them'" (Gen. 19:5). Lot, unwilling to let the mob get his guests offers his two daughters instead. The men of Sodom, however, are not interested in his daughters and actually get aggravated when Lot, a nonnative, tries to bargain with them: "'Out of our way! This man has come and settled here as an alien, and does he now take it upon himself to judge us? We will treat you worse than them'" (Gen. 19:9). The men attack Lot and try to break into his house, but the divine guests strike the men with blindness and rescue their host. They transfer Lot and his family away from the city before God lets "fire and brimstone" rain down (Gen. 19:24).

This narrative is reminiscent of a genre also known elsewhere, with the theme of the virtue of hospitality. A deity in human appearance arrives in a hostile city, where some friendly citizen gives him lodging. Later on, the guest thanks his host by rescuing him from the devastation of the city.[41] The story comes from the so-called Yahwist, who has used an older story that follows a similar formula. The Yahwist has supplemented the basic text, for instance, in verses 5, 7–8, and his description of the people of Sodom makes their behavior sound especially rude.[42] The date of the Yahwist is debated; here it is sufficient to conclude that the Yahwist's text originates from the exilic period at the latest and that it employs older sources.[43]

In English, the term "sodomy" (verb, "sodomize") has traditionally had the meaning "homosexual (anal) intercourse," and a "sodomite" is a person who engages in it. This semantic development, which has its roots in the translations of the Bible,[44] reveals the one aspect of the story of Sodom the Christian tradition has underscored. For thousands of years readers have been offended most by the fact that the men of Sodom tried to attack the male visitors. Thus, the core of the Sodomites' sin, as it has been conceived, was "homosexuality." This has naturally had a massive impact on how homosexuals have been treated in Western countries, where the Bible has been read as the moral guideline. For this reason, it is important to examine the role same-sex interaction plays in the story of Sodom and in its early interpretations.

The men of Sodom wanted to lie with, that is, rape Lot's male visitors, according to our text. The root meaning of the verb used here, *yādaʿ*, is "to know." In the Yahwist's texts or in its sources the verb is used as an expression for intercourse (e.g., Gen. 4:1, 17, 25; 24:16; 38:26). Because the verb indisputably signifies sexual "knowing" only in about a dozen of its almost one thousand occurrences,[45] D. Sherwin Bailey has rejected the verb's sexual connotation in the story of Sodom. Bailey argues that sexual intercourse is usually expressed with a verb *šākab*, "to lie, to sleep." Therefore, the verb *yādaʿ* would imply nothing more than that the men of Sodom wanted to "get to know" Lot's guests, to find out who they were, to examine their credentials.[46] In this interpretation, the story of Sodom says not a word about a (homo)sexual rape attempt.

Although Bailey's interpretation of the verb *yādaʿ* has met with some approval,[47] the theory ultimately fails. Lot tries to appease the troublemakers by offering them his daughters (Gen. 19:8), saying that his daughters are virgins, or, as the Hebrew text puts it, "they do not know of man" (*lōʾ yādĕʿû ʾîš*).[48] In this context the verb *yādaʿ* is used with an explicitly sexual meaning—only a couple of lines after the previous similar use. Bailey's explanation, that the daughters were only a tempting bribe to calm down the mob,[49] may be correct but this does not alter the sexual connotation of *yādaʿ*.

Distressed, Lot then offers the men his own daughters as a better object to satisfy their urge to rape. This violent trade of women makes a contemporary reader shiver, but the Yahwist commends Lot: he considered hospitality so sacred that he was willing to sacrifice even his daughters' virginity for the sake of his guests. This was a significant cost; in the narrator's world, when a daughter lost her virginity, it put her father to shame (Deut. 22:20–21).

The sexual aspect of the actions of the men of Sodom cannot be gainsaid. The Yahwist has deliberately placed the sexual offense before the catastrophe—as he did earlier, in the context of the flood: the final offense that impelled God to let the waters flow was when the sons of gods mingled with the daughters of the people (Gen. 6:1–7).[50]

Surprisingly, the earliest interpretations of the story of Sodom do not emphasize the sexual nature of the sin of Sodom. This sexual theme reappears only in a story of a rape in Gibeah (Judg. 19). Elsewhere in the Hebrew Bible, frequent references to Sodom are made, always as a negative warning.[51] Whenever the sins of the Sodomites are described in more detail, it is their pride, xenophobia, and judicial offenses that get the main attention. For instance, in Ezek. 16:49:

This was the iniquity (or: pride *gā'ôn*) of your sister Sodom: she and her daughters had pride of wealth and food in plenty, comfort and ease, and yet she never helped the poor and wretched. (NEB)

That the sexual aspect is missing here is important to observe also because the same chapter describes the behavior of "sister" Jerusalem with clearly pornographic expressions.[52] There is no need to assume that the authors of the prophetic writings would not have heard about the attempted sexual assault in Sodom; rather, they never considered it an issue of sexual immorality in its own right but "a synecdoche for the violence of the Sodomites."[53]

The Apocrypha mentions Sodom only a couple of times, with no clear references to same-sex activity.[54] Sirach, after mentioning the giants of Gen. 6:4, tells how Lot was horrified by their arrogance (16:8);[55] it is possible that Sirach links the giants and Lot because of a sexual association. The Wisdom of Solomon accuses the people of Sodom of abandoning wisdom and of "leaving their lives as a monument to folly" (10:6–8). The xenophobia of the Sodomites becomes apparent elsewhere in the Wisdom of Solomon, where the text compares the people of Sodom with the Egyptians (19:13–15 [Eng. 14–17]):

There had been others [Sodomites] who refused to welcome strangers when they came to them, but these made slaves of guests who were their benefactors. There is indeed a judgement awaiting those who treated foreigners as enemies; but these, after a festal welcome, oppressed with hard labour men who had earlier shared their rights. They were struck with blindness also, like the men at the door of the one good man . . . (NEB)

References in the New Testament follow the same course.[56] Sodom is the symbol of corruption, and its fate is a warning example for people waiting for the end time. In the Jesus tradition the sin of Sodom is an example of the lack of hospitality. In a passage originally belonging to the so called Q source (Q refers to the words of Jesus common to Matthew and Luke but not in Mark), Jesus, when giving travel instructions, speaks of cities that do not receive his disciples: "I tell you, it will be more bearable for Sodom on the great day than for that town" (Luke 10:12, cf. Matt. 10:15).[57]

Already in the Hellenistic age, however, (homo)sexual aspects were observed in the sin of Sodom. There are traits of this kind of interpretation in the pseudepigraphal literature, and Josephus and Philo represent it explicitly (see below pp. 93–95). The Qur'an also assumes this line of interpretation.[58]

Nevertheless, it is relevant to ask why the earliest references to Sodom did not especially emphasize the sexual aspect of its sin, even though the narrative seems to give good reason to do so. The answer lies in the story itself: The attempted homosexual rape is not the main theme in the story. The Sodomites' behavior is characterized by excessive arrogance, xenophobia, and contempt of hospitality. The transgression of Sodom is particularly grave because it offends God's emissaries and thus God. Abraham's (18:1–5) and Lot's (19:1–3) exemplary hospitality are the opposite of the outrageous behavior of the Sodomites.[59]

This is the background for understanding the Sodomite men's rape attempt. George R. Edwards got to the heart of the matter by defining the Sodomite's activity as phallic aggression generated by xenophobic arrogance.[60]

In a patriarchal society manly honor largely is equivalent to human value, to offend which is a grave shame. Gang rape of a man has always been an extreme means to disgrace one's enemies and put them in their place. Its purpose is to disgrace one's manly honor, to reduce one to a woman's role, which inevitably has a homoerotic aspect. It is not a matter of exercising one's homosexual orientation or looking for erotic pleasure but simply of protecting or threatening one's masculinity. Rape—homosexual or heterosexual—is the ultimate means of subjugation and domination, the reverse side of which is the fear of being raped.[61]

Even today, gang rape is an extreme way to humiliate another man. Literature, films, and life itself give abundant evidence of this. Homosexual rape has been a traditional way of establishing the relation with captured enemies and foes.[62] Anthropological material offers numerous examples of how those regarded as soft, strangers, newcomers, or travelers have been sexually disgraced by people of their own sex, including forced anal intercourse.[63] A Greek picture on a red-figure oinochoe portrays the victory of Athens by the river Eurymedon in 460 B.C.E.[64] In the picture, a man dressed in Persian fashion is half bent down, looking terrified, trying to reject his attacker. A Greek is approaching him, holding his erected penis in his hand, ready to embarrass his defeated enemy completely. The picture includes a text: "I am Eurymedon. I have bent down."[65] It proclaims to the Athenians of the time their real virility in contrast to the "sissy" Persians.[66] Also the Egyptian myth of the power struggle between Horus and Seth, discussed above, as well as Assyrian legal and omen texts depict the act of forcing another man to have sex as a way of asserting one's supremacy.

Priapus, a god of Phrygian origin whose portraits are dominated by his enormous penis, was one of the phallic symbols with which the Greeks and Romans repelled strangers in the Hellenistic age. His statue often guarded the Greeks' houses and gardens, his penis ready to confront the potential intruders.[67] In Rome, the Priapic figure was perceived as a personified phallus, the symbol of a threatening male. This imagery of phallic aggression found its expression in the large collection of Priapic poetry (*Carmina*

Priapea),[68] in which the phallus is an effective weapon; both men and women could become its victims.[69]

Modern interpreters of the story of Sodom may thus have erred in speculating about the homosexual motives of the Sodomite men. There is no need to assume that Lot's guests would have been handsome young men for whom the Sodomite men felt erotic attraction.[70] The men were motivated not to satisfy their sexual lust but to show their supremacy and power over the guests—and ultimately over Lot himself, a resident alien to whom a lesson was to be taught about the place of a foreigner in the city of Sodom. Lot's daughters, therefore, were not a satisfactory substitute.[71] The story centers on the attempt to disgrace the guests, not the homoerotic means of doing it—which, of course, is condemned as part of the bad behavior of the Sodomite scoundrels.

The extent to which the Sodom narrative is relevant to the issue of "homosexuality" depends on the question whether same-sex rape should be seen as an aspect of it. This is a modern problem that is not inherent in the narrative itself. It is, therefore, misleading to speak of the "author's antagonism towards homosexuality" or claim that "he condemns homosexuality." Homoeroticism appears in the story of Sodom only as one aspect of hostile sexual aggression toward strangers. Other than that, the Yahwist's attitude towards same-sex interaction remains unknown.

GIBEAH: JUDGES 19

"In those days when no king ruled in Israel"—so begins the story of Judges 19—it happened that a certain Levite, who lived in the hill country of Ephraim, stopped at the Benjaminite town of Gibeah. He was accompanied by his (anonymous) wife of secondary rank,[72] whom he had recaptured from her refuge in Bethlehem at her father's house. The Gibeahites were unfriendly toward travelers; only by late evening did an old man accommodate them. The man, also from the hill country of Ephraim, invited them to his house and showed them great hospitality. But then suddenly something horrible happened:

> While they were enjoying themselves, some of the worst scoundrels in the town surrounded the house, hurling themselves against the door and shouting to the old man who owned the house, "Bring out the man who has gone into our house, for us to have intercourse *(yāda')* with him." (19:22, NEB)

The old man wanted to protect his guest and offered his own daughter and his guest's wife instead. When this did not appease the scoundrels, the Levite gave his wife up to the men, who then fell on her sexually *(yāda')* and "assaulted and abused her all night till the morning" (19:25). The woman died of her injuries, and the incident led to a war between the Benjaminites and other tribes of Israel (Judg. 20–21).

There is so much correspondence between the stories in Genesis 19:1–11 and Judges 19 that the latter actually sounds like a repetition of the former. The following common features are striking:[73] (1) The city is unfriendly toward visitors. (2) The guests are prepared to spend a night in the streets, but there is one friendly man in the city who shows them hospitality. (3) The friendly host is not a native in the town. (4) The house comes to be surrounded by aggressive men from the city. (5) The men demand that the guest or guests come out, because they want to have sex (*yādaʿ*) with him or them. (6) The host is horrified by this demand: "Please, dear men, do not commit such an evil deed!"[74] (7) Virgin daughters are offered as a substitute. (8) The hostility of the people of the city and the hospitality of the man are juxtaposed. Both stories are preceded by an experience of special hospitality (Abraham in Gen. 18:1–5; the father of the Levite's wife in Judg. 19:3–10).

The story of Gibeah does not mention Sodom, nor do later interpretations generally link these two stories together. Josephus, who associates the behavior of the Sodomites with Greek pederasty (*Ant.* 1:200), does not mention anything equivalent in this context (*Ant.* 5:143–148);[75] the first writer to notice the parallel seems to be Pseudo-Philo, in approximately the first century B.C.E.[76] The many similarities, however, raise the question whether the literary history of the story of Gibeah is connected with that of the story of Sodom. The considerable number of links between the texts makes a literary dependence possible, but it is difficult to determine which story has literary priority. This problem cannot be solved simply by a comparison of the two stories, because the dates and mutual relationship of the Yahwist and the Deuteronomistic history, to which the stories belong, are heavily debated questions that go far beyond the scope of the present study.[77]

If there is a literary dependence of Judges 19 on Genesis 19, as is assumed more often than not,[78] then the story of the fate of the Levite's wife is itself an additional example of how the Sodomites' xenophobic offense against the honor of a male guest and his host has been interpreted. The men of Gibeah are represented as "homosexuals" no more than the men of Sodom.[79] Judges 19 involves a homoerotic aspect (the verb *yādaʿ* and the corresponding intended action) almost in the same form and place as in the story of Sodom. The main difference between the stories is that in Judges 19 a rape actually takes place—a rape not of the Levite but of his nameless wife.[80] This focuses the attention on the question of gender and power, a theme equally dominant in the story of Sodom.[81]

The main cause for offense in the story of Gibeah is the heterosexual assault on the Levite's wife. Perhaps not surprisingly, no later interpreter of the story, ancient or modern, has condemned heterosexual behavior because of this text, although it is structurally equivalent to the story of Sodom, which has been used to condemn homosexuality. The interpreters apparently consider the rape of a woman, condemnable as such, to be less outrageous than that of a man, because it involves a form of sexual assault in which the boundaries of gender roles are not transgressed. The subordinate status of the woman is taken for granted in the story; she is given no voice and she is handed to the rapists on the unilateral decision of her husband.[82] Moreover, even in the deadly sexual assault on the woman, it is really the Levite's honor that is at stake. He (and through him also his host) is the ultimate object of the defaming act of the men of Gibeah; the narrative shows this by making the men intend to rape him in the first place. Even if "only" his wife is abused physically, his socially defined male role, including his control over his wife, is severely challenged; thus, he is raped by proxy, through the rape of his wife.[83] Also his host, the old man, is defamed as not being able to protect the honor of his guest and thus fulfill the demands of hospitality.

The narrator depicts the dishonored Levite not as an innocent victim but as a coward. The Levite of the story does not even mention the fact that he also almost got raped and that he himself handed his wife over to the brutes (20:4–7) and thus initiated a chain of events that almost lead to the annihilation of the tribe of Benjamin. Thus, the Levite's manly honor is challenged not only by the men of Gibeah but also by the narrator, who uses this horrifying incident as an example of the anarchy that allegedly prevailed in Israel before the monarchy was established. Judges 19 is a part of a larger collection of narratives (Judges 17–21), which has been positioned as a kind of link between the stories of the "judges" and of the kings as leaders of Israel. Within this macrocontext, the narrative serves as an example of the corruption of Israel without a proper government. "No such thing has ever happened or been seen before" since the days when the Israelites left Egypt (19:30). This and many other misdeeds occur during the period when "there was no king in Israel and every man did what was right in his own eyes" (17:6; 21:25). The condition of anarchy called for change, and soon a prophet was born in the hills of Ephraim, Samuel (1 Sam. 1), who restored order and prepared the way for the first king of Israel, Saul (1 Sam. 8–12). All things considered, the stories at the end of the book of Judges are positioned to serve as the background and rationale for monarchy, which is consistent with the first Deuteronomist historian's (DtrH) positive attitude toward the Davidic monarchy in Israel.[84] It is also possible that the pattern of the Yahwist (cf. Gen. 6:1–7; 19:1–11) influenced the decision to present a sexual offense as a culmination of events leading to a dramatic turn, this time to civil war.

HAM AND NOAH: GENESIS 9:20–27

According to the Bible, all humankind has descended from Noah and his three sons, who were saved from the flood. Noah's sons, Shem, Ham, and Japheth, are the ancestors of different nations that are grouped so that Shem is the ancestor of the Israelites and Arameans; Ham of the Canaanites, Egyptians, and Nubians; and Japheth of the Greeks and the people of Asia Minor (Gen. 10). Before the genealogical account begins, however, a dramatic incident is narrated (Gen. 9:20–25):

> Noah, a man of the soil, began the planting of vineyards. He drank some of the wine, became drunk and lay naked inside his tent. When Ham, father of Canaan, saw his father naked, he told his two brothers outside. So Shem and Japheth took a cloak, put it on their shoulders and walked backwards, and so covered their father's naked body; their faces turned the other way, so that they did not see their father naked. When Noah woke from his drunken sleep, he learnt what his youngest son had done to him, and said, "Cursed be Canaan, slave of slaves shall he be to his brothers." (NEB)

A reader might wonder why Ham's apparently innocent behavior brings about such a bitter curse—and on his son! After all, the Bible, with no trace of moralizing, later tells how Lot's daughters get their father drunk and make him impregnate them in order to have descendants (Gen. 19:31–38). "Seeing" Noah's "nakedness" (his genitals) obviously is an expurgated expression for something that the narrator wishes not to put into words. According to the Holiness Code it is shameful and punishable for a man to take his sister as his wife and for them to "see one another naked." According to the Hebrew expression, "the man has revealed the nakedness of his sister" and deserves punishment (Lev. 20:17; cf. vv. 18,19). Both seeing nudity (*rā'â 'erwâ*) and revealing it (*gālâ 'erwâ*) are, without a doubt, circumlocutions for sexual intercourse, as many translations (the NEB, among others) actually put it. Thus, interpreting the euphemism, one can assume that Ham did something more than just get a glimpse of his naked father.[85] The text says that Noah, once sober, "learned what his youngest son had *done* to him (*'āśâ lô*)" (9:24), probably implying an act where Ham is the assaulting partner.[86] To this may be added that "uncovering the nakedness" of a woman also connotes the man's jurisdiction over the woman's sexual function.[87] By analogy, what Ham did can be interpreted as taking jurisdiction over what normally is a female sexual function—putting his father in a woman's sexual role.

The story sets Ham's deed against Shem's and Japheth's respectful behavior toward Noah: they take care not to see his nudity in any way. Shem, the ancestor of the Israelites, then stands morally higher than Ham, the ancestor of the Canaanites. The text appears to be written by the Yahwist, and its actual ambition is to curse Canaan and to reduce his descendants to the class of slaves. For this purpose, Ham is relegated to the status of the youngest son, in contrast with the order mentioned elsewhere (Gen. 7:13; 9:18; 10:1). The Yahwist's motivation is understandable in light of the assertion that Ham's descendants include both the Egyptians and the Canaanites. The former put the Israelites into slavery while the latter inhabited the promised land. It may be that the Yahwist wanted to criticize the dominance of Egypt—or his contemporary oppressors—and reverse the role of master and slave.[88]

What did the Yahwist take to be Ham's motivation? Apparently Ham aspired to dominance among post-flood humanity and attempted to show his superiority by disgracing his father sexually. In this sense the case of Ham and Noah is reminiscent of the Egyptian myth of the power struggle between the gods Seth and Horus, and it brings to mind also the Mesopotamian omen that promises power to a man who unites with another man. From this same attitude arise also the attempts of the men of Sodom and Gibeah to show who is master in the house. If Noah's disgrace involves incest, it does not speak of Ham's homosexual orientation but his hunger for power.

DAVID AND JONATHAN:
1 SAMUEL 18–20; 2 SAMUEL 1:26

A few passages of the Hebrew Bible have occasionally been used as biblical arguments for a positive attitude toward homoeroticism, notably those that describe the friendship of David and Jonathan in a way that easily generates a homoerotic association in the eyes of a modern reader. How is the relationship between the two young men portrayed in the Deuteronomistic history?

The episodes about David and Jonathan belong to the story of David's ascent to power, which is commonly regarded as one of the sources of the Deuteronomistic history, and to its later additions.[89] Jonathan is the son of Saul, the first king of Israel; he becomes friendly with David in undefined circumstances:

> That same day, when Saul had finished talking with David, he kept
> him and would not let him return any more to his father's house, for
> he saw that Jonathan had given his heart to David and had grown to
> love him as himself. So Jonathan and David made a solemn compact
> because they loved the other as dearly as himself. And Jonathan
> stripped off the cloak he was wearing and his tunic, and gave them to
> David, together with his sword, his bow, and his belt. (1 Sam. 18:1–4,
> NEB)

David is impressively successful in the war against the Philistines.
Therefore Saul, who has taken David into his care, begins to fear and be
jealous of the young man he had taken under his protection (18:5–16).
Finally Saul attempts to get David out of the way by getting him killed. For
this purpose Saul offers his daughter to David to marry, if David would
bring him one hundred foreskins of the Philistines as a dowry; Saul's intent
is to get David into the hands of the enemy. David, however, returns, alive,
with the required foreskins and wins Michal as his wife, a woman who
loves David and later would rescue him from Saul's attempt at murder
(18:17–29; 19:9–17). Jonathan, also, who is very fond of David, ends up
rescuing him and talks his father out of his plan to kill David (19:1–8).

Because of Saul's persecution, David finds it better to hide and learns
from Jonathan about Saul's intentions. Jonathan does not want to believe
that Saul, without telling him, would harbor thoughts of killing David, but
David alleges that Saul knows about their friendship and therefore keeps
his undertakings hidden from Jonathan. The two men connive to find out
more about Saul's intentions and swear to each other eternal friendship,
which would encompass both families. So "Jonathan pledged himself
afresh to David because of his love for him, for he loved him as himself"
(20:16–17).[90]

The men execute their scheme. The next day and the day following,
David misses the meal of the new moon. When Saul inquires about the reason for his absence, Jonathan answers that he had given David permission
to attend a family celebration in Bethlehem. This infuriates Saul, who roars
(20:30):

> You son of a crooked and unfaithful mother! You have made friends
> with the son of Jesse only to bring shame on yourself and dishonour
> on your mother; I see how it will be. (NEB)

Jonathan is so offended by his father's words that he leaves the table
without eating a bite. The next day he goes with his servant boy outside the
city and, by shooting an arrow according to their plan, informs David, who
is hiding, of Saul's murderous attempts. Then he lets his servant go. The
episode ends with a heartbreaking farewell (20:41–42).[91]

When the boy had gone, David got up from behind the mound and bowed humbly three times. Then they kissed one another and shed tears together, until David's grief was even greater than Jonathan's. (NEB)

David spends the following years in the mountains and in Philistine cities, hiding from Saul, accompanied by a group of runaways (22:2). Once more he meets Jonathan in the mountains of Judah and makes with him a solemn compact (23:16–18).[92] After this, David and Jonathan will not meet again. Finally, Saul and his three sons are killed in a battle against the Philistines (1 Samuel 31). When David learns of this, he laments for Jonathan:

How are the men of war fallen, fallen on the field! O Jonathan, laid low in death! I grieve for you, Jonathan my brother; dear and delightful you were to me; your love (*'ahābâ*) for me was wonderful, surpassing the love (*'ahābâ*) of women. (2 Sam. 1:25–26, NEB)

These texts suggest the nature of the relationship of David and Jonathan, which was extremely close. More than once or twice the text reports how Jonathan loves (*'āhab*) David as himself (*kĕnapšô*). This love, which David calls more wonderful than the love of women, is expressed also physically. When David takes his tender farewell of Jonathan—unlike the parting from his wife—the men kiss each other as they shed tears.

These considerations make it conceivable to interpret David's and Jonathan's relationship as homoerotic.[93] This becomes even more plausible from Saul's exclamation to his son at the dinner table, words that can be translated more accurately than is generally the case: "I know you have chosen the son of Jesse—which is a disgrace to yourself and to the nakedness of your mother!" The "choosing" *bāḥar* indicates a permanent choice and a firm relationship.[94] The mentioning of disgracing one's mother's "nakedness" (*'erwâ*) conveys a negative sexual nuance and gives the impression that Saul saw something indecent in Jonathan's and David's relationship. What could Saul have seen as so shameful in an ordinary friendship of his son and the young man under his care?

Surely the relationship of David and Jonathan can be interpreted also from another perspective than that of homoeroticism.[95] Saul's reaction can be taken as an oriental outburst of rage, which commonly involved obscene language, even to the point of disgracing one's mother.[96] It is also possible to interpret David's and Jonathan's love as an intimate camaraderie of two young soldiers with no sexual involvement. What is striking in this relationship is the equality of the two men. There is not a trace of the distinction, elsewhere so central, between the active and the passive role. Perhaps for this very reason Jonathan's love was for David dearer than woman's love![97] Nothing indicates that David and Jonathan slept together "as one sleeps with a woman." Neither of the men are described as having problems in their heterosexual sex life. David had an abundance of wives and concubines (2 Sam. 5:13) and suffered impotence only as an old man (1 Kings 1:1–4).

The text thus leaves the possible homoerotic associations to the reader's imagination. The story of David and Jonathan was being told at the time when the Holiness Code with its commands and prohibitions of sexual contact between males regulated the Israelites' sexual morality.[98] However, those who added to the story have augmented its intensity by making the men meet one another again and again, restating their love, and reinforcing their friendship with a pledge. This was hardly considered particularly inappropriate, and it raises the question whether a modern reader is more prone than an ancient to find a homoerotic aspect in the story. The editors of the Deuteronomistic history, in spite of the negative attitudes toward homoerotic contact expressed in Leviticus 18:22 and 20:13, found nothing to be censored in the story of the relationship between the two men.[99] Their mutual love was certainly regarded by the editors as faithful and passionate, but evidently without unseemly allusions to forbidden practices. We do not know how far Israelite men could go in expressing their mutual attachment. In any case, emotional and even physical closeness of two males does not seem to concern the editors of the story of David and Jonathan, nor was such a relationship prohibited by Leviticus 18:22 and 20:13.

Modern readers probably see homoeroticism in the story of David and Jonathan more easily than did the ancients. In the contemporary Western world, men's mutual expressions of feelings are more restricted than they were in the biblical world. Men's homosociability[100] apparently was not part of the sexual taboo in the biblical world any more than it is in today's Christian and Islamic cultures around the Mediterranean. Physical expressions of feelings belong to homosocial contacts and seem strange to Western people, who understand the eroticism of gestures in their own way, categorizing people accordingly as homosexuals or heterosexuals.

The relationship of David and Jonathan can be taken as an example of ancient oriental homosociability, which permits even intimate feelings to be expressed. In this sense it can be compared to the love of Achilles and Patroclus (in Homer's *Iliad*) or the love of Gilgameš and Enkidu.[101] In these relationships emotional partnership is emphasized, whereas erotic expressions of love are left in the background and only to be imagined, and there is no distinction between active and passive sexual roles. Perhaps these homosocial relationships, based on love and equality, are more comparable with modern homosexual people's experience of themselves than those texts that explicitly speak of homosexual acts that are aggressive, violent expressions of domination and subjection.

4

CLASSICAL ANTIQUITY

GREEK MALE HOMOEROTICISM

It is common knowledge that a particular form of homoerotic relations between men was a custom maintained for centuries in ancient Greece. Conventionally these relations have been known as *pederasty* (Greek, *paiderastia*, "love for boys"), because their basic form was erotic-social interaction between adult men and boys. For centuries it was accepted behavior in Greek culture, with some variations depending on the time and the place. Pederasty flourished during the classical age before and after Plato (428–347 B.C.E.), but it can be traced already to an earlier time,[1] and it was still practiced at the beginning of the Common Era.

Most of the existing information about the pederasty of the ancient Greeks comes from Athens and Sparta in the classical age, although Crete also had a strong pederastic tradition.[2] Forms of pederasty and people's attitudes toward it varied in different parts of ancient Greece. Plato asserts that Elis and Boeotia accepted pederasty completely, whereas in Ionia some cities did not tolerate it. In Athens the situation was, according to Plato, more "complicated";[3] what this means will be discussed below.

The following overview of pederasty applies expressly to Athens, which offers the most source material. What follows is largely drawn from sources that reflect philosophical, idealistic, and elite attitudes and may not be in complete accordance with common customs and opinions. What is said about pederasty in this chapter, based on the writings of Plato and other philosophers, should therefore be balanced with the analysis and caveats presented in the last part of this chapter.

The origins of pederasty are disputed, and it is not possible here to examine that discussion in detail. Some scholars regard pederasty as a local, exceptional phenomenon brought about by a specific historical-social development[4] or as an expression of a primeval homosexual tradition.[5] Many see it as derived from the male initiation rites of primitive societies.[6] The Greeks themselves justified pederasty from their belief that also their gods practiced it.[7] Greek mythology gives abundant examples of gods' relationships with young male humans. The most famous, perhaps, of these human lovers is Ganymedes, a handsome young man, whom Zeus, in the appearance of an eagle, came to fetch to Olympus with him.[8] Also Iolaos left his father to become Heracles' student and beloved. It would be impossible to list all the lovers of Heracles, claims Plutarch.[9]

Greek pederasty needs to be understood in its own social context. The sexual and social aspects of pederasty were based on a subtle system of sex and gender, different from modern Western cultures. In Greek culture, public homoerotic behavior did not represent a subculture that challenged mainstream values, as often is the case in the modern Western world, but rather resulted from and supported the basic, accepted values of the community. Pederastic relationships were at times an essential part in raising young men to be full-fledged members of society (*agōgē*); those who prefer the terms of Greenberg (1988) would perhaps prefer the expression "transgenerational homosexuality." It was truly a matter of initiation, in which a boy, with the guidance of an adult, would mature into a man in both sexual and social senses.[10] The goal was to maximize men's spiritual capacity and moral virtue (*aretē*).

In Athens pederasty was associated with cultural institutions: the aesthetic ambience of philosophy, music, arts, and physical exercise. Pederasty was a part of elite upbringing, which did not aim at learning the skills for making a living.[11] In Sparta and some other states pederasty had an established connection with military culture. Because "only lovers can die for one another,"[12] military troops were sometimes arranged according to pederastic relations, so that a man and a boy would fight side by side, the older serving as a model and prodding the younger to heroic actions.[13]

It is impossible to understand a pederastic relationship without appreciating its essential role structure and, especially, its distinction of active and passive roles. A boy ("beloved," *erōmenos*) was a passive partner who was taught and brought up by an adult ("lover," *erastēs*), an active partner, not primarily in the art of physical love but also and first of all in a cultural sense.[14] In Sparta, where the community was regarded as more important than the family, an *erastēs* basically fulfilled the tasks that usually belonged to a father.[15]

As a formational relationship, pederasty aimed to develop youths into brave, cultivated men who would defend and serve their community in a manly way. In Plato's view, men should be brought up with regard to the benefit of the state; children belonged more to the state than to their parents.[16] He also said that a city would be easier to rule if its citizens were men living in pederastic relations.[17] The central idea is that love would inspire a man and a boy to compete in courage and virtues; the older one was to serve as an example, to win the admiration of the younger, and to give his protecting affection to the younger. In return, he would gain admiration and sexual satisfaction from the young man:[18]

> When an older lover *(erastēs)* and a young man *(paidika)* come together and each obeys the principle appropriate to him—when the lover realizes that he is justified in doing anything for a loved one who grants him favors, and when the young man understands that he is justified in performing any service for a lover who can make him wise and virtuous—and when the lover is able to help the young man become wise and better, and the young man is eager to be taught and improved by his lover—then, and only then, when these two principles coincide absolutely, is it ever honorable for a young man to accept the lover.

This excerpt well describes the Greek view of ideal pederasty and the conditions for an acceptable pederastic relationship, as Plato depicts them in the *Symposium* and in *Phaedrus*. These works are philosophical dialogues of aristocratic men. The party Plato describes in his *Symposium* takes place at the house of Agathon, where guests give speeches in honor of Eros, with mostly homoerotic themes. Most vocal are Socrates and Pausanias, Agathon's lover, who, on the basis of his behavior, could be considered a homosexual according to our classification. A modern reader would easily identify also Plato's own sexual orientation as predominantly homosexual; he never married and never praises women with erotic expressions.[19] The issue at stake in the dialogues is not homosexuality or sexual orientation, however, but love—*eros* or *philia.* The homoerotic aspect turns out to be inseparable from this theme.

Plato appreciated the pederastic relationship as the noblest of all human relations and as the embodiment of the purest love. As a relationship, it was more intimate and closer than marriage, which lacked its cultural purpose.[20] Authentic pederasty was seen essentially as a part of philosophical upbringing in which the older guided the younger.[21] It represented a Platonic relationship in the most original sense of the word. Plato had in his mind a "higher," nonphysical love in which carnal needs are sublimated to a spiritual level so that the thoughts are turned from an *erōmenos* to love itself.[22] Socrates recounts what priestess Diotima taught him about love:[23]

> That is what it is to go aright, or be lead by another, into the mystery of Love: one goes always upwards for the sake of this Beauty, starting out from beautiful things and using them like rising stairs: from one body to two and from two to all beautiful bodies, then from beau-

tiful bodies to beautiful customs, and from customs to learning beautiful things, and from these lessons he arrives in the end at this lesson,
which is learning of this very Beauty, so that in the end he comes to
know just what it is to be beautiful.

Sexual activity, according to Plato, is necessary for procreation only.
Erotic expressions, or sexual acts, do not necessarily corrupt the pederastic relationship, which without saying involves caresses and physical contact. It cannot be said, thus, that even Plato would describe a pederastic
relationship as nonerotic.[24] By "rendering a service" (*hypourgein*) or by
"granting a favor" (*charizesthai*), a boy gave bodily contact to an older
male as a reward for his teaching.[25] Under the best circumstances, however,
the man and the boy would refrain from excessive expressions of physical
love. By this they could enslave the sources of moral destruction and
release the good powers of virtue.[26] The best example of chaste continence
(*enkrateia*) is Socrates himself, who slept under the same cloak with his
beloved Alcibiades, but did not respond to his attempts of seduction any
more than he would have responded to his own father or brother.[27]
Alcibiades' amazement, however, indicates that Socrates' behavior was
exceptional and would not have occurred under "normal" circumstances.[28]

A lover's responsibility for his lover was permanent and was to lead to
friendship for life. An inferior *erastēs*, whose love was purely physical,
quickly lost his interest in his beloved, whereas a good *erastēs* remained a
friend forever.[29] Also society benefited from this, because the boys who had
had this kind of relationship became the best politicians, men who served
their society.

It belonged to a man's course of life to find himself first as a beloved
and then, after the initiation, as a lover. Naturally, his life was to include
also marriage and sex with a woman. A man could continue his pederastic
relationship throughout his life, but ordinarily that became rare once he got
married.[30] Pederasty thus meant a homoerotic relationship in which the
partners were not, at least in principle, homosexuals in the modern sense of
the word. It would be more appropriate to speak of institutionalized bisexual role behavior, in which the partners expressed their sexuality from quite
a different basis and in ways different from modern concepts of homosexuality.[31] This model of thought and behavior did not distinguish between
people with homosexual, bisexual, or heterosexual orientation, but
assumed that everyone was able to love both genders.[32] Pederasty was not
a biological but a social, pedagogical, and ethical phenomenon, in which
social identity was more central than sexual identity. At the same time, it
also reflected patriarchal society's considerable mistrust of women's spiritual capacity, as will be observed later. All this raises the question whether
the term "homosexuality" is relevant here at all. At the least, as an expres-

sion for sexual orientation, the term does not correspond with the cultural construction of Greek pederasty.[33]

In Greek culture it was understandable for people to fall in love with either of the sexes, and men's public expressions of homoerotic feelings were not seen as inappropriate but rather were tolerated perhaps more than public erotic behavior between a man and a woman. A reason for a man's attraction to a young boy was seen in human nature (*physis*) itself.[34] Plato, in Aristophanes' mouth, gives a mythological rationale for the fact that different people love different sexes. In the beginning there were three kinds of human beings: male, female, and androgynous, and the shape of each human being was completely round with two faces, four hands, two sets of sexual organs, etc. These "human" beings had great ambitions, and they even tried to ascend to heaven to attack the gods. Zeus cut them in two to make them lose their strength. Since then each one has longed for its own other half:[35]

> Each of us, then, is a "matching half" of a human whole, because each was sliced like a flatfish, two out of one, and each of us is always seeking the half that matches him. That's why a man who is split from the double sort (which used to be called "androgynous") runs after women. Many lecherous men have come from this class, and so do the lecherous women who run after men. Women who are split from a woman, however, pay no attention at all to men; they are more oriented towards women, and lesbians (*hetairistriai*) come from this class. People who are split from a male are male-oriented. While they are boys, because they are chips off the male block, they love men and enjoy lying with men and being embraced by men; those are the best of boys and lads, because they are the most manly in their nature. Of course, some say such boys are shameless, but they're lying. It's not because they have no shame that such boys do this, you see, but because they are bold and brave and masculine, they tend to cherish what is like themselves. Do you want me to prove it? Look, these are the only kind of boys who grow up to be politicians. When they're grown men, they are lovers of young men, and they naturally (*physei*) pay no attention to marriage or to making babies, except insofar as they are required by local custom (*nomos*). They, however, are quite satisfied to live their lives with one another unmarried. In every way, then, this sort of man grows up as a lover of young men and a lover of Love, always rejoicing in his own kind.

This myth seems to foreshadow the modern understanding that people from their birth, regardless of their will, are oriented either as heterosexuals or homosexuals. This kind of distinction of sexual orientation, however, is anachronistic and does not correspond even with Plato's model of pederasty;[36] presumably Plato is not even suggesting that the myth represented his own view.[37] Neither do other ancient sources imply that this myth conveys a generally known and accepted anthropological theory. In any case, this myth in the present literary context shows not only that it was taken for granted that different sexual preferences exist but also that an authoritative justification was needed for manifestly homoerotic practices which, after all, were not without moral concern.

General moral ideals and restrictions regarding sexual life applied to homoerotic relations as well. The appropriate use of pleasure (*chrēsis aphrodisiōn*), which included self-control (*enkrateia*) and moderation (*sōphrosynē*), was the philosophical ideal.[38] Plato's *Symposium* lists four virtues of Eros: justice (*dikaiosynē*), rationality (*sōphrosynē*), courageousness (*andreia*), and wisdom (*sophia*).[39] Sexual life was treated by the Greeks in the classical age in both positive and negative terms. Sexuality was regarded as divine and good (*aphrodisia*), on the one hand, and as tainted with shame (*aischrourgia*), on the other. Socrates, according to Xenophon (*c.* 430–357 B.C.E.), considered it a blessing that people, unlike animals, were sexually active throughout the year. Yet it was proper for a husband and a wife to express their erotic desire only in the privacy of their home; it would have been shameful if done in public.[40] Adultery (*moicheia*) was a grave transgression, and adulterers deserved severe punishment.[41] Sometimes adultery was judged as a worse offense even than rape. [42]

Both arts and literature reveal a certain tightening of sexual norms throughout the classical age.[43] Sexual self-control (*enkrateia*) and related training (*askēsis*) were regarded as philosophical ideals. Erotic desire naturally needed to be satisfied, but people were not to indulge in it, and desire itself was not to become a value. All activity that aimed solely to satisfy one's own desires, whether regarding food, wine, sex, or gambling, became a target of philosophical suspicion.[44] Some even argued that one should have sexual intercourse only when the physical pressure grew unbearable and, even then, one was to find satisfaction with the least possible effort, without investing one's soul in it.[45] Obviously these austere ideals of the philosophers surpassed people's everyday behavior. General attitudes toward sexual life hardly diverged much from the modern outlook that sex is an acceptable source of enjoyment as long as certain moral boundaries are not transgressed.

Classical Greek culture, however, differed from modern Western cultures in two interrelated respects: first, regarding the relationship of man and woman, and, second, regarding homoeroticism.

Greek social life was characterized by a separation of the worlds of men and women.[46] Men and boys moved and worked outside their homes; they fought and exercised in gymnasiums and were educated to develop their bodies as well as their spirits. Men's environment was *polis*, society.

Women and girls took care of the household and gave birth to and nurtured children. Their dominion was *oikos*, the household. "For the woman it is more honourable to remain indoors than to be outside; for the man it is more disgraceful to remain indoors than to attend to business outside."[47] Women were not to go around the city; it was the duty of the household slaves to run errands in public places. Houses were divided into men's (*andrōnitis*) and women's (*gynaikonitis*) sides.[48] Women's rooms were situated as far as possible from the streets, preferably upstairs, inaccessible to strangers. Girls' chastity was carefully protected, and young Greeks had scant opportunities to socialize with the opposite sex. The segregation of the sexes should not, however, be exaggerated; women were not cloistered in their houses without social contacts. In general, the strict separation was hardly as thoroughgoing in practice as it was in theory; extant sources document women's activities and employment outside the household.[49] At the least, women and girls from the lower social classes had to maintain social and economical contacts with the outside world—they had no slaves to send on their errands.

What is said above refers to the basic setting throughout the classical age, despite some local differences (for instance, Spartan women were more independent than their Athenian sisters).[50] By the Hellenistic age, with the increasing influence of Rome, the social status and influence of women, at least of those from upper classes, were increased—a development displeasing to certain conservative philosophers.[51]

Although adultery was severely condemned, men were freer in their sexual conduct than women. For example, it was not adultery for a man to have sexual contact with a woman who did not belong to another man's household (no other man's rights were violated). Especially a man of wealth had plenty opportunities to satisfy his sexual needs with the opposite sex.[52] As Demosthenes is claimed to have said:[53]

> Mistresses *(hetairas)* we keep for the sake of pleasure, concubines for the daily care of our bodies, but wives to bear us legitimate children and to be faithful guardians of our households.

Concubines and slaves were a regular part of the household of a wealthy man, and he could use also prostitutes or dancing girls and musicians to entertain himself in festivities.[54] A rich man could also keep a female "companion," a *hetaira*. This custom did not clash with general morality, nor was it regarded as distorting family life, at least in principle.[55] *Hetairas* actually were the most independent (and most famous) women in both the classical and the Hellenistic ages. Best known of them are Neaera,[56] known from the orations of Demosthenes, and Aspasia, whom Socrates himself valued as his teacher in rhetoric.[57] The common constraints of wives did not apply to *hetairas*, who often had both independent wealth and cultivation, both luxuries beyond the reach of ordinary house-wives.[58] Prostitutes and *hetairas* thus formed their own class of women who enjoyed more respect and had a different social status from that of wives, confined to their homes.[59]

Greek literature, even from one and the same author, exhibits both appreciating and demeaning attitudes toward women.[60] Plato, in his utopian works (*State* and *Laws*), frequently emphasizes the equality of men and women, more so than any of his contemporaries. He diverges in this respect especially from Aristotle, his student and contemporary.[61] This, however, does not prevent him from voicing misogynist statements through the words of characters in his dialogues.[62] For his part, Xenophon, in his dia-logue *Oeconomicus*, strongly stresses the significant role of women in tak-ing care of the *oikos* and as productive members of society. This emphasis, however, was still far from the recognition of women's repression and need for liberation. Xenophon presented detailed arguments about the separation of virtues and different areas of activity for woman and man. Governance and activity in the public sphere belonged to men, while women's activity was restricted to the private sphere, and their virtue was obedience.[63]

Greek literature reflects contemporaneous characteristic images of woman and her spiritual capacities. Generally speaking, this literature, written by men, regarded woman as both physically and spiritually weaker than man. Whereas man was "dry," that is, self-possessed and cool, woman was seen as "wet," that is, fickle, superstitious, incapable of persistent reflection, susceptible to emotional outbursts, and so forth. Woman, it was assumed, enjoyed sexual intercourse more than man, which made woman by nature prone to adultery.[64] Perhaps even more revealing than this straightforward negative image of woman are the "complimentary" remarks on woman's abilities in "manly" activities: "By Hera, Ischomachus, you show that your wife has a masculine intelligence (*andrikē dianoia*)."[65] A definite male perspective dominates the sources, which portray women from the point of view of the established philosophy. In practice and in private life, women's status and esteem may have been considerably higher than the male writers suggest.[66]

The Greeks regarded it impossible for a man to have a deep, all-encompassing love relationship with a woman. This was possible only between two men, and such was the aim of pederastic relations. If a man desired the company of a cultivated woman, he could look for a *hetaira* if he could afford it. Marriage was a highly respected institution, and the importance of a wife as the caretaker of the *oikos* was emphasized.[67] Sexually, however, a wife was needed primarily for procreation and the sat-isfaction of the sexual appetite;[68] for the latter purpose the rich could use also concubines. Mutual love between spouses is rarely highlighted, although it doubtlessly existed.[69] Physical eroticism could take both heterosexual and homosexual forms, but spiritual love was something that happened between men only. Without this fact, it is impossible to understand what ancient pederasty was all about.

Pederasty thus was a homoerotic expression of a dominant male culture. It was nothing like the same sex interaction that is seen even today under coercion and need, for instance, in prisons, barracks, or otherwise isolated circumstances where women are lacking (although in Sparta pederasty was an intentional part of the military training).[70] The issue was not whether women were available. The woman—a wife, a slave, or a prostitute—was the obverse of pederasty. With her a man could enjoy as much physical pleasure as he wanted, but spiritual satisfaction and deep friendship were sought elsewhere.

In Greek pederasty the partners were not equal, and it was not intended that they should be. Sexual satisfaction belonged to the active partner, whereas the passive partner was not allowed to have sexual satisfaction or even aspire to it. In its Athenian conception, nevertheless, the relationship was to occur between two free citizens, that is, between two equal men. Unlike later Rome, a pederastic relationship with a slave was not tolerated in Greece.[71] The model of pederastic education excluded slaves, as well as women and foreigners.

A social environment that promoted pederasty was the *gymnasion*; it offered men a place to meet young boys and find their own lovers. In gymnasiums boys performed their physical exercises naked, which doubtlessly eroticized the atmosphere and made it necessary to limit adult men's access to the training rooms. A young, trained male body represented the ideal of beauty of the time, and the boys with good bodies were naturally the most popular. There are numerous accounts of the stir and flirtation caused by a particularly handsome boy entering a room full of adult men.[72] Because upper class women stayed away from public places, young boys performed the role that in modern culture belongs to models and cover girls.[73] The sources even mention boys' beauty contests.[74] The ideal boy of the early classical age was not slight and feminine but rather athletic.[75] However, already from the end of the classical age, the image of a boy lover changed toward a more feminine direction. This development can be seen both in literature and arts.[76]

For adolescent boys, pederasty offered an alternative to dating girls, which at least among upper class people was virtually impossible.[77] Slave girls were available, but they could not satisfy the boys' need to be loved. Because daughters from good families were unreachable, attention focused on adult young men. This was so not only because girls were not available but also because social mores actively supported pederastic relations. Boys' pederastic relations correlate, in some respect, with adolescents' dating customs in modern Western cultures. By its structure, pederastic courting and dating resembled heterosexual models known from a variety of cultures. In courtship the suitor was put off, and accepted only after long resistance to his advances, thus demonstrating the youth's chastity and how difficult he was to approach.[78] Moral values regarding pederasty are reminiscent of those of today; courtship was allowed as long as one's partner had a good reputation and the couple did not rush into a sexual relationship. Pederastic dating had its advantages: parents did not need to worry about unwanted pregnancy. It was also an advantage if an *erastēs* was a well-known, wealthy, and generous man. Nevertheless, the sexual purity of the boy was a matter of honor and shame, and a pederastic relationship always involved danger in this respect.

Naturally, therefore, parents wanted to control their sons' relationships and tried to protect them from exploitation and suspicious company. A *paidagōgos*, a male slave, was to accompany boys and repel possible molesters on the way to school.[79] Gymnasiums could be kept open only during the daylight hours, and adults were not allowed to participate in boys' physical exercises.[80] Their dance teacher was to be more than forty years old, mature enough not to get excited about the bodies of naked boys.[81]

The age difference between the partners in a pederastic relationship varied, but normally the *erōmenos* was a boy in his puberty, between twelve and seventeen years old, and the *erastēs* was a mature man and normally still single.[82] In Sparta the pederastic upbringing started as the boy reached the age of twelve.[83] At the beginning of the relationship, the boy's awareness of his own sexuality was still in its bud and developed in the relationship.[84] An epigram of Strato reads:[85]

> I delight in the prime of a boy of twelve, but one of thirteen is much more desirable. He who is fourteen is a still sweeter flower of the Loves, and one who is just beginning his fifteenth year is yet more delightful. The sixteenth year is that of the gods, and as for the seventeenth it is not for me, but for Zeus, to seek it. But if one has a desire for those still older, he no longer plays, but now seeks "And answering him back."

The beginning of the growth of the beard may have signified that the boy (*pais*) had matured into a youth (*meirakion* or *neaniskos*) and was ready to shift from the passive to the active role.[86] Once gaining body hair, the boys lost their appeal in the eyes of adult men. The boys who were too choosy were cautioned that their beard could start to grow earlier than they would guess:[87]

Thy beard will come, the last of evils but the greatest, and then thou
shalt know what scarcity of friends is.

There were many exceptions to these rules. For instance, the age difference of the pederastic couple could be quite small: a *neaniskos* could
have a boy just a couple of years younger than himself.[88] And it may not
have been impossible for the same young man simultaneously to be a lover
of a boy younger than himself and a beloved of an older man.[89] However,
people were likely to try to avoid this kind of exceptional relationship.

Marriage did not necessarily mean that men would abandon their boy
lovers, and heterosexual sex life did not end pederastic relations; Socrates,
Pausanias, and Aeschines (see below) are examples of this. Moreover, all
homoerotic relationships were not pederastic; some, like Pausanias's lover,
Agathon, continued in their passive role even as adults.[90] The reverse age
order nevertheless stirred annoyance and scorn; the roles within the same
relationship could not change.[91]

A popular boy could be surrounded by many lovers with good reputation and choose his lover from several rivals. Dramas of jealousy were not
uncommon, as the boys were indeed the objects of competition.[92] It is
revealing that the literature uses hunting metaphors for the pursuit of the
boys—they were literally chased.[93] The gifts the boys received were also
related to hunting metaphors. Those gifts, not valuable in themselves, were
often game animals that served as erotic symbols.[94] Innumerable pictures
portray a man handing a rabbit, fish, or another small animal to a boy as a
token of his affection. The boy in the picture gestures to suggest whether
he finds the gift or its giver pleasing or whether he rejects the flirtation.
Pederasty thus was part of competitive Greek culture for men. A boy with
a good reputation was considered a good catch.[95]

Plato's portrait of pederasty as a training ideal, in which eroticism was
secondary, may be over-idealistic and at odds with ordinary life. The
sources—pottery paintings and literature[96]—demonstrate the strongly
erotic nature of pederastic relations. The subject in the paintings is often
men's erotic encounter or sexual activity. The pictures also illustrate the
difference between the active and passive partners—the cornerstone of the
(homo)sexual relationship—and its different nuances. In some pictures an
adult offers a boy a gift as a symbol of his affection. Another common
scene is an adult touching the face of a boy with his one hand and his genitals with the other.[97]

The vase paintings describe sexual contact either as anal intercourse,
in which the active partner approaches from behind the passive partner,
who is bending down, or as intercourse in which both partners are standing and the active partner bends over the straight-standing passive partner,

rubbing himself between his thighs. In the former position (anal inter-course) also a woman may take the passive role, but the latter (intercrural contact) occurs only between two men. There is a moral distinction between the positions. Anal intercourse subjugates the passive partner both in terms of the position and the mode of penetration. Thus, in addition to pictures, it is used in old comedy, which mocks pederasty. In intercrural contact, however, there is no penetration, nor does the position of the pas-sive partner express subjection. This setting coincides with Platonic ideals of the nature of pederastic eroticism.[98]

In many of the pictures that depict intercrural intercourse, the passive partner is staring off in the distance without seeing the face of the active partner.[99] A woman, however, when facing a man in intercourse, looks the man in the eyes and obviously enjoys the act. This is appropriate for a woman, who was presumed to enjoy sex more than a man. But an honor-able *erōmenos* would not expect any physical pleasure for himself, would not allow himself to be penetrated in any part of his body, and would not subject himself to positions that express subjection, that is, positions proper for women. The ideal attitude is demonstrated also by picturing the passive partner's genital as flaccid even when the active partner has an erection.[100]

There were two kind of boys, it was believed: good boys (*agathoi*), with whom men could develop pederastic relationships, and call boys (*pornoi*), who were used as "one-night stands."[101] A similar difference can be seen between the concepts *erōmenos* and *kinaidos*. Whereas *erōmenos* is an honorable name, with no shameful implication, for the passive part-ner in a pederastic relationship, *kinaidos* carries the stigma of effeminacy and the desire to be penetrated by other men.[102] It was important that an *erōmenos* was protected from being labeled a *kinaidos*.

It was not proper for a decent boy to aspire to sexual satisfaction from a pederastic relationship. His role was to "render a service" (*hypourgein*) or to "grant a favor" (*charizesthai*) to the older male. It would have been shameful for a boy to assume a passive role deliberately, to take money for it, or to show any sexual initiative. If a free man or a boy voluntarily sub-jected himself in this way, under the arbitrary domination (*hybris*)[103] of another man, he identified himself with a woman, slave, prostitute, or for-eigner. A man once fallen into prostitution would lose forever his moral honor in the eyes of other men and would be barred from public office. This happened whether the boy himself had chosen prostitution or had drifted into it unwillingly, through coercion; social consequences out-weighed personal motives. Getting a bad reputation could make one's social status difficult, and the most popular and handsome boys were in the greatest danger in this respect.[104]

The accepted limits of pederastic relations are well documented in a text that dates back to 346 B.C.E. In this text Aeschines demands the death penalty for an Athenian politician called Timarchus, accusing him of having practiced prostitution (*hetairēsis*) in his adolescent years. Aeschines quotes several laws that govern honorable behavior. These quotations clarify how male prostitutes lost their rights to serve in public offices and to participate in citizens' meetings.[105] Prostitution itself was not illegal: prostitutes paid taxes and free citizens were entitled to visit brothels.[106] Male (homosexual) prostitution was accepted in principle as long as a free man did not work as a prostitute or as a pimp.[107] It was essential that a free citizen should not take a role that would lead to subjection to another man. Non-Athenians had nothing to loose, nor did those Athenians who did not regard their citizenship as indispensable.[108] The use of prostitutes as such neither was punishable nor shameful to a free citizen. An active partner broke no moral norms if his behavior was not excessively debauched. But assuming a passive role outside the limits of honorable pederasty meant breaking the rules of society and was thus to be punished. Male and female roles were not to be mingled by putting a boy or another man in the role of a woman.[109]

Aeschines' accusations do not point to pederasty itself. He says that he himself had been and still was (at the age of forty-five) an *erastēs*, that he had written love poems to boys, and that he even had taken part in jealous fights over boys.[110] What is decisive is that the pederastic relationship be decent, the roles of the partners correct, and no money exchanged. Aeschines' speech reveals also the reverse side of the coin: not everybody followed these ideals but acted from less noble motives. Maybe this was in Pausanias's mind in Plato's *Symposium* when he referred to pederasty as a "complex" matter (*poikilos*): pederasty was accepted in a certain ideal form (*nomos*), yet the reality did not always correspond with the ideal and its limits.[111] This "complexity" means that it is difficult to decipher the general values amid the diversity of judgments surrounding homoerotic behavior. Relationships with boys was a delicate issue managed with a subtle moral code.[112] The problem with these relationships was not so much the homoerotic aspects as the boys' honor as freeborn citizens.

ROMAN MALE HOMOEROTICISM

Sources from Republican and early imperial Rome are both historically and culturally closer to the New Testament and other sources of the early church than are Greek documents from the classical age. It is therefore appropriate to examine Rome separately, where the exterior forms of homoeroticism and the moral foundation differ considerably from classical Greek ideals—at least as these are presented by Plato or Xenophon.

Homoerotic behavior was quite common also in Rome. Under certain conditions it was accepted, but it was never such a celebrated institution in Rome as it had been in Athens or Sparta. Homoerotic relationships of famous men like consuls and emperors are well known. Nero's homoerotic behavior could be explained from his frivolousness,[113] but the same cannot be said of such a reputable emperor as Hadrian, who kept a young Greek, Antinous, as his lover and commissioned sculptures of him.[114] It has even been claimed that, of the first fifteen emperors, only Claudius led an exclusively heterosexual life.[115] Of the Roman poets, Catullus especially, but also Virgil, Horace, and, with more reservations, Ovid, wrote bisexual verses that may more or less indicate their actual preferences.[116] Already Plautus (c. 250–184 B.C.E.) employed homoerotic themes in his plays.[117]

Homoerotic relationships between free men, however, were not generally accepted and may have been even prohibited by law. In this context the sources (for instance, Cicero, Suetonius, and Juvenal) usually refer to *Lex Sca(n)tinia*, the exact wording of which has not been preserved. It is not clear, however, whether this law prohibited homoerotic relations of free men as such[118] or same-sex sexual offenses, such as *stuprum cum puero*, raping a freeborn boy.[119] Valerius Maximus also lists sexual offenses, half of which are homosexual and half heterosexual; again, it is not clear that a homoerotic relation itself would have been forbidden—quite the contrary.[120] According to Cicero, to act "as a woman among men and as a man among women" (a condition attributable to the passive partner of a homoerotic relationship) was against good mores (*contra fas*)—an opinion he does not ground on any written law.[121] Cicero, to be sure, claimed that homoeroticism originated in Greece; he deemed that it was born in the gymnasiums where young boys exercised naked (the Romans loathed nakedness).[122] However, Cicero's view is probably based on his learning in classic literature rather than on any particular historical knowledge of the roots of Roman customs.

Prostitution, including male homosexual prostitution, was a common, legal, and tolerated phenomenon in the Roman streets and baths.[123] That male prostitution was legal becomes irrefutably clear from the fact that in the Augustan era male prostitutes, adult men and boys, paid taxes and were even entitled to an annual vacation day on the 26th of April.[124] Homosexual prostitution involved mainly slaves and foreigners. A free Roman citizen was not to become a prostitute; prostitutes, male or female, enjoyed no social respect.

What was common to both Roman and Greek homoeroticism was the basic structure that required an active and a passive partner. As in Greece, this often meant adult men's relationships with young boys (*pueri deli-*

cati). A crucial difference is that in Rome homoerotic relationships normally occurred between a slave and a master.[125] In Plautus's plays, for instance, this is a rule with few exceptions. A slave could be called *puer*, "boy," even as an adult. Slaves could also be freed and patronized by wealthy men with whom they continued to live in a kind of permanent concubinage.[126] In Greece, erotic relations between a slave and a master were considered improper; pederasty was permissible only between free citizens, a practice that was disapproved in Rome, at least in the early years.[127] This reveals the different attitudes of the Greeks and the Romans toward pederasty. The Greek ideal of pederastic upbringing, which aimed at developing good, manly citizens, required that the partners come from the same social class. The Romans did not maintain this pedagogical goal, nor was homoeroticism at any point motivated by social or political reasons. Instead, the sexual dimension of the relationship was more emphasized than in Greece.[128]

To generalize, it is conceivable that Roman homoeroticism was more physical and had more elements of subordination than what the Greek ideal would have condoned. A Roman slave did not enjoy the respect of a Greek *erōmenos*. The Roman ideal of masculinity involved aggression, also in sexual life, as is demonstrated by the Priapic poetry.[129] Sexual activity was a manifestation of virile potency, and penetration was a symbol of masculinity, the expression of male body-language as such. The submissive role of the Greek *erōmenos* would have been contrary to the Roman virtue of virility, which manifested itself in the subordination of slaves to the passive sexual role:[130]

> Losing one's virtue is a crime for the freeborn, a necessity in a slave,
> a duty for the freedman.

Young male slaves in Rome could serve as long-term beloved. In that capacity they always assumed a passive role, in which they had to subject themselves to their masters. Men could practice sex with slaves before getting married, and emotional bonds were not always excluded. However, once married, these relationships became less allowable:[131]

> You are said to find it hard,
> Perfumed bridegroom, to give up
> Smooth-skinned boys, but give them up. . .
> We realize you've only known
> Permitted pleasures: husbands, though
> Have no right to the same pleasures.

The poem of Catullus suggests that getting married required a change in a man's sex life: giving up boys and getting used to a female partner. This did not mean a change of roles, since the man in both phases is represented as the active partner; in any case, marriage required a "process of genital sorting-out"[132] of those who had had a male beloved before marriage. How well the men fulfilled this demand may be doubted to some extent; as far as one can believe the satirists, it was not unusual for a married man to keep a *puer*. This, of course, caused problems for the marital relationship.[133]

For a free Roman citizen the passive role was shameful, as it involved the loss of one's manly honor. In these cases the active partner also was condemned. Attempts to rape a free citizen and to force him into a passive role called forth severe punishment, but also the penetrated had to suffer: for him the rape caused an *infamia*, which meant that he would be struck off the list of "equestrians," the prerequisite of full civil rights.[134] Apparently the rape of a free male citizen sometimes even brought the death penalty to Roman soldiers.[135] If the passive partner, however, was not a free citizen but, for instance, a slave or a prostitute, the active partner was not culpable of any punishable transgression.

In Rome, an essential part of the passive role was a feminine appearance. Horace, for instance, praises beautiful boys and their long, wavy hair, calling them *mollis*, a term that describes girlishness.[136] This kind of role was acceptable also for a young boy, if he was not forced into the relationship and did not do it for money.[137] Certainly the families of free citizens did not regard pederastic relations as desirable and tried to protect their boys from sexual exploitation,[138] especially from becoming a *cinaedus*,[139] a man who permanently, even as an adult, assumed the role of the passive partner, with effeminate mannerisms.[140] For a *cinaedus*, this role implied availability for other men—not necessarily always as the passive party in physical sexual contact, even if this belonged to their role in general.[141] As males by anatomy, the *cinaedi* were physically intact, unlike the *galli*, the emasculated priests of Cybele, who also were associated with promiscuous sexual activity with males.[142] The *cinaedi,* who frequented the public baths, brothels, and private homes, were an urban phenomenon, while the *galli* apparently lived as devotees of the Goddess in their own religious communities, which were not bound to cities.

As in Greece, also in Rome the satirists mocked men who assumed a feminine appearance and passive sexual roles and were, for this reason, permanently stigmatized. Juvenal, for instance,[143] who regarded the Romans' sexual life by and large as perverted and chaotic, belittles with no pity those men who have forsaken their virile roles by feminizing their outlook and behavior.[144] Regardless of its exaggeration, Juvenal's satire (first century C.E.) gives us to understand that during the imperial period the passive male role became increasingly common, and the *cinaedi* formed a subculture with more or less fixed forms of social behavior. This does not mean, however, that the passive role would have gained any more esteem. The stereotype of the effeminate, sexually passive male in different genres of literature illustrates this fact clearly enough.[145]

Even homoerotic relationships of the pederastic kind, in which both parties were free citizens, are not completely missing. They are mostly described by the poets—Martial[146] and Tibullus,[147] for example. In these poems the active partner is always the narrator, the *puer* never. Also Catullus in a number of his poems[148] describes his relationship to Juventius, who was apparently a free young man from a good family.[149] Catullus, however, no more than the other poets, hardly represents especially strict moral norms. Besides, he rebutted sternly, albeit with a humorous tone, his friends' accusations that he himself would have been a *mollis*, that is, in a passive role inappropriate for a virile, adult man:[150]

> I'll bugger you and stuff your gobs.
> Aurelius Kink and Poofter Furius.
> For thinking me, because my verses
> Are rather sissy, not quite decent.
> For the true poet should be chaste
> Himself, his verses need not be.

Both Roman and Greek literary sources usually illustrate the customs and morals of upper class men, whereas they tell hardly anything and only indirectly about women and people from the lower classes. Therefore, there is less information regarding the homoerotic practices of "ordinary people." However, there are some sources that indicate that pederasty was not confined to the upper class. The best sources for this are the Pompeian graffiti, scribbled by ordinary, uneducated people.[151] They include several writings with a clearly homosexual content and some that leave it doubtful whether they speak of a girl or a boy. Typical of the homosexual writings is that they are written by an active partner, who boasts about his masculinity and either ridicules or praises his passive boy partner.

To conclude, Roman homoeroticism was not prohibited in principle, yet it did not hold any moral value. In its accepted form, however, it had its limits. Tolerance did not extend to those cases in which a free adult man had become the passive partner. A homoerotic relationship with a slave or a prostitute was acceptable; it disgraced only the passive partner. By and large, it was the passive partner who endured the scorn. The young boys praised by the poets were, of course, an exception to this rule, but the poets wrote their verses partially under Greek literary influence and were free to write about preferences and feelings, fancied or experienced, that did not necessarily represent the generally respected moral ideals.

Figure 1. Ištar, Gilgameš, the Bull of Heaven, and Enkidu. BM 89435

Figure 2. A eunuch, recognizable by his beardlessness, worshipping the warlike Ištar, who is standing on a panther with a bow and arrows in her hand. The palm trees and ibexes are emblems of the goddess. BM 89769

Figure 3. "I am Eurymedon. I have bent down." A Greek soldier approaches a horrified Persian soldier with intent to rape him. The picture portrays the victory of the Athenians over the Persians by the river Eurymedon in 460 B.C.E.

Figure 4. Zeus tries to grab hold of the beautiful but resisting Ganymedes.

Figure 5a. The young lyre player entertains the guests, one of them flirting with a boy who is crowning him with a garland. Note the presence of women (*hetairai*?) and the muscular bodies of the male persons.

Figure 5b. Two men (a lover and his beloved?) enjoying each others' company in a banquet.

Figure 6. Three men courting a handsome boy who embodies the masculine ideal of the sixth century B.C.E. The second man from the left stands in the typical courtship position, touching the genitals of the boy with his right hand. The boy has grasped his left hand, preventing him from touching his face. The man on the right is bringing an animal as an expression of his affection for the boy.

Figure 7. A Greek boy whose appearance represents in every detail the ideal of beauty of the Classical period: broad shoulders, muscular chest, well-developed belly, narrow pelvis and small genitals.

Figure 8. An example of a courtship: the man offers the boy a rooster as an indication of his affection. The boy, however, shows reservation.

Figure 9a. The courtship has been successful: the boy has accepted the gift (a bag of fruit?), and his gestures suggest that he is ready for the man's caresses. Note the childish appearance and small genitals of the boy, whose decency is shown by the loss of erection.

Figure 9b. An intercrural intercourse: a man, bent over his boy partner, rubs himself between the boy's thighs. The boy, standing straight, passively seems to allow it.

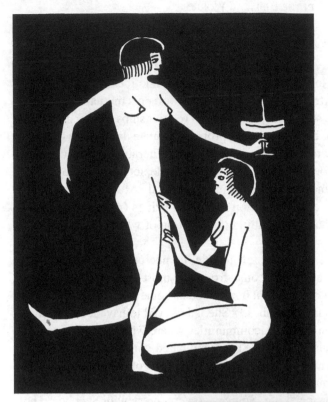

Figure 10a. Two nude women having erotic contact—a motif not very common in the paintings of the Classical period. The woman sitting on her heels caresses the clitoris of the standing woman with her right hand, while her left hand is holding her inner thigh.

Figure 10b. The woman has a basket full of artificial phalli (*olisboi*) for erotic dance or masturbation.

FEMALE HOMOEROTICISM

As mentioned above, ancient sources describe well the life of upper class men but have little to say about the life, morals, and ideals of women. As a result, there are extremely few references to women's mutual sexual relations. They disclose sufficiently that lesbian relationships did occur both in Greece and in Rome but do not give a proper, adequate description of them. The absence of the topic is conspicuous in the literature of the classical age. Women's homoerotic relationships are not depicted in the comedies, and Plato, for instance, refers to women's mutual sexual attraction only once, in his myth about the creation of human beings (mentioned above). In addition to this, he includes it in his definition of what is against nature (*Laws* 636C).

The strongest expressions of female homoeroticism and the only sources written by a woman come from the most famous female poet, Sappho. Sappho was an aristocrat born in the last quarter of the seventh century B.C.E. on the island of Lesbos.[152] She is believed to have led communities of young women (*thiasoi*), communities where women learned poetry, dance, and music, and which have been compared with the Athenian gymnasiums, both in terms of education and the homoerotic customs they fostered. In these communities of erotic atmosphere, young women were educated and trained for social life. Sources contemporary with Sappho do not mention her school; thus the existing data are drawn from later sources.[153]

Sappho's poems have been preserved poorly. They are known only from papyrus fragments and quotations in the texts of writers who came after her. The remaining material, however, is enough to show that Sappho wrote glowing verses to and about women. Her language resembles that of the pederastic texts, but in her poems the object of love or jealousy is a woman (fragm. 31):[154]

> To me it seems
> that man has the fortune of gods,
> whoever sits beside you, and close
> who listens to you sweetly speaking
> and laughing temptingly;
> my heart flutters in my breast,
> whenever I look quickly, for a moment—
> I say nothing, my tongue broken,
> a delicate fire runs under my skin,
> my eyes see nothing, my ears roar,
> cold sweat rushes down me,
> trembling seizes me,
> I am greener than grass,
> to myself I seem

needing but little to die.
But all must be endured, since . . .

The erotic nature of Sappho's relationships to women was generally recognized in the Hellenistic age, if not earlier.[155] Sappho's own sexual orientation has been debated, along with the modern understanding of "homosexuality." Sappho is said to have had a husband called Cercylas from
Andros and a daughter called Cleis, but the sources that mention this are
late.[156] She might have been married, whether this information is historically reliable or not, but this does not really tell us anything about her sexual preferences. Since "Sappho as a poet is not a historian documenting her
own life but rather a creative participant in the erotic-lyric tradition,"[157]
even homoerotic verses as such do not necessarily disclose that she herself
was a homosexual. On the other hand, their great number in Sappho's
poetry suggests that more than just a literary device is at stake.

Sappho's poems sparkle with passionate, even ecstatic love, and
although she does not always name the object of her love, enough women's
names (Atthis, Gongyla, etc.) are mentioned to prove that women's mutual
love was a reality in her world. All this indicates that women-to-women
love and relationships had a significant part in the life of Sappho and her
Lesbian women's community. "To admit that Sappho's discourse is lesbian
but insist that she herself was not seems quixotic."[158] In one of her poems
(fragm. 1) she even mentions her own name, which would seem strange if
her poems would not express her true life experiences and feelings. There
is not much to conclude about the nature and dimensions of women's eroticism, but at least Sappho lets her readers understand that physical contacts
were not unheard of.[159] At the same time, supposedly, the young women
were trained also to attract men, because at least some of them later got
married. The above quoted fragm. 31 is not the only source that expresses
the longing and jealousy a marrying member of the community leaves
behind her.[160]

Another producer of poetry with erotic tones, to some degree comparable to Sappho's poetry, was Alcman, who lived in Sparta at the turn of the
sixth century B.C.E. and whose *partheneion* songs celebrate young
women's beauty.[161] These songs were performed in festivities by girl choirs,
which possibly provided an opportunity for homoerotic interaction. It may
be because of institutions like these girl choirs that Plutarch claims that in
Sparta "good and decent" women, after the model set by men, kept girls
(*parthenoi*) as their lovers and protegees.[162] This may have meant a certain
kind of initiation for girls who were getting married.[163]

It is possible that the sources from Sparta and Lesbos reflect women's
more independent status in these states compared to Athens, where

women's mutual love was not discussed openly.[164] The Athenians seem to have regarded a lesbian relationship as a taboo and did not consider it appropriate to refer to them in discussions and plays. Perhaps this is why the sources prefer not to mention directly even Sappho's homoerotic habits, although she most certainly was known in Athens also.[165] Comedies, however, mention the women of Lesbos as examples of sexual shameless-ness, and the verb *lesbiazein* is associated with flirtation and, especially, fellatio.[166]

Sappho lived before the political society of the classical age. Her soci-ety was not the *polis* of Plato or Aristotle, the sophisticated system of sex and gender that established roles and functions for men and women.[167] Sappho participated in a different erotic-lyric tradition, and the way she and her tradition perceived the relationships between males and females may have been outdated or even scandalous in the eyes of the (exclusively male) writers of the classical age. This is true also for later interpretations of Sappho that flourished in the Roman period: while being greatly appre-ciated as a poet, Sappho's erotic inclinations were a matter of constant pre-occupation and were at times also used against cultural achievements of women.[168]

The silence of the Athenians on lesbian relationships may be due to the fact that its structure was considered strange. Sappho's poems are interest-ing in that they use a vocabulary that resembles that of pederasty but do not express an analogous division of roles. Sappho's women do not seem to have any social hierarchy with respective roles at all. The distinction between the active and passive, dominant and submissive roles, which was so essential in pederasty, cannot be found in Sappho's texts. Sappho's love relationships are mutual; both partners behave in a similar manner: woo-ing, bribing, repelling, and lusting.[169] Nor is the erotic relationship peda-gogically accentuated, as it was in the Platonic model of the pederastic relationship. Instead, Sappho focuses on the emotional intensity of love and does not even polarize the sexes by the implication that women follow their passions and desires while men are guided by reason.[170]

If erotic relations between women really were like this, it could indeed have caused confusion in a culture where women were considered by nature to have passive and submissive roles. It might have been difficult to understand a relationship of two passive partners. Men could perceive it only in term of one of the women assuming an active role and impersonat-ing a man. This thought was found offensive, as evidenced in the rare later texts that mention sex between women.

One of the few cases in point is the *Interpretation of Dreams* (*Oneirokritika*) by Artemidorus of Daldis, from the second century C.E.[171] In the first book, chapters 78–80,[172] he creates a distinction between three classes of sexual acts that may occur in dreams: those "according to convention" (*kata nomon*), meaning sexual relations of a man with almost anybody,[173] those "against convention" (*para nomon*), such as incest, and those "against nature" (*para physin*). The last category includes all positions except the "natural" face-to-face position with the man extended in full length on top of the woman; oral eroticism; relations with dead bodies, gods, and animals; self-fellation—and "a woman penetrating a woman." Whatever is meant by "convention" and "nature" here, sex between women clearly represented something quite anomalous for Artemidorus—unlike relations between men that appear mostly as acts "according to convention." The reason for this is obvious: a woman cannot perform the act of penetration, which Artemidorus calls "entering into the secrets" (*mystēria*), by any "natural" means and thus cannot take an active sexual role. Artificial emulation of penetration breaks the balance of social status and sexual hierarchy, and this is what makes sexual contact between women "unnatural."[174]

On the same basis, the Roman sources repudiate women's homoerotic relations. In Roman literature "love between women is in the first place against nature, and in the second place criminal."[175] For married women this sort of relationship is analogous to adultery, and especially bothering is the thought of a woman abandoning her "natural" passive role and assuming male behavior.[176] These women are given a detesting label, *tribas*, which was borrowed from Greek; indeed, the Roman writers generally preferred to associate "tribadism" with alien and unnatural Greek behavior, the actual existence of which in Rome they were reluctant to admit.[177]

Seneca (4–64 C.E.) refers to such a role change indirectly when he talks about women who "even rival men in their lusts . . . although born to be passive."[178] The masculine role of some women is an explicit theme in several epigrams of Martial (*c*. 40–104 C.E.), which, using vulgar and exaggerated imagery, reflect male disgust at this inverted and ridiculous role structure.[179] One of the epigrams is addressed to a woman named Bassa (1:90) and two to Philaenis, "the *tribad* of the very *tribads*" (7:67, 70). Bassa, once thought to be especially chaste by Martial because she had seemingly no interest in men, turns out to be a *fututor* (obscenity for *male* sexual activity), whose "monstrous lust imitates a man." This refers to her masculine role in a female coupling. Philaenis, then, is a woman who behaves in a macho way or as a sadomasochist and is sexually aggressive toward both boys and girls. She plays the active role in intercourse with girls, the "middles" of which she "devours," because fellatio is not "manly enough" for her. She is also said to have "the erection of a husband," which would mean that she is depicted as capable of physical penetration of some kind. For Martial all this means that Philaenis has ceased being a woman without finally succeeding in becoming a real man either.

Ovid, who was not startled by men's homoeroticism, considered lesbian relations strange. His *Metamorphoses* (9:666–797) includes a story of the love between two women, Iphis and Ianthe.[180] Iphis is a girl, whose mother, on the advice of the goddess Isis, hid her gender in order to save herself from the wrath of her father, who had hoped for a boy. She is betrothed to Ianthe, with whom she falls madly in love. They are desperate, because their relationship is against nature—after all, it is not possible for a woman to burn with love for another woman any more than it is for mares or cows to burn for one another![181] Iphis wishes that, if the gods in any case would destroy her, they would at least give her an evil which is natural and customary instead of her unprecedented and monstrous (*prodigiosa*) love for Ianthe. The story has a happy ending, however, at least from the perspective of the implied readers: Isis transforms Iphis into a man, and the marriage can be fulfilled.

Lucian (third century C.E.) tells of a lesbian, Megilla, who covered her shaved head with a wig and deliberately assumed a male role: "I was born as a woman like the rest of you, but my mind, desire, and everything else in me are that of a man."[182] Megilla kept a courtesan, Leaena, at her house and loved her like a man. Leaena, however, confessed that she was ashamed because she considered their relationship "strange" (*allokotos*). She found Megilla "scaringly masculine" (*hē deinōs andrikē*).[183] Even without the male organ, Megilla was a phallic character whose masculine self-presentation Lucian depicted as shameful.

In a source from an even later period (fourth century C.E.), Pseudo-Lucian's dialogue *Affairs of the Heart*, Charicles, arguing for the love of women, says that if pederasty, which he derides, is accepted, so also should relations between women.[184] Although Charicles's attitude toward women's mutual sexual contacts is bitter, he eventually considers them better than feminizing a man, because it would be even more degrading for a man to take the passive role than for a woman to take the active role.

According to this argument, women's homoeroticism was considered abnormal in a men's world. Feelings of abhorrence are manifest in a rare description of lesbian eroticism, in which women presumably used artificial penises—after all, how else could they have imitated intercourse?[185]

> Let them strap to themselves cunningly contrived instruments of lechery, those mysterious monstrosities devoid of seed, and let woman lie with woman as does a man.

Artificial penises (*olisboi*), used in erotic dance and masturbation, are known from both texts and pictures.[186] It was possible also for two women, facing each other, to use an *olisbos*. According to the comic poets, the *olisboi* were used by women whose sexual needs were frustrated by the absence of husbands (or adulterers).[187] Artificial phalli may have been involved also in the case of Bassa and Philaenis in the above mentioned epigrams of Martial.[188] This is, however, a purely masculine view on women's mutual eroticism or autoeroticism, the abhorrence of women who tried to imitate men by strapping on the most important signifier of masculinity.

The scanty and scattered sources available do not allow us to conclude much about women's homoeroticism in the ancient world. A common feature that unites the sources from Sappho to Greek vase-paintings and male authors of the Roman period is the relative equality of status of the two women involved in an erotic relationship. Even though the male writers understand these relationships, like all erotic encounters, as an interplay of the active and passive partners, the female couples always consist of two adult women. Evidently, female homoeroticism was not perceived as another kind of pederasty but as a coupling of two equals that did not conform to the hierarchical concept of sexual roles and, for this reason, was a matter of moral concern.

Interestingly enough, the only positive descriptions of women's eroticism (and the only sources written by women) come from Sappho, whereas men generally oppose women's mutual erotic relations regardless of what they think of homoeroticism between men. Men viewed women's relationships from a male perspective and ultimately made female homoeroticism a matter of male honor and shame. From this perspective, the supposed active role of one of the two parties in a female homoerotic relationship was considered a grave transgression of established gender role boundaries. It was worse than the passive role of a man, which brought shame only upon the individual, while the active role of a woman was an attack on manliness itself, threatening to lower its status and undermine the male privilege of penetration. Male and female homoeroticism, therefore, were not just symmetrical sides of the same coin but represented different kinds of sexual practices that required different treatment by male writers.[189]

CRITIQUES OF HOMOEROTICISM

Attitudes toward homoeroticism in antiquity were not based on an assumption of two distinct identities and orientations, "homosexuality" and "heterosexuality," between which one should have made a moral choice. The issue nevertheless was the object of intense moral preoccupation, because it involved some of the strongest values of classical antiquity: virility, self-control, and the appropriate use of pleasure. Because masculinity was not a birthright but rather an achieved state of paramount moral significance,[190] there was always the danger of losing it. As stated above, homoerotic relationships were a delicate issue, managed by a subtle moral code, the honor of a free-born citizen being its primary concern. Thus, "what might appear at first sight as tolerance reveals, in fact, the comprehensiveness of the codes adopted by the elites."[191]

Homoeroticism had hardly ever totally matched its Platonic ideal but, by the beginning of the Common Era at the latest, it had become an increasingly debated phenomenon. When the Roman tradition emerged to the side of and beyond the Greek tradition, homoerotic relations developed such brutal traits that they would never have been tolerated in Plato's symposia. Thus many Greeks and Romans, especially philosophers oriented toward Stoicism, bitterly castigated men's homoerotic relations. Literary works also, such as plays and novels, present homoeroticism in a less than ideal light.

During the classical age, the femininity of the passive partner was belittled, especially in comedies, which exhibited a respectful attitude toward heterosexual sexual life but rarely depicted homoeroticism without a pejorative coloration. For instance, Aristophanes in his plays treats homoeroticism with quite a different tone from that of Plato in his *Symposium*.[192] Sexually passive males were a particular target of mockery. In *Clouds* they are given an extremely obscene epithet, *euryprōktoi*,[193] and they symbolize the corruption of the once grand and masculine Athens.[194] Aristophanes also refers to the practice of giving animals as gifts to the beloved boy and considers this to be not essentially different from prostitution.[195]

Aristophanes' satire is overtly heterosexual and finds its target in beautiful Agathon, the beloved of Pausanias, who was known for his passive role even in adulthood. Aristophanes portrays Agathon as a transvestite with a female hairdo and clothing and even a female voice,[196] who always carried along a mirror and a razor for shaving his body hair.[197] Aeschines indirectly accuses Demosthenes of homosexual conduct, as he changes Demosthenes' nickname Battalos ("the stammerer") to Batalos ("ass"), and chides him for his unmanly and effeminate behavior and clothing.[198]

Satire resembling that of Aristophanes comes later from Athenaeus, who narrates how Diogenes jeered men who shaved their hair and smelled of perfume.[199] Another voice utters a direct warning to those who support pederasty: "So beware, you philosophers, who indulge in passion contrary to nature (*para physin*), who sin against the goddess of love . . ."[200] Ironically, Athenaeus aims his criticism at the hypocritical Stoics, who expressly strove towards "natural" in every aspect of their lives.

In later Hellenistic love novels, homoeroticism is conspicuous by its absence.[201] However, in Longus's *Daphnis and Chloe*, for instance, the desire of a certain man, Gnathon, for a young shepherd named Daphnis is depicted as a repulsive custom of city people.[202] Gnathon is "a lover of boys by nature" (*physei paiderastēs*) and also a *parasitos*, a drinker and an eater, "nothing other than a gaping jaw and a stomach and the parts below the stomach" (4:11).[203] He was "educated in all love's mythology at the symposia of wanton men" (4:17) and, according to Lamon, the father of Daphnis, he wanted to take him to Mytilene (the capital of Lesbos) "to do the woman's service" (*gynaikon erga*) (4:19). Particularly disgusting in Gnathon's lust for Daphnis are Gnathon's intemperate lifestyle, his lack of self-possession, and the fact that he is a parasite who eats from the table of the rich, whereas Daphnis genuinely belongs to the upper social class, even though he plays a shepherd. These factors weigh more in the story than does homoeroticism, which has significance largely because Gnathon is a character opposite to Daphnis's beloved, Chloe.

The reader is not made to choose between homosexual or heterosexual love; the purpose is to awaken sympathy for the young couple and their love, threatened by the attempts of Gnathon (and also Dorkon and Lampis, men enamored of Chloe). It is notable that the romance of Daphnis and Chloe is actually outside the social conventions of courtship—this is a romance of a fifteen-year-old boy and a thirteen-year-old girl and of their mutual learning of the skills of love, without any clear role distinction.[204]

The inconvenient aspects of homoeroticism were criticized also by the philosophers of the classical age. Aristotle's (384–322 B.C.E.) sparse comments on homoeroticism express disinclination, although he does not condemn it in principle. In his *Nicomachean Ethics* he categorizes men's mutual sexual behavior among things that are not naturally pleasant, but which become pleasant "either as a result of arrested development or from habit, or in some cases owing to natural depravity." After stating that some unnatural propensities (such as cannibalism) are due to bestial character while others are due to disease or insanity, he continues:[205]

> Other morbid propensities are acquired by habit, for instance, plucking out the hair, biting the nails, eating cinders and earth, and also that of love of men *(hē tōn aphrodisiōn tois arresin)*. These practices result in some cases from natural disposition *(physei)*, and in others from habit *(ex ethous)*, as with those who have been abused from childhood.

According to Aristotle there is both "natural" and learned homosexuality, and the latter type he clearly disapproves of. And yet he does not appear to be much concerned about the issue, regarding male homoeroticism as anomalous as pulling one's hair or biting one's nails.

Plato's works give an idealistic and positive picture of pederasty, which does not mean that he would not have seen any negative or ridiculous aspects of sex between men. Socrates criticizes a man who runs after girlish boys:[206]

> He will be seen pursuing someone soft *(malthakos)* rather than tough, brought up in a shadowed light rather than in the full light of the sun, unversed in manly exertions and harsh, sweated labour, but fully versed in a soft and effeminate *(anandros)* way of life, decking himself out in borrowed colours and ornaments for lack of his own, and resorting to all other practices that go along with these. . . .

Criticism is directed at adult men who seek weak, submissive boys *(kinaidoi)* and satisfy their lust in a way inappropriate to the ideal relationship. These cases blatantly reveal the inequality of the active and passive partners:[207]

> The older man does not willingly let the younger one leave his company by day or by night, but is driven by a frenzied compulsion which draws him on by giving him continual pleasures, as he sees, hears, touches, experiences his loved one through all the senses, so that pleasure makes him press his services on him; but as for his loved one, what kind of solace or what pleasures will he give him, and so prevent him when he is with him over an equal period of time from experiencing extreme disgust, as he sees a face which is old and past its prime, and with everything else that follows on that, which it is no pleasure even to hear talked about, let alone to be continually compelled as well to deal with them in practice.

Surprisingly enough, Plato in his later work *Laws* also adopts the view that homoerotic physical contact, be it between males or females, is something "against nature." In later discussions this was to become an important argument against pederastic relations. The Athenian utters:[208]

> When male unites with female for procreation, the pleasure experienced is held to be due to nature *(kata physin)*, but contrary to nature *(para physin)* when male mates with male or female with female.

How is it possible that Plato ended up with a view that seems to clash with his earlier ideals? The contradiction is not as striking as it seems at first glance. Plato speaks expressly about improper use of pleasure, a sexual act motivated by desire, something his earlier works did not recommend either. In *Laws*, Plato delineates a utopian society, where everything would be in "natural" harmony. Plato regarded sexual acts that result from physical desire as by and large avoidable[209] and as natural only when they lead to procreation, which was necessary for society.[210]

As the case of Timarchus suggests (see above), not all homoerotic behavior was tolerated, and the abuse of pederasty was severely condemned. The line between "genuine" pederasty and prostitution seems to have been subtle and well realized already then. Attitudes toward the passive partner and his behavior and character reveal also that even those who accepted homoeroticism in principle and practiced it openly found it disturbing that in the passive role one's manhood came to be questioned. If a man was an *erōmenos* in his adolescence, in a decent "Platonic" relationship with his lover, and in time moved from the passive role to the active and behaved in a manly way in other respects also, then his role was acceptable. Deviation from this pattern, especially to continue in the passive role and maintain an effeminate look even as an adult, led both to moral criticism and to ridicule. Homoerotic relations were not a credit to a man serving in public office if he continued in the passive role even in adulthood and if his acceptance of such a role had originally occurred under suspicious circumstances.

Later in Rome, the *cinaedi* were the target of constant scorn. Their body-language and stereotypical mannerisms of self-presentation—voice, walk, gestures, dressing and cosmetology—were manifestly effeminate and thus diametrically opposed to the Roman concept of masculinity. Manliness, according to the Roman understanding, did not automatically follow from anatomical sex but was an achieved state that had to be embodied and shown by culturally determined signs, a "symbolic language" of masculinity, which in every respect was contrary to the self-presentation of the *cinaedi*.[211] Manliness was a matter of honor and shame. To retain his honor a man had to prove his masculinity, otherwise his moral and social status was on shaky ground. The most important cultural signifier of the role difference between "real" men and *cinaedi* was without doubt physical sexual penetration, which ultimately and concretely manifested the difference between the active, penetrating male and the passive, receptive female role. Sexual penetrability of a man was shameful, and it was also regarded as *impudicitia*, "unchastity,"[212] a word with a negative moral connotation.

Given this perspective of honor, shame, and morality, it is no wonder that facts or rumors about the sexual behavior of male Roman citizens could be used as an effective moral and political weapon—especially because their behavior did not always conform to the generally accepted norm. Juvenal wrote merciless satire about the sexual lives of the Roman upper-class, but criticism was not limited to the satirists. Sexual invective and lampoons—true or not—were also used in the Roman political forum.[213] Mark Antony, Cleopatra's famous lover, got an earful from Cicero, who claims that Mark in his youth had served as an ordinary prostitute (*vulgare scortum*) and even lived in the house of his lover, Curio, as his wife (*in matrimonio stabili et certo*).[214] Cicero attacked similarly also consul Gabius and tribune Clodius[215] and, in one of the senate sessions, he even reminded Julius Caesar himself about his relationship with King Nicomedes of Bithynia.[216] The target of his criticism was not so much the homoerotic relationship itself but the related sexual desire and the abhorrence connected with a free Roman citizen accepting a passive role or even prostitution.

Seneca (4–64 C.E.), the famous Stoic statesman, philosopher, and Emperor Nero's tutor, despised feminine male slaves and their masters, who could think only of drinking and lust. He was especially irked by the slave who at the orgies served wine, who was dressed in feminine clothing, and whose beard and body hair had been shaved or plucked. This kind of pathetic slave had to stay awake all night long to satisfy his master's lust for drinking and sex. In the bedroom he was expected to act as a man, but at parties as a boy (*in cubiculo vir, in convivio puer*).[217] Seneca saw his pupil Nero as an outrageous example of immoderate homoeroticism: Nero had his favorite slave, Sporus, castrated, gave him a woman's name and clothes, and took him as wife in a festive wedding ceremony.[218]

Plutarch, a Greek biographer and moral philosopher (50–125 C.E.), addresses men's homoeroticism in his work *Dialogue on Love*. In this dialogue[219] young men debate whether Bacchon, a handsome youth, should marry a rich widow, Ismenodora. The decision is left to other young men. Anthemnion and Daphnaeus argue for the marriage, Pisias and Protogenes against it. The opponents' point is that a man could find no sexual joy with a respectable woman. Protogenes says pederasty is pure and uncorrupted, proceeds from love, and advances virtues and friendship—unlike lust for women! "True love has nothing to do with the women's quarters," he believes. In real life, men do not love women any more than flies love milk, bees honey, or cooks the animals they have fattened.[220] Love of women in particular is womanish (*thēlys*), because lying in woman's arms softens man and makes him flabby.

Daphnaeus then argues for marriage as follows:[221]

> But I count this a great argument in favour of women: if union contrary to nature (*hē para physin homilia*) with males does not destroy or curtail a lover's tenderness, it stands no reason that the love between men and women, being normal and natural (*tē physei chromenon*), will be conducive to friendship developing in due course from favour (*charis*). . . . But to consort with males (whether without consent, in which case it involves violence and brigandage; or if with consent, there is still weakness [*malakia*] and effeminacy [*thēlytēs*] on the part of those who, contrary to nature [*para physin*], allow themselves in Plato's words "to be covered and mounted like cattle")—this is a completely ill-favoured favour (*acharis charis*), indecent, an unlovely affront to Aphrodite.

In other words, Daphnaeus here makes a distinction between those homoerotic relations into which the other partner is coerced and those into which both enter voluntarily. Even in the latter case he nevertheless regards as weak and womanish those who acquiesce in the passive role; in this context he appeals to Plato. Daphnaeus suspects that the high virtue and friendship of pederastic relations is often mere bluff. In the dusk of the evening and once the guardian is gone, the ulterior sexual motives of the lover become overt: "Sweet is the harvest when the guard is away."[222]

Plutarch also criticizes pederastic relations as temporary and considers permanent pederastic relationships rare.[223] This was perceived as a problem already in the classical age: when an adult man falls in love with a new boy, his old beloved is abandoned and mistreated.[224] Also jealousy between lovers was common, as Aeschines admits from his own experience.[225]

Plutarch resolves the discussion in favor of marriage. Through Daphnaeus's words he asserts the unnatural nature of pederasty. He defines a pederastic relationship as sexual intercourse that is "against nature" (*hē para physin homilia*), whereas he highly respects marriage and love for a woman. Plutarch, to be sure, shares the Aristotelian concepts of the imperfection of the female body and the woman's total receptiveness in conception; for him, as for Xenophon, ruling belonged to men and obedience to women.[226] However, unlike Xenophon, he does not value a woman only in a functional sense as the one who gives birth to children and takes care of the household. For him, women and men have basically the same virtues. He introduces a distinction between one woman and another and sees love as directed expressly to the person of a woman. He also emphasizes the need for mutual affection, virtue, and self-control, even mutuality of property, friends, and social relations in marriage.[227] *Charis* emerges as a central concept, signifying mutual friendship and affection between the spouses, who are in a relationship in which also the woman is willing and consenting and not merely an involuntary object of her husband's desires. *Charis* constitutes the main distinction between pederasty and marriage, between the love of women and the love of boys. According to Plutarch, there is no *charis* in the pederastic relationship, which makes it less valuable and ultimately a form of love to be rejected.[228]

Plutarch's discussion does not compare homosexual and heterosexual orientations but pederasty and marriage. The option of loving both sexes remains for everyone. It is a matter of two different forms of love, one between an *erastēs* and an *erōmenos*, the other between a husband and a wife. Behind this distinction lies the rejection of the traditional view of two types of love: first, sensual and physical attraction based on lust (*epithymia*), which is common to human beings and animals and is manifested, according to those supporting pederasty, when a man loves a woman; second, pure, spiritual, "true" love that is free from physical passion, and which is possible only in a pederastic relationship. Plutarch wants to acknowledge only one Eros, which is ruled by *charis* and which includes also physical expressions of love. According to him, physical union with a lawful wife is the beginning of friendship (*philia*) and a daily source of respect (*timē*), kindness (*charis*), mutual affection (*agapēsis*), and loyalty (*pistis*).[229] Plutarch thus elevates marriage, even with its physical sexual aspects, to what in Platonic ideology belonged to pederastic relationships of personal development.

Plutarch elsewhere, however, writes about Spartan men's pederastic upbringing in a positive tone, suggesting that it advanced their masculinity and deepened their friendships.[230] Is Plutarch idealizing here the good old times and their uncorrupted homoeroticism, of which he found no traces in his day?[231] At least it seems that Plutarch does not condemn pederasty as such but regards it as an inadequate form of love and thus less valuable than marriage.

Dio Chrysostom (d. *c.* 112 C.E.), also a Stoic thinker, has a less philosophical approach to homoeroticism. He bluntly links homoerotic relations with lechery and drinking. He held tavern keepers responsible for the fact that people ended up in sexual relationships without love and affection, or that were based on the lust for money.[232] Dio, like Plutarch's Daphnaeus, deems that prostitution belittles Aphrodite, "whose name stands for normal (*kata physin*) intercourse and union of the male and female."[233] Prostitution, according to him, corrupts not only young women but also young men. Once men no longer find enough satisfaction from women, they look to homoerotic relations for a change in their sex life. These kinds of men are like alcoholics to whom wine has become repugnant and who have to satisfy their thirst artificially.[234] This leads men to make boys into women, frivolously, even though there were enough real women available. As a result, "a far worse and more unfortunate breed is created, weaker than the female and more effeminate."[235] Dio's view is thus diametrically opposite to the thought that men's homoerotic relations were caused by the lack of women.

Another example of the Stoic philosophers is Epictetus (d. *c.* 125/130 C.E.), who also mocked feminine men. In one of his discussions, Epictetus speaks of a man who, to please women, shaves his body hair and transforms himself into a woman. According to Epictetus, this kind of man acts against his nature (*physis*) and behaves like a playboy (*kinaidos*), whom he compares with the Corinthians.[236] Epictetus speaks here, perhaps with irony, only about pleasing women, but he clearly means the behavior of the passive partner in a pederastic relationship, namely, the well-known relationship of Socrates and Alcibiades:[237]

> But observe what Socrates says to Alcibiades, the most handsome and youthfully beautiful of men: "Try, then, to be beautiful." What does he tell him? "Dress your locks and pluck the hairs out of your legs?"

God forbid! No, he says: "Make beautiful your moral purpose, eradicate your worthless opinions."

The list of the critics could be extended, but these examples are enough to demonstrate that sex between men was also viewed negatively in the Greco-Roman world at the beginning of the Common Era. Homosexual or bisexual behavior was not generally condemned in every form, but its specific characteristics were criticized time and again.

1. As was the case already in the classical age, homosexual prostitution was viewed negatively, and the character of a free man who engaged in it as a boy or an adult was questioned. The line between prostitution and free choice in homoerotic relations, however, was thin. Prostitution could entail any temporary relationship in which the main motive was to satisfy sexual desires. Criticism was directed especially at the passive partner, who was considered to have sold his manliness and human dignity by subjecting himself to satisfy somebody else's sexual appetites, The active partner, that is, the "customer" of a male prostitute, usually avoided this accusation. The prostitute, female or male, was the one to be denounced, not the customer or the institution itself. In Roman culture, however, the passive role belonged most often to slaves, whose human dignity was already in a different category from that of free men; using slaves was not necessarily regarded as an evil thing. There were some exceptions, of course, as Seneca's above mentioned example points out.

2. Another point of criticism was the effeminacy of the passive partner, whether he was a prostitute or not. Typical in this line of argumentation is the concern over men's masculinity and virility rather than over women's dignity or obligation to procreate. The unmanliness or effeminacy of a man was regarded as a moral problem; the ideal required a self-presentation corresponding to symbols of masculinity, and effeminacy was linked with lack of self-control and willingness to yield to pleasure. The girlishness or "sissiness" of the passive partner provoked contempt and plain disgust. The critics failed to see this as an expression of, say, a transvestite's need. They saw it rather as a deliberate or forced renouncing of one's masculinity and as the submission of oneself, against nature, to the role of an animal that has to be served. They found the inequality of the active and passive partners offensive because the passive partner, too, was a man.

Opponents of pederasty differed radically from those who regarded homoerotic relations as manly and relationships with women as leading to softness. Whereas the critics concentrated on the nonmasculine sexual role of the passive partner, those who argued for pederasty emphasized the perfect nature of the relationship between two men, the depth of their friendship, and the purity of their motives. They could see women only as sex objects, necessary to satisfy sexual needs but unfit for serious relationships.

3. Plutarch's comments for and against pederasty display the discrepancy between two different ways of thought. The advocates of pederasty make a sharp distinction between two different and even antithetical kinds of love, attributing the spiritual kind to pederasty and the physical to love of women. Those against pederasty aspire toward a monistic understanding of love, which includes sensual pleasure, but the highest expression of which is mutual affection, *charis*.[238] "In marriage, to love is a greater boon than to be loved."[239]

4. Criticism of prostitution and fear of effeminacy were associated equally with homosexual and heterosexual relations. The philosophically charged criterion of "against nature," however, was applied more to homoeroticism, even though it was used also with regard to heterosexual relations, probably only as a counter-argument.[240] Sex between men (and between women) was regarded as "against nature" for two reasons: (1) It did not lead to procreation. Plato's definition (*Laws* 1:636C) is in this respect unambiguous and applies apparently to the later writers. What is at stake here, however, is not only the anatomical necessity, but also (2) the breakdown of the role structure that had been considered "natural." For men this meant that the passive partner's masculine role was changed into a feminine role—the submissive role of the male passive party that was considered "unnatural." For women what was involved was just the opposite— they went beyond the passive role that was considered "natural" for them.

By and large, by the Hellenistic age and at the beginning of the Common Era, homoerotic relations increasingly had taken forms that would hardly have been tolerated in the classical age. Thus it is no wonder that the issue was discussed by moral philosophers, which inevitably influenced both Jewish and Christian circles—especially if the criticism of homoeroticism could be harmonized with the Jewish tradition. During the formative period of the early church, Greco-Roman philosophical models prepared the soil and conceptual basis for Jewish and Christian condemnation of homoerotic relations.

5

⚬∽⚬

JUDAISM

APOCRYPHA AND PSEUDEPIGRAPHA

The so-called Apocrypha and Pseudepigrapha are Jewish writings that never became part of the Hebrew canon.[1] Deriving from roughly 200 B.C.E.—100 C.E., these writings illuminate various aspects of Judaism in the Hellenistic era as well as the Jewish background of early Christianity. The Apocrypha and Pseudepigrapha include a number of texts that seem to touch on homoeroticism. Most often these fragments warn the Jews about the Gentiles' illicit behavior. The depravity of the Gentiles is claimed to manifest itself especially in their corrupt sex life—especially in homosexual relations and incest:[2]

> The majority of other men defile themselves in their relationships, thereby committing a serious offense, and lands and whole cities take pride in it: they not only procure the males, they also defile mothers and daughters. We are quite separated from these practices. (*Letter of Aristeas* 152)

Sodom is mentioned often as the quintessence of a perverted lifestyle and abandonment of God's law. For instance, in the *Book of Jubilees*[3] Sodom is frequently represented as the symbol of corruption, fornication, and idolatry (13:17; 16:5–6; 20:5; 22:22; 36:10). These writings, more than those of the Hebrew Bible, see clear sexual nuances in the sin of Sodom.[4] Quite often there is apprehension about heterosexual recklessness. Sodom's fornication is associated with lechery with women (*Test. Benj.* 9:1). Adultery, prostitution, and marrying a Gentile woman are also included among the sins of Sodom and are seen as transgressions of the Torah (*Test. Levi* 14:6–7). There are no unambiguous references to homoeroticism, which has to be read between the lines from statements that leave room for diverse interpretations.

The corrupt sexual practices are generally seen as deriving from idolatry. In Wisdom of Solomon 13–15, for instance, all possible immorality is explained as stemming from the worship of idols: "The invention of idols is the root of immorality; they are a contrivance which has blighted human life" (Wis. 14:12). "Immorality" (*porneia*) here may be a figurative expression like those used in the Hebrew prophets, who often label idolatry as fornication. However, Wisdom later offers a list of vices in which sexual lapses are discussed in quite concrete fashion (Wis. 14:22–27):

> Then, not content with gross error in their knowledge of God, men live in the constant warfare of ignorance and call this monstrous evil peace. They perform ritual murders of children and secret ceremonies and the frenzied orgies of unnatural cults; the purity of life and marriage is abandoned; and a man treacherously murders his neighbour or corrupts his wife and breaks his heart. All is in chaos—bloody murder, theft and fraud, corruption, treachery, riot, perjury, honest men driven to distraction; ingratitude, moral corruption, sexual perversion, breakdown of marriage, adultery, debauchery. For the worship of idols, whose name it is wrong even to mention, is the beginning, cause, and end of every evil. (NEB)

The writer, versed in biblical tradition, includes a number of elements from both the Decalogue and the Holiness Code, with its list of sexual offenses (including child sacrifices!). The words "sexual perversion" are a translation of the Greek *geneseōs enallagē*, which literally means changing one's origin of birth or breed. In principle this can refer to any change in what is considered customary—to homoeroticism, among other things. By itself this expression does not contain a direct reference to same-sex conduct, but the following components of the list suggest that sexual issues are indeed at stake here.[5]

The key term "changing" (*enallagē*) and other words derived from the same root relate to sexual offenses, but not necessarily homosexual ones, also elsewhere in Jewish literature. "Changing" is a broad term that seems to denote various kinds of peculiar and repudiated forms of sexual activity. For instance, Aquila[6] translates the Hebrew term *qĕdēšîm* with the Greek *en(di)ēllagmenos* (fem. -*menē*), which, without a specifically homosexual nuance, links "changing" with disapproved sexual behavior.[7]

Sexual "changing" gets an interesting dimension in the *Testament of Naphtali*[8] which like the above mentioned excerpt from the Wisdom of Solomon brings together idolatry, sexual behavior, and "changing." There the patriarch Naphtali teaches his children to be obedient to the law of God and admonishes them as follows:[9]

Sun, moon and stars do not alter their order; thus you should not alter the Law of God by the disorder of your actions. The gentiles, because they wandered astray and forsook the Lord, have changed the order *(ēlloiōsan tēn taxin autōn)* and have devoted themselves to stones and sticks, patterning themselves after wandering spirits. But you, my children, shall not be like that: In the firmament, in the earth, and in the sea, in all the products of his workmanship discern the Lord who made all things, so that you do not become like Sodom, which departed from [lit. "changed"] the order of nature *(enēllaxe taxin physeōs autēs)*. Likewise the Watchers departed from [lit. "changed"] nature's order *(enēllaxan taxin physeōs autōn);* the Lord pronounced a curse on them at the Flood. On their account he ordered that the earth be without dweller or produce. *(Test. Naph.* 3:2–5)

The Sodomites' "changing the order of nature" may allude to the Yahwist account about the homosexual rape attempt in Gen. 19:1–11,[10] although by the time of the Pseudepigrapha the Sodomites had gathered about them plenty of other corrupt traits. Interesting in this context is the comparing of the Sodomites with the "Watchers" *(hoi egrēgoroi)*, angelic creatures who copulated with human daughters:[11]

When mankind began to increase and to spread all over the earth and daughters were born to them, the sons of the gods saw that the daughters of men were beautiful; so they took for themselves such women as they chose. . . . In those days, when the sons of the gods had intercourse with the daughters of men and got children by them, the Nephilim [giants] were on earth. They were the heroes of old, men of renown. (Gen. 6:1–2, 4, NEB)

Ancient interpreters of this myth often demonstrate strong repugnance toward intercourse between the Watchers and the human daughters. Intercourse between godly creatures and humans disturbs the natural order and transgresses the fixed border between divine and human. *Genesis Apocryphon* tells how Noah's father, Lamech, feared that his son was not his own but conceived by the Watchers or the giants. Lamech would not believe his wife's affirmation that the semen was indeed his, but inquired about this of his grandfather, Enoch. Unfortunately the remaining text, including Enoch's reply, is missing.[12]

In *1 Enoch*, which has no connection to the above mentioned story,[13] the deeds of the Watchers are condemned as against the law, because they have occurred "not of the spirit but of the flesh" (106:14,17). Intercourse between the Watchers and humans is compared to the intercourse of a man and a woman during the woman's menstruation (which is considered unnatural), and the children born from it are called "children of fornication." The angel Gabriel is assigned to cause these to destroy one another, whereas Michael is told to tie up the Watchers, the fallen angels, to await the day of judgment (10:9–11).

Intercourse between divine beings and humans, according to the Yahwist, was the last straw, which finally provoked God to destroy humanity by the flood—just as a sexual transgression preceded the destruction of Sodom and Gomorrah. Quite possibly already the Yahwist had deliberately constructed his story this way;[14] at least subsequent interpreters treat the Sodomites and the Watchers (or with the giants they procreated) as parallels also in other sources besides the *Testament of Naphtali*. Sirach has these two in sequence: "There was no pardon for the giants of old, who revolted in all their strength. There was no reprieve for Lot's adopted home, abhorrent in its arrogance" (Sir. 16:7–8, NEB). In some texts the parallel is even more direct. In *Jubilees* the Watchers are mentioned in quotations from *1 Enoch* (*Jub.* 7:21), and their descendants are included with the Sodomites among the condemned:[15]

> And he told them the judgement of the giants and the judgement of
> the Sodomites just as they had been judged on account of their evil.
> And on account of their fornication and impurity and the corruption
> among themselves with fornication they died. (*Jub.* 20:5)

The tradition of the Watchers and their fate has found its way from *1 Enoch* also to later parts of the New Testament, Jude (v. 6) and, through Jude, to 2 Peter (2:4–5).[16] These texts again link the Watchers to the people of Sodom and Gomorrah:

> Remember too the angels, how some of them were not content to
> keep the dominion given to them but abandoned their proper home;
> and God has reserved them for judgement on the great Day, bound
> beneath the darkness in everlasting chains. Remember Sodom and
> Gomorrah and the neighbouring towns; like the angels, they commit-
> ted fornication and followed unnatural lusts (*opisō sarkos heteras*);
> and they paid the penalty in eternal fire, an example for all to see.
> (Jude 6–7, NEB)

> God did not spare the angels who sinned, but consigned them to the
> dark pits of hell, where they are reserved for the judgement. . . . The
> cities of Sodom and Gomorrah God burned to ashes, and condemned
> them to total destruction, making them an object-lesson for godless
> men in future days. (2 Pet. 2:4, 6, NEB)

The reason for paralleling the Sodomites and the Watchers (or the giants) is sexual transgression. The letter of Jude uses a term "other" or "other kind of flesh" (*hetera sarx*) for this, with the same nuance of meaning as the term "changing" in other texts. The nature of the transgression of the Watchers and the human daughters is clear: it is unnatural sexual contact between angelic beings and humans. But how is sexual transgression to be interpreted in connection with Sodom? Lot's guests were angels (*mal'ākîm*, Gen. 19:1), creatures of nonhuman origin. The Sodomites' attempt to rape them was seen as aspiration for "another kind of flesh," similar to the intercourse between the Watchers and the human daughters. The sin of Sodom is viewed not as males violating other males but as mortals violating immortals.[17] It is therefore quite understandable that the texts speak of the Watchers, giants, and Sodom in the same breath. Homoeroticism is not the issue in these texts.

What has same-sex eroticism, then, to do with the polemic regarding the Gentiles, the Watchers, and the Sodomites? These texts are obscure inasmuch as same-sex conduct is an independent concept in them but rather looms behind a variety of terms that have different intentions and interpretations. Based on these concepts, it is possible to understand same-sex sexual behavior as one way to "change" the ordinary to the unordinary, to change divinely based life orders to illicit ones. Ultimately all this is regarded as paganism, an expression and result of idolatry. It will become apparent below how this mode of thought had a crucial influence on Paul's arguments.

JOSEPHUS, PHILO, AND PSEUDO-PHOCYLIDES

Notable Jewish writers from the time of the New Testament, the historian Flavius Josephus and the philosopher Philo of Alexandria, interpret the story of Sodom in their own ways. These writers put more stress on the homosexual aspect of the behavior of the Sodomites, and they do this with less ambiguity than any of their contemporaries. Josephus and Philo read into the story of Sodom the kind of homoerotic behavior they knew from their own context, namely, pederasty and other kinds of sexual interaction between active and passive males.[18] These learned men, who were profoundly influenced by Hellenistic philosophy, used the familiar term *physis* ("nature"), defining homoerotic behavior as against nature (*para physin*).[19] Josephus, in his *Jewish Antiquities*, writes that the Sodomites' arrogance and hatred of strangers were the reasons for the destruction of their city, thus recapitulating the customary Jewish argument (*Ant.* 1.194–204).[20] New in Josephus's interpretation is that he—like many modern scholars— thinks that Lot's guests were handsome young men (*neaniskoi*) who aroused erotic passions in the Sodomite men:[21]

> But the Sodomites on seeing these young men of remarkably fair appearance whom Lot had taken under his roof, were bent only on violence and outrage to their youthful beauty. (*Ant.* 1.200)

In Josephus's mind, then, the Sodomites' attempt to rape the men had pederastic elements. Yet when commenting on the case of Gibeah (*Ant.* 5.143, regarding Judg. 19:22) Josephus tells of the rape of the Levite's wife, but says not a word about the Gibeahites' desire to attack a man. Possibly Josephus did not want to smear the reputation of the Benjaminites, who were part of the people of Israel (King Saul himself originated from this tribe).[22] It was undoubtedly easier to bring up a sin like this with Sodom, the mother of all pollution. Josephus seems unwilling to admit that his own people would ever have engaged in homoerotic relations. Instead, he actually boasts about the Jews' homophobia and their death penalty for homosexual relationships (*Against Apion* 2.199):[23]

> What are our marriage laws? The Law recognizes no sexual connections, except the natural *(kata physin)* union of man and wife, and that only for the procreation of children. The sexual connection of a man with another man it abhors, and punishes any guilty of such assault with death.

Josephus's arguments are reminiscent of the *Letter of Aristeas* 152, cited above, and proves that he also regarded homosexual relations as a Gentile vice with which Israel has absolutely nothing to do. According to Josephus, the Greeks found an excuse for their unnatural *(para physin)* enjoyment from their belief that their gods behaved that way also (*Against Apion* 2:273–275). He was not totally wrong here, because the pederasty of the gods surely entitled people to pursue similar relations.[24] Furthermore, Josephus was aware of prominent persons who had practiced pederasty. Mark Antony's fondness for boys was well-known, also by Josephus. He tells how Antony suggested that Herod send Aristobulos, a sixteen-year-old boy, to Rome. Herod did not consider this safe, because he perceived the young man to be in danger of becoming sexually abused by his protector (*Ant.* 15.28–29). In his criticism Josephus joins contemporary influential Gentiles—Cicero also criticized the same man for the same penchant (*Phil.* 2.44–45).

Philo's treatment of homoerotic behavior is broader and more philosophical than that of Josephus. He accuses the Sodomites not only of uncontrollable coveting of each others' women but also of their men's mutual relationships that, according to him, led to infertility, men's effeminacy, and venereal diseases.[25] According to Philo (*On Abraham* 135–136), the Sodomites[26]

> threw off from their necks the law of nature *(ton tēs physeōs nomon)* and applied themselves to deep drinking of strong liquor and dainty feeding and forbidden forms of intercourse. Not only in their mad lust for women did they violate the marriages of their neighbours, but also

men mounted males without respect for the sex nature which the active partner shares with the passive;[27] and so when they tried to beget children they were discovered to be incapable of any but a sterile seed. Yet the discovery availed them not, so much stronger was the force of the lust which mastered them. Then, as little by little they accustomed those who were by nature men *(tous andres gennēthentas)* to submit to play the part of women, they saddled them with the formidable curse of a female disease. For not only did they emasculate their bodies by luxury and voluptuousness but they worked a further degeneration in their soul and, as far as in them lay, were corrupting the whole mankind. Certainly, had Greeks and barbarians joined together in affecting such unions, city after city would have become a desert, as though depopulated by a pestilential sickness.

Philo connects here homoerotic relations and procreation, which is important in his thinking elsewhere also. Same-sex contacts he considers as a threat to the reproduction of humankind—not only because they make sexual contacts between men and women rare, but also because they actually cause sterility, destroy the semen, and cause lethal "women's" illnesses, that is, probably, venereal diseases.[28]

Philo condemns sexual relations between men and boys, because they convert men to women and distort sex life, the sole purpose of which he sees to be procreation. He condemns Plato's and Xenophon's "symposia" as pederastic debauchery *(On the Contemplative Life* 59–62). In this context it becomes evident that the terms *erastēs*, *paiderastēs*, and *erōmenos* are familiar to Philo who, in addition, likes to name the passive partner in a pederastic relationship as an *androgynous*, a man-woman.

Philo interprets Lev. 18:22 and 20:13 *(Laws* 3:37–42) straightforwardly from the perspective of pederasty, distinguishing between the active and the passive partner. The latter, according to him, is a perfumed boy prostitute with a feminine hairdo and makeup and deserves the appellation *androgynous*. These boys, some of whom are even castrated, have spread everywhere and have gained a remarkable status in the Greek societies.[29] The boys' lovers boast about their behavior, and the girlish boys openly strut along—actually the alteration of a masculine nature into a feminine is considered an art form, and it no longer even makes people blush. However, the Torah prescribes the death penalty for both the boys and their lovers.

Philo's disgust for homoerotic relations has two sides. He is repulsed by the changing or transforming of a masculine role into a feminine, which seems to be characteristic of the passive partner in the form of pederasty he knew. This already is "against nature" *(para physin)*, according to Philo, but even more so because of the squandered semen. Homoerotic relationships destroy the whole purpose of procreation because they do not generate children, thus causing cities to become uninhabited and deserted.

Just before discussing pederasty, Philo had examined some other forbidden forms of sex life (*Laws* 3:32–36). People are not to waste sperm for improper desire, not even in heterosexual intercourse. Intercourse is prohibited during menstruation, which cleans the womb and prepares it for a successful insemination. A man is to be the farmer who waits for the rain before planting the seed and unites with his wife in a fitting time. A man who knowingly marries an infertile woman is compared by Philo to a farmer who ploughs hard, stony land, knowing well that his efforts are futile. This kind of man, then, has intercourse just for the sake of lust. Philo considers them as debauchees who have sex like pigs and goats, and who are God's enemies. However, when moving from this topic to pederasty, Philo deems the latter even a graver vice.

In addition to Josephus and Philo, the sentences of *Pseudo-Phocylides* also show Greek influences, especially Stoic philosophy. This collection of the Jewish ethical sentences from the beginning of the Common Era is written either to win "sympathizers" for the Jews in the Hellenistic world or—more likely—to demonstrate to the Jews that there was no fundamental difference between Jewish and Greek ethics.[30] The sentences place a heavy emphasis on sexual matters. In Stoic fashion, they emphasize sexual chastity, forbid castration and (twice) homosexual relations, and advise on how to protect young boys from sexual abuse:

> Do not cut a youth's masculine procreative faculty.[31]
> Neither commit adultery nor rouse homosexual passion.[32]
> Do not transgress with unlawful sex the limits set by nature. For even
> animals are not pleased by intercourse of male with male.[33]
> Guard the youthful prime of life of a comely boy, because many rage
> for intercourse with a man.[34]

This collection contains also a rare reference to women's active sexual role:

> And let women not imitate the sexual role of men.[35]

This sentence suggests that the Jews imagined women's erotic encounters as the Greeks and Romans did, that one of the women assumed the role of a man. Another kind of warning about violating the role boundaries concerns young boys, who are admonished not to have long, braided, or knotted hair, because "long hair is not fit for boys, but for voluptuous women."[36]

Philo, Josephus, and *Pseudo-Phocylides* argue against homoeroticism by traditional Jewish reasoning. However, they, more than others, are clearly thinking of the most common form of homoeroticism of their time, pederasty, and express their explicit opinions about it. Yet their criticism does not arise solely from their Jewish context, because they all aim to build a bridge between Jewish and Hellenistic cultures. It is quite clear that especially Philo agrees in detail with those moral philosophers who reproach homoerotic relations and the effeminacy of the passive partner in particular. In assessing pederasty, it was easy for Hellenistic Jews to join the similar criticism of their most famous contemporary moral philosophers. "Here again the Jewish writers were not simply at variance with Greek morality, but could be seen as taking sides in widespread Greek debate."[37] But they gave the Greek concepts new contents adapted to Jewish tradition.[38] In terms of homoeroticism this meant a more categorical refutation than the Greeks thought necessary. This was no doubt influenced by the fact that the Hellenistic Jewish Diaspora was a minority society, the identity of which required defending their own particularity against the dominant culture.

The Hellenistic Jewish argument will become manifest again in Paul's writing.

RABBINIC LITERATURE

The Torah already at the beginning of the Common Era had privileged status in Judaism as the cornerstone of holy scripture. Because it was forbidden to add anything to the Torah, new rabbinic interpretations and teachings (*hǎlākâ*) emerged on its side, as a "fence for the Torah." They clarified and specified points in the Torah, applied its teaching in different life situations, and defined circumstances that could lead people to break the law. All this was considered to be the "oral Torah," which was esteemed as a revelation of Moses as much as the written Torah. Alongside of the oral Torah there were traditions (*haggādâ*) that supplemented the Torah's interpretations with stories and folk wisdom.

A number of works emerged from the rabbis' interpretations, for instance, the *Mishnah*, the Palestinian and Babylonian *Talmuds* that explained it, a parallel work, the *Tosefta*, and the *Midrash*ic literature, which explained and complemented the Bible. These works retain a pivotal position even in modern Judaism, and it is impossible to think of Jewish biblical interpretation without them. Rabbinic texts cannot be expected to shed much light on the background of the New Testament, because most of the material is either contemporaneous with or later than the New Testament—an important caveat in what follows. Roughly speaking, it is possible to see Rabbinic literature as affected by the same cultural influences as the New Testament and other texts of the early church.

The speculative character of the Rabbinic sources must be kept in mind. These texts explain the Torah as if the temple of Jerusalem were still standing and the Jewish state still existing. The texts of *Mishnah* and *Talmud* give detailed directives about the temple services and order punishments, the execution of which apparently was beyond the jurisdiction of the Jewish community.

Rabbinic texts sometimes refer to homoerotic behavior, mostly focusing their discourse on male relationships in which one partner sexually penetrates the other.[39] This concern apparently comes from the Torah, the relevant sentences of which (Lev. 18:22 and 20:139) the rabbis interpret; but in the background of their discussion is also the Greek and Roman cultural milieu with its pederastic and other male-to-male sexual practices. Other points from the Hebrew Bible rarely surface. For instance, Sodom is epitomized in traditional fashion as an example of arrogance and injustice (the "Sodomitic rule" means justice without charity),[40] whereas only a few Midrashic stories allude to the sexual offenses of Sodom.[41] Occasionally some other texts emerge, for instance, the Egyptian courtier Potiphar is said to have taken Joseph as his slave because of his erotic interest and, for this reason, to have been castrated by the angel Gabriel (b. *Sotah* 13b; cf. Gen. 39:1–6); another text tells how Ham had sexually abused his drunken father Noah (b. *Sanhedrin* 70a; cf., Gen. 9:20–22).[42]

In Rabbinic literature, homosexual relations are categorized along with incest, adultery, and bestiality. These, together with idolatry, mockery, wrongdoing, murdering, and stealing were forbidden in the so-called Noachian commandments, that is, the commandments God gave after the flood. The Noachian commandments identified certain minimal moral requirements that supposedly applied also to Gentiles.[43]

The Rabbinic texts have no term for "homosexuality" any more than the Hebrew Bible has. These texts are concerned with the blurring of gender roles and the penetration of a male rather than same-sex desire or "homosexuality." The rabbinic concept "lying of a man" (*miškab zākûr*) has clear counterparts in the biblical expressions "lying with a woman" (male anal intercourse[44] *miškĕbê 'iššâ* Lev. 18:22; 20:13) and "lying with a man" (*miškab zākār* Num. 31:17–18, 35; Judg. 21:11–12).[45] These expressions clearly imply a role distinction between the active and the passive partners—a distinction well recognized and reflected by the rabbis especially from the point of view of the passive male.[46] It seems that it was the actual penetration that caused the problem, not just any erotic interaction.[47]

The *Mishnah* explains the Torah's death penalty by ordering a man who is found guilty of lying with another man and of other sexual crimes to be stoned (m. *Sanhedrin* 7:4).[48] The interpretation of the Babylonian

Talmud is more detailed. It makes a distinction between an active and a passive partner and pays attention to the age of the guilty one (b. *Sanhedrin* 54ab).[49] A problem arises, however, because the rabbis see the prohibition, "Do not lie with a man as you lie with a woman," to pertain only to the active partner, whereas the punishment applies to both. This clashes with rabbinic logic, and a solution is sought elsewhere, from Deut. 23:18. This verse supposedly deals with ordinary prostitution and assumes that a male prostitute, as the word *qādēš* is interpreted, would be looking for men,[50] thus making also the passive partner guilty.

The Talmud's interpretation of the Torah reflects the cultural background of contemporary Roman society with its male-to-male sexual practices, which the rabbis knew—or at least interpreted—as prostitution and the feminization of males, manifested in the self-representation of *cinaedi*. Fully in line with Roman morality, the rabbis consider the passive sexual role a woman's role, humiliating for a male, especially if penetration took place (y. *Qiddushin* 1:7.61a). Being penetrated by another male was sacrificing one's maleness, and with it the authority and power attached to the male role in society.[51] The rabbinic attitude toward the active partner differs from the Roman view, according to which the behavior of the active partner was generally not condemned. Following the Torah, the rabbis prohibit the penetration of another male, considering it a manifestation of arrogance and hedonism, comparable even to bestiality.[52] Both partners are guilty of transgressing divinely constituted gender boundaries.[53]

The Rabbinic sources do not confine spousal sex life to procreation only, but allow it also for people's sexual needs and pleasure (b. *Nedarim* 15b).[54] Procreation, however, is the main purpose of sexuality and, because it is possible only through heterosexual intercourse, rabbis perceive all other forms of sex life as a transgression of the natural order and the wasting of semen (b. *Niddah* 13a).[55] Rabbi Akiba interprets the statement from the paradise narrative, "That is why a man leaves his father and mother and is united to his wife, and the two become one flesh" (Gen. 2:24), to exclude both men's homosexual relations and incest, adultery, and bestiality:

> His "father" means "his father's wife"; "his mother" is literally meant.[56] "And he shall cleave," but not to a male; "to his wife," but not to his neighbour's wife; "and they shall be as one flesh," applying to those that can become one flesh, thus excluding cattle and beasts. (b. *Sanhedrin* 58a)

Homoerotic behavior, like other sexual peculiarities, is habitually judged as a pagan vice.[57] Jewish boys are cautioned not to fraternize with pagans, to avoid becoming objects of their pederastic lusts (b. *Shabbath* 17b). Also, Jews are forbidden to leave their animals in pagan inns for fear that their hosts might use them for sexual purposes (t. *Abodah Zarah* 3:2; 10:2). These fears probably stem more from tradition than actual events. The Torah's teaching about the corrupted customs of other people (Lev. 18:1–3 and elsewhere) is taken literally, and close attention is paid to whatever support for this view is found in concrete contexts. The motivation, however, is the same as that of the formation of the Holiness Code: a smaller group living in the grip of a dominant group has to provide for its continued existence and preserve its identity.

The Talmud includes only one story that assumes that there might be some sexual interaction between Jewish men: Once when Rabbi Judah ben Pazzi climbed to the attic of a school building, he caught two men in a sexual act. These two replied to their teacher simply, "Rabbi, please take note that you are one and we are two" (y. *Sanhedrin* 6.4, 23c).[58] This small story communicates how difficult it was to disclose possible homosexual relationships: according to Jewish law, two witnesses were required for valid proof. The story suggests, however, that homoeroticism nevertheless was to some extent a reality also in Jewish communities. Although the interpretations of the Torah are mainly speculative, the stories imbedded in them arise from real life. Nevertheless, one story among a vast mass of texts does not justify broad generalizations.

Also the *Mishnah* takes into consideration, at least in theory, that a man could feel erotically drawn toward another man or a boy. This possibility is mentioned in those interpretations of laws regarding sexual and marital life that aim to eliminate situations that might lead an individual to forbidden sexual relations. First a reference is made to dangerous heterosexual situations, then to homosexual temptations:[59]

> A man should not remain alone with two women, but a woman may remain alone with two men. Rabbi Simeon says: "Also: One may stay alone with two women, when his wife is with him. And he sleeps with them in the same inn, because his wife keeps watch over him." A man may stay alone with his mother or with his daughter. And he sleeps with them with flesh touching. But if they [the son who is with the mother, the daughter with the father] grew up, this one sleeps in her garment, and that one sleeps in his garment.
>
> An unmarried man may not teach scribes. Nor may a woman teach scribes. Rabbi Eliezer says: "Also: He who has no wife[60] may not teach scribes." Rabbi Judah says: "An unmarried man may not herd cattle. And two unmarried men may not sleep in the same cloak." And sages permit it. (m. *Qiddushin* 4:12–14)

Both boys and cattle were seen to bring about dangerous situations for a man who did not have an opportunity for a regular sexual life with a woman. Because "the sages," that is, the prevalent opinion of the rabbis, do not consider all the restrictions necessary, this danger was probably not taken overly seriously. One of the interpretations of this point states forthrightly, "Israel is not suspected" (t. *Qiddushin* 5:10). In other words, this was not considered a real threat in a Jewish community. Was homoeroticism, then, totally absent or unknown in the Jewish communities? Presumably not, even if references to it are rare, considering the quantity of Rabbinic literature. Apparently it was not considered a particularly grave problem; in any event, it did not stimulate nearly as much moral discussion as did heterosexual relations. It is possible that, because of the stern prohibition, homoerotic relations, if existing, were closeted.

Rabbinic sources pay even less attention to women's homoerotic relations.[61] The reason may be, on the one hand, that Torah does not include a related prohibition and, on the other hand, that the men who interpreted the Torah did not comprehend this dimension of women's sexual life.[62] Moreover, female homoeroticism was not comparable with the main concern of the rabbis, the prohibition of male anal intercourse, because no penetration took place.[63] The masculinized women abhorred by some Roman writers do not seem to have attracted the rabbi's attention. A female marriage is included in a list of imaginative "laws" of the Egyptians and Canaanites (Lev. 18:3) which should not be followed.[64] There is one (condemning) reference to a woman using an artificial penis (b. *Abodah Zarah* 44a).

By and large, lesbian relations were not considered overly threatening, although, in principle, they may have been disapproved of by some of the rabbis. At least this conclusion follows the rabbis' reasoning about the command in the Torah that a harlot (*zônâ*) could not qualify to be a priest's wife.[65] Rabbi Eleazar surmises that this means a woman who has previously slept with a man, but not a woman who has had a sexual contact with another woman. The latter, according to him, would be plain levity (*pěrîṣût*), which would not be an obstacle for marrying a priest (b. *Yebamoth* 76a).[66] In the Palestinian Talmud, the rabbis disagree on this matter: If two women "rub" each other, the school of Shammai forbids and the school of Hillel allows the woman in question to marry a priest (y. *Gittin* 8:10, 49c).[67]

In the context of homoeroticism it is also interesting to follow the rabbis' pondering about those people whose gender is ambiguous or not clear.[68] The Mishnah (*Bikkurim* 1:5) mentions women, "persons of doubtful sex" (*ṭumṭum*), and "androgynes" (*androginos*) among those who may bring the Lord the first fruit of the harvest (Ex. 23:19), but who are not allowed to utter the appropriate declaration (Deut. 26:5–11). The explanation (*Bikkurim* 4)[69] describes an androgyne as a person who is "in some things like to men and in some things like to women, and in some things like both to men and to women, and in some things like neither to men nor to women."[70] Rabbi Jose believes "an androgynous is a creature by itself, and the sages could not resolve whether it was a man or a woman. But it is not so with one of doubtful sex, since such a person is at times a man and at times a woman."[71] It is difficult to discern what the rabbis actually had in mind when they spoke of androgynes or of people of doubtful sex. An androgyne has a man's appearance: he dresses and cuts his hair like a man and he can also take a wife. An androgyne supposedly both ejaculates and menstruates. Perhaps the rabbis are thinking here of a hermaphrodite, the existence of which is taken into account elsewhere; sexual relations with them are equated with those with a male person (m. Y*ebamoth* 8:6; cf. b. *Yebamoth* 83b; t. *Yebamoth* 10:2; y. *Yebamoth* 8:6, 9d). Those of "doubtful sex" are in their own category, because they alter their sexual appearance. This might indicate an unusual gender role in the fashion of the *hijra* or *assinnu* (see chapter 2, above). Eunuchs, whether those by birth (*sārîs ḥammâ*[72]) or castrated by men (*sārîs ʾādām*), form yet another category, discussed by the rabbis mainly in terms of their being allowed to make heave offerings and marry women (m. *Yebamoth* 8:1–6).

The connection to androgynes and those with ambiguous sex and gender remains blurry. It is not impossible that a person with homoerotic behavior could be categorized in either group: an androgyne was forbidden to stay alone with either a man or a woman, a command intended to eliminate sexual temptations. They are not mentioned, however, in the texts that address explicitly homoerotic contacts. The rabbis' main concern was not to define gender but to clarify how the law could be applied to different people.

6

THE NEW TESTAMENT

PAUL AND THE UNNATURAL: ROMANS 1:26-27

The only New Testament author who addresses the issue of homoeroticism is Paul, whose writings have had considerable authority wherever the interpretation of the Bible has influenced moral codes and social structures. In various Christian communities, what Paul once wrote has subsequently been perceived as the word of God. Paul himself was flesh and blood, an educated male of Hellenistic Jewish origin whose worldview and moral standards, even after his conversion to Jesus Christ, had much to do with his cultural environment. Paul was a man of considerable self-awareness, whose letters were meant to be authoritative, indeed; nevertheless, when writing his letter to the Romans, he was scarcely aware that he was participating in the making of Holy Scripture. His words in Romans 1:26–27 concerning female and male same-sex interaction, however, continue to affect the lives of lesbian and gay persons at the turn of the third millennium C.E. As the most influential—and, in fact, the only clear and direct—reference to homoeroticism in the New Testament, Romans 1:26–27 has also been the object of intensive study from multifaceted perspectives.[1]

In Romans 1, Paul refers to persons who, among other things, were involved in same-sex conduct—both male and female. According to Paul, exchanging the true God for images resulted in the parallel alteration of their sexual behavior from "natural" to "unnatural":

> For we see divine retribution revealed from heaven and falling upon all the godless wickedness of men. In their wickedness they are stifling the truth. For all that may be known of God by men lies plain before their eyes; indeed God himself has disclosed it to them. His invisible attributes, that is to say his everlasting power and deity, have been visible, ever since the world began *(apo ktiseōs kosmou)*, to the

eye of reason, in the things he has made. There is therefore no possible defence for their conduct; knowing God, they have refused to honour him as God, or to render him thanks. Hence all their thinking has ended in futility, and their misguided minds are plunged in darkness. They boast of their wisdom, but they have made fools of themselves, exchanging *(ēllaxan)* the splendour of immortal God for an image shaped like mortal man, even for images like birds, beasts, and creeping things. For this reason God has given them up to the vileness of their own desires and the consequent degradation of their bodies, because they have bartered away *(metēllaxan)* the true God for a false one, and have offered reverence and worship to created things instead of to the Creator, who is blessed for ever, amen. In consequence, I say God has given them up to shameful passions. Their women have exchanged *(metēllaxan)* natural intercourse *(tēn physikēn khrēsin)* for unnatural *(para physin),* and their men in turn, giving up natural relations *(tēn physikēn khrēsin)* with women, burn with lust for one another; males behave indecently with males, and are thus receiving a due recompense of their error *(planē)* among themselves. (Rom. 1:18–27, NEB, the last clause trans. by the author)

Paul's way of describing the people in question, especially the exchanging of God for images, gives the impression that he is talking about Gentiles, that is, non-Jews. Although he does not use the word "Gentile," he depicts the people involved with language that easily suggests traditional Jewish attitudes toward non-Jews, much in the spirit of the Wisdom of Solomon (see above, chapter 5). Paul's rhetorical strategy lets this connotation arise in the implied reader's mind, but, as the text proceeds, the reader is shown that, in this respect, Jews have no advantage, and what has been said in 1:18–32 applies to them as well (Rom. 2:1). Everyone, not only the Gentiles, is sinful (3:9), and all humankind therefore needs justification by faith in Jesus Christ (3:21–31). The purpose of this strategy may at least partly have been to play down the difference between Gentile Christians and those of Jewish origin, both of whom were represented in the Christian community or communities in Rome.[2]

Greco-Roman and Jewish sources are a good basis for examining the arguments of Paul, who clearly shares with Josephus, Philo, and others Jewish repugnance toward homoeroticism. Paul's language is deeply rooted in the Hellenistic Jewish tradition of his time, influenced by Stoic philosophy. For example, expressions like *akatharsia* ("impurity," 1:24) or *askhēmosynē* ("shamelessness," 1:27) belong to the Jewish terminology of purity,[3] while *epithymia* (1:24), *pathē* (1:26) and *orexis* (1:27), all of which denote passion and desire, as well as *ta (mē) kathēkonta* (1:28), "things that should (not) be done," are part and parcel of Stoic language and thought.[4] It can be presumed that Paul expected this language to be understood by the addressees of his letter, whether they were of Jewish or non-Jewish background.

The crucial expression *para physin* ("against nature") is familiar to us from Greek and Jewish sources (see chapters 4–5, above). The question arises whether the word *physis* is part of Paul's own deliberate theological terminology or whether he more spontaneously follows convention here.[5] In either case, it is necessary to distinguish between a modern and an ancient concept of "nature." In antiquity, *physis* expresses a fundamental cultural rule or a conventional, proper, or inborn character or appearance, or the true being of a person or a thing rather than "nature" in a genetic-biological sense, as a modern reader would perceive it. Accordingly, "unnatural" is a synonym for "(seriously) unconventional."[6] In Stoic philosophy as well as in Philo, *physis* belongs essentially to the laws according to which people must live.[7] For Seneca, for example, hot baths, potted plants, banquets after sunset, and a man's passive sexual role were all "against nature," *contra naturam*.[8]

According to Paul, nature teaches that "while flowing locks disgrace a man, they are a woman's glory" (1 Cor. 11:14–15, NEB); this suggests the way Paul understood natural and unnatural. It is a matter of the common order of things as Paul had learned it: the Jews regarded a man with long hair as effeminate.[9] A Jew is a Jew "by nature" (Gal. 2:15: *hēmeis physei Ioudaioi*) and a Gentile is "uncircumcised in his natural state" (Rom. 2:27: *ek physeōs akrobystia*), who "by the light of nature" can do what the law requires (Rom. 2:14: *physei*). God, "against all nature," prunes the Gentiles from a wild olive tree, where they grow in their natural state, and implants them onto a cultivated tree (Rom. 11:24). The "unnatural" or "against nature" thus deviates from the ordinary order either in a good or a bad sense, as something that goes beyond the ordinary realm of experience.

On the same grounds, ancient Greeks could have defended homoeroticism as "natural": from their perspective it was not unusual or against common moral sense. The Greeks had practiced pederasty from generation to generation; thus it was "natural" to them.[10] As noted above, however, the Greeks also used the expression *para physin* when dealing with certain aspects of homoeroticism, and the Jews, under their influence, interpreted the term much more strictly and categorically than did the Greeks. Paul's argument about the "unnatural" is thus not his own creation but grows from his Hellenistic Jewish background. Also, it does not represent any specifically new Christian morality.[11] Presumably Paul in Romans 1:19–32 freely reproduces the teaching of the Hellenistic Jewish synagogue, agreeing with and molding it from his own perspective.[12]

In light of the Jewish texts mentioned above, it is not surprising that Paul depicts homoeroticism in a way reminiscent of Jewish polemics against idolatry. Josephus, Philo, and Paul each represent a Hellenistic Jewish attitude that goes back to the Torah (Leviticus 18 and 20), according to which sexual vices in particular were characteristic of the Gentiles and linked with idolatry. "For the worship of idols, whose names it is wrong even to mention, is the beginning, cause, and end of every evil" (Wis. 14:27). Paul's letter to the Romans brings nothing essentially new to these thoughts. It can be assumed that Paul has Leviticus in mind; even though he does not quote the prohibitions of male-male intercourse, there are enough common points between Romans 1:26–32 and Leviticus 18 and 20 to make this probable.[13] It is unknown how familiar Paul was with Josephus or Philo; supposedly he knew at least the Wisdom of Solomon, where the expression *geneseōs enallagē* (change of one's origin, Wis. 14:26) resonates with Paul's thought.[14]

"Changing" (*allassō* or *metallassō*), the key term for sexual transgressions in Jewish thought, is a fundamental term also in Paul's argumentation. His starting point is the exchanging of the one and only God for images, as stated in Ps. 106:20: "They exchanged their Glory for the image of a bull that feeds on grass."[15] The language here matches the *Testament of Naphtali*, which speaks of "changing nature" with a sexual connotation. This text resembles Paul's thoughts in a striking way:

> Sun, moon and stars do not alter their order; thus you should not alter the Law of God by the disorder of your actions. The gentiles, because they wandered astray and forsook the Lord, have changed the order and have devoted themselves to stones and sticks, patterning themselves after wandering spirits. But you, my children, shall not be like that: In the firmament, in the earth, and in the sea, in all the products of his workmanship discern the Lord who made all things, so that you do not become like Sodom, which departed from [lit., "changed"] the order of nature. (*Test. Naph.* 3:1–5)

Paul's thoughts follow the same logic. Changing the Creator to a creature leads to the altering of conventional orders, which is manifest in disordered sexual behavior, among other ways. Actually, Paul seems to have chosen same-sex sexual relations as an example of an indecent life precisely for the reason that they best rhetorically illustrate the exchanging of God for idols— even more clearly than the later mentioned transgressions, like rapacity, envy, arrogance, lack of affection and pity, etc. (Rom. 1:29–31). The natural order is the divine order,[16] and to change the Creator to a creature means converting order to disorder, for example, exchanging "natural intercourse" (*physikē khrēsis*) for "unnatural" (*para physin*).

Paul does not specify what he means by "natural intercourse"; it can only be discerned from his argumentation that he has in mind a heterosexual act. Often in this context scholars speak of an order of creation, referring to the gender difference and the complementarity of sexes constituted by God at the beginning (Gen. 1:27). *Physis* (nature), however, is not a synonym for *ktisis* (creation); creation and nature are not interchangeable concepts in Paul's theology.[17] The criterion for the "unnatural" or "against nature" (*para physin*) does not by itself imply any distinct theology of creation; these expressions instead relate to the concept of the "law of nature" (*nomos physeōs*) identical with the law of God.[18] Creation is mentioned explicitly because of God, so that God's "invisible attributes, everlasting power and divinity," which have been made known to all people, would make it stupid and reprehensible to serve a creature instead of the Creator (1:20), the result of which is turning the normal order of things upside down. Paul does not refer to the creation narratives (Genesis 1–3) when describing the errors of the people, and he does not explain their apostasy on the basis of Adam's fall.[19] Adam's transgression and the "groaning" of creation are discussed only later (Rom. 5:12–21; 8:18–25) in totally different contexts. Even if the idea of creation is not absent from our text, its moral implications are clearly subordinated to Hellenistic Jewish ideas of the law of nature, according to which the order and purpose of creation are visible in conventional patterns[20]—like heterosexuality. This theology of creation is not primarily drawn from Genesis 1–3 but from the thinking of Paul's contemporaries.

Evidently, "natural intercourse" implies not only gender difference and the complementarity of sexes but also gender roles. That Paul refers to the women as "their women" (1:26) is a clear indication of an implied gender role structure.[21] Paul's understanding of the naturalness of men's and women's gender roles is not a matter of genital formation and their functional purpose, which today is considered the main criterion for the unnatural.[22] A man and a woman each have their own place and role, which are not to be exchanged. According to 1 Corinthians 11:3–16, strict gender differentiation, based on the hierarchical ladder, God-Christ-man-woman, and manifested in different headdresses and hair styles, is a matter of shame and honor before God and thus becomes a theological issue.[23] This hierarchical pattern was not invented by Paul but belonged firmly to his culture. Gender role categories in the eastern Mediterranean, with culturally defined concepts of maleness and femaleness, masculinity and effeminacy, are already familiar to us from the previously discussed sources. They are not determined by anatomical sex only but also by an appropriate self-presentation and conformity to established gender roles. In spite of his conviction that in Jesus Christ there is no male and female (Gal. 3:28), Paul did not question the prevailing gender system. That was a radical view—but not radical enough to demolish the societal gender hierarchy altogether.[24]

Paul brings the transgressions of gender role boundaries under the concept of "impurity" (*akatharsia* 1:24).[25] Why has Paul chosen such a word? If he is paraphrasing traditional Jewish teaching, the word may be borrowed in order to persuade implied readers from a Jewish background. In any case, the choice of words is intentional. Even if Paul does not require non-Jews to adopt the Jewish purity code, he, by calling gender transgressions *akatharsia*, places them into the realm of the forbidden, condemnable, and corrupt.[26] While Paul in general was ready to break with Jewish proscriptions based on impurity, such as the dietary laws, he seems not to have been willing to give up the aspect of impurity when gender roles are at stake.

That Paul mentions expressly *women* "changing" their "natural" intercourse into "unnatural," even before he mentions men, deserves special attention. Women's alleged "unnatural" relations may have annoyed Paul especially because he could hardly accept women exercising their sexual energy in any other way than with their husbands—not to mention the possibility that a woman would assume a man's role as an active partner.[27] It is possible that Paul mentions women's homoerotic relations first in order to make men's comparable acts appear particularly "unnatural."[28] In Jewish literature, female homoeroticism is not even listed among Gentile vices. Paul does not give any concrete details about the "unnatural" things practiced by women.[29] It is generally assumed, by analogy to the following description of erotic desire between males, that he expressly means women's mutual sexual contacts. This assumption is conceivable, but not conclusive, because there is more at stake here than sexual contact only. As noted earlier (see above, pp. 76–79), the scandalous aspect of women's homoerotic relations in Paul's world was first of all the crossing of gender role boundaries. It was women's active sexual role that was regarded as truly "contrary to nature." This, together with 1 Corinthians 11:2–16, constitutes the interpretative background of the reference to women "exchanging natural relations for unnatural."

The patriarchal role structure was disturbed also by the female role assumed by the passive partner in a homosexual relationship of two men. This is something Paul cannot possibly have been unaware of, even if he does not mention it explicitly. Even if Paul's point of reference cannot be restricted to pederasty,[30] there is no reason to believe that the common structure of a male-male sexual relationship as an interplay of active and passive roles would not be the first thing that would occur in the minds of Paul's readers.[31] Effeminacy was one of the main themes of Greek and Roman critics of homoeroticism, as well as of Philo, who, as has been noted earlier, not only used the expression *para physin* and claimed that men involved in homoerotic acts had shaken off the yoke of natural law (*ho tēs physeōs nomos*) but also condemned men's feminine hair styles and likened homoerotic behavior to "the formidable curse of a female disease" (*On Abraham* 135–136).

The last mentioned statement of Philo has sometimes been connected with Romans 1:27, where Paul says that the male Gentiles involved in homoeroticism "receive the due recompense of their *planē* among themselves." The word *planē* ("error") is often understood as referring precisely to homoeroticism, which brings punishment to those involved—venereal disease, for example. It is more probable, however, that *planē* is not just a sexual lapse on the part of some individuals but a much broader phenomenon that applies to all the people in question (*en heautois*), namely, idolatry. The *planē* of the people is thus expressed already in the verse 1:21: "Knowing God they have refused to honour him as God, or to render him thanks." To "exchange" one's sexual behavior as such is due recompense for this fundamental error, especially since God has left people to the consequences of their passions. This is where divine retribution, the wrath of God (*orgē theou*, 1:18), has been revealed.[32]

Discussion about active "changing" of sexual behavior has raised the question whether Paul in his letter to the Romans actually speaks at all about homosexual orientation or homosexual persons. Strictly on a textual level, and with regard to the meaning of these modern concepts, the answer is negative.[33] The text speaks of people who deliberately turn their natural sexual orientation upside down and take an adversary role in it. To use modern terms, Paul refers to heterosexual people who knowingly and voluntarily make themselves homosexuals. In this case criticism would be directed not to homosexuals but to heterosexuals who practice homoeroticism. However, the categories of sexual orientation play no role here. Paul's criticism does not focus on homosexuals or heterosexuals but more generally on persons who participate in same-sex erotic acts. The distinction between sexual orientations is clearly an anachronism that does not help to understand Paul's line of argumentation.[34] Paul does not mention *tribades* or *kinaidoi*, that is, female and male persons who were habitually involved in homoerotic relationships; but if he knew about them (and there is every reason to believe he did), it is difficult to think that, because of their apparent "orientation," he would *not* have included them in Romans 1:26–27.

It is likely also that Paul considered "changing" one's sexual behavior a voluntary act. Admittedly, Paul compared such changing to idolatry, and it is unlikely that Paul would assume that every single Gentile deliberately substituted idols for the God of Israel.[35] However, he argues that every human being is able to perceive God by observing things in one's milieu, so that "all that may be known of God by men lies plain before their eyes," and thus they have no defense (1:19–20).[36] Moral transgressions mentioned later (1:29–31) are also traced back to the act of trading God for idols, and yet Paul doubtlessly considered them intentional acts: "They know well enough the just decree of God, that those who behave like this deserve to die, and yet they do it; not only so, they actually applaud such practices" (1:32, NEB). People commit these acts knowing that they are doing wrong; they therefore are responsible, not victims of high-handed divine hardening.[37] The "foolishness" (1:21–22) of idolatry and the subsequent distorted behavior do not free them from responsibility.

It is essential to notice that Paul speaks of homoeroticism precisely as a practice (*khrēsis*) that transgresses the boundaries of "nature" (*physis*).[38] For him, there is no individual inversion or inclination that would make this conduct less culpable. Paul asserts that God has left people "to the vileness of their own desires" (*epithymia* 1:24) because of the "changing," but also that they follow their desires deliberately and hence are responsible for their acts. Same-sex conduct is then "an integral if unpleasingly dirty aspect of Gentile culture"[39] and stands out as a touchstone, because the changing involved in sexual behavior is a particularly illustrative analogy to substituting idols for the one God.

What kind of conduct might Paul, then, have had in mind? The reference to women itself indicates that Paul's criticism should not be restricted to pederasty, although it is definitely one of the phenomena in the background.[40] He probably wrote his letter to the Romans in Corinth, an international seaport with the mores of a port city, to judge from Epictetus's references to the Corinthians of Paul's time.[41] Paul may have witnessed homoeroticism in a less than ideal form. Quite possibly the Greeks under Roman hegemony were exposed to a Roman understanding of homosexual relations, in which slaves rather than free young men assumed the passive role. Perhaps Paul himself had encountered such abused slaves.[42] Furthermore, it is not impossible that homoerotic behavior was associated with real or imaginary pagan cults—after all, "degradation of their bodies" and idolatry are juxtaposed (1:24).[43] All this is only speculation, however, because Paul does not give specific details about his objections.

Paul's description may be intentionally indeterminate. Coming from a Jewish background with a prevalent disgust for same-sex sexual interaction, he may have found a detailed explication unnecessary or even unsuited for his purpose. The persons he describes in Romans 1:18–32 are presented as a group with no faces, without a single concrete hint at what they actually do and the circumstances under which their actions take place. His vague presentation, which is reminiscent of the propagandist defamation of false teachers and enemies elsewhere in the New Testament (e.g., 2 Tim. 3:1–9; 2 Pet. 2; Jude 3–16), may also be simply a part of Paul's rhetorical strategy. Therefore, it is wise to refrain from drawing detailed conclusions from Paul's terminology about the nature of the same-sex conduct in Romans 1.

But neither should Paul's arguments be overgeneralized. Paul argues on the basis of his experience and the Hellenistic Jewish tradition. There is no reason to assume that he would speak of a "generic homosexuality" on a theoretical level beyond his experience and without a cultural context. Paul, like his contemporaries, could not possibly take into consideration homosexual orientation or identity. He only knew people who "change the order of their nature." Whatever he knew about the slave pederasty and boy-prostitution of the Romans he utilized to confirm his views about the nature of homoerotic relations. Paul's strong negative expressions, like *atimazesthai* (disgrace), *pathē atimias* (shameful lusts), *orexis* (desire), and *askhēmosynē* (obscenity), lead in the same direction, marking the semantic environment of the word *akatharsia* (impurity). In line with Jewish teaching, Paul labeled homoerotic behavior as a whole as debauchery, lustful deeds, and abnormal transgressions of gender boundaries, that is, "unnatural" acts performed by "normal" people. Already John Chrysostom in his commentary on the Romans remarks that Paul speaks here not of love but of lust.[44]

To speculate about the concrete phenomena behind Paul's description of homoeroticism may miss the actual point in question in his letter to the Romans as a whole. Romans 1:18–32 belongs to a textual world that functions under its own conditions and does not necessarily reflect the actual historical world. Paul's words about homoeroticism need to be read in the context of his letter to the Romans. Surely Paul does more than just repeat the clichés he learned from his Jewish tradition; he actually uses Jewish weapons against the Jews themselves. What matters here is the theology of justification by faith, not homoeroticism as such. Paul's rhetorical strategy in Romans 1–2 seems to be to stimulate his readers' moral indignation by listing sins traditionally associated with Gentiles, in conventional Jewish wordings—but this is a rhetorical trap: Paul turns the force of his criticism against his potential readers.[45]

The description of the corruption of humankind in Romans 1 is an introduction to chapters 2 and 3, where Paul proceeds to assert that the Jews are really no better off than the Gentiles if they imagine that they can be saved because of the Law and circumcision (3:9). "You therefore have no defense—you who sit in judgement, whoever, you may be—for in judging your fellow-man you condemn yourself, since you, the judge, are equally guilty" (2:1, NEB). To the Jews, who abhorred homoeroticism, this must have sounded harsh, but equally sharp is Paul's focus and realization: "It is God's way of righting wrong, effective through faith in Christ for all who have such faith—all, without distinction. For all alike have sinned, and are deprived of the divine splendour, and all are justified by God's free grace alone, through his act of liberation in the person of Christ Jesus" (3:22–24, NEB). Only now has he reached his actual point, which motivates all that has been mentioned thus far. Simultaneously he returns to the theme of 1:16–17: "For I am not ashamed of the Gospel. It is the saving power of God for everyone who has faith—the Jew, first, but the Greek also—because here is revealed God's way of righting wrong, a way that starts from faith and ends in faith; as Scripture says, 'He shall gain life who is justified through faith'" (NEB).

The first chapters of Paul's letter to the Romans, then, address the theology of justification by faith, not homoeroticism. Paul does not list individual sins that would rouse God's wrath. The deeds he mentions are not provocations of the wrath of God but manifestations, symptoms, and results of the one root sin, exchanging God for idols, which inevitably leads to "unnatural" practices (*para physin*).[46] It is of no help if people amend the wicked habits that rule their lives, since even a "natural" way of life (*kata physin*), that is, a life according to the Law of God, does not bring salvation; only faith in Christ can remedy the situation. Those practicing homoeroticism, like everybody else, need God's grace, which, because of Christ, they can receive by faith. They are in the same position as those, who are "without natural affection and without pity" (1:31).

Presumably nothing would have made Paul approve homoerotic behavior. Clearly, Paul, to whom marriage was the only acceptable venue for sexual life, could not have approved any same-sex interaction that even resembled sex between a man and a woman. But condemning "homosexuality" is not Paul's main concern. His words about same-sex conduct in Romans 1:26–27 are one example he chose from his tradition to illustrate how badly the world needs grace and, at the same time, to set a trap for anyone who would read his words with feelings of moral superiority or religious bigotry.

Paul's criticism of homoeroticism in his letter to the Romans can be summarized as follows:

1. The actual goal of Paul's argumentation is justification by faith. The reference to homoeroticism is a rhetoric illustration that serves this goal and demonstrates the root sin of exchanging God for idols.

2. Paul's thoughts have a background in Hellenistic Jewish tradition and language, which was significantly influenced by Greco-Roman philosophy. In his criticism of homoeroticism as such, he does not present any independent ideas.

3. Paul is likely to have been familiar with some forms of homosexual behavior, although he does not disclose exactly what kind of homoeroticism he has in mind. His mention of women shows that his arguments are

not limited to pederasty. His references to "homosexuality," however, do not come from outside his experience and world. Therefore, his statements cannot be understood as if they deal with "homosexuality" theoretically and generally.

4. Paul does not speak of gender identity or sexual orientation nor does he speak of homoerotic relationships based on mutual love; instead, he considers homoeroticism to involve lustful sexual acts and unchaste behavior, in which men's and women's "natural" roles are confused. For Paul, same-sex relations are not a matter of personal identity, but they certainly are a matter of accepted gender roles, the confusing of which, for him, is "against nature."

MEN WHO SLEEP—WITH WHOM?
1 CORINTHIANS 6:9 AND 1 TIMOTHY 1:10

Two further passages of the New Testament have been traditionally associated with the issue of homoeroticism, 1 Corinthians 6:9 and 1 Timothy 1:10. Both verses include the Greek word *arsenokoitēs*, and 1 Corinthians 6:9 includes also the word *malakos*. Both words have been generally interpreted to denote homosexual men. Thus, the statement of 1 Corinthians 6:9 that *malakoi* and *arsenokoitai*, among other transgressors, "will never come into possession of the kingdom of God," has been interpreted to mean that all homosexuals will be eternally damned.[47] This verse has had a deep influence in the way homosexuals have been treated in Christian communities, in spite of the fact that the actual meaning of these two words is ambiguous and their homosexual interpretation has been challenged.

In both cases we have to do with a list of vices that resembles those in Romans and in the Wisdom of Solomon. Lists of virtues and vices are a literary genre known from both Greco-Roman and Jewish literature. Hellenistic Jews adopted this genre from Greek popular philosophers and have ever since applied it in their moral teaching. Lists of virtues and vices found their way from there also to Paul and his followers (cf. Rom. 1:29–31; Gal. 5:19–23; Col. 3:18—4:1; Eph. 5:21—6:9; 2 Tim. 3:1-5, etc.).[48]

All vice lists appear as summaries, rarely referring to the actual context of the vices or to the real people to whom the text is directed.[49] Compilers of such lists are not particularly selective about their content but use them to describe all the evil people could potentially do. The longer the list, the more weight it has; Philo lists no less than one hundred forty-seven vices![50] It is hard to know whether Paul in his list in 1 Corinthians wants to underscore any particular point, although he doubtlessly concurs with the items in it. It is equally difficult to know whether any vice mentioned in the list was an especially real problem in the Corinthian congregation.

There are three vice lists in close proximity in 1 Corinthians. Paul appears to aim at rhetorical climax by expanding his list each time.[51] The first list (5:10) mentions those "who lead loose lives or are grabbers and swindlers or idolaters." The second list (5:11) is extended, admonishing against "any so-called Christian who leads a loose life, or is grasping, or idolatrous, a slanderer, a drunkard, or a swindler." The third list (6:9–10) adds to all of the above also adulterers and thieves, as well as *malakoi* and *arsenokoitai*, which in the English Bible translations are translated as "homosexuals" (RSV, 1st ed.), "sexual perverts" (RSV, 2d ed.), "guilty. . . of homosexual perversion" (NEB), "male prostitutes" and "sodomites" (NRSV), and so forth.

Nothing else in 1 Corinthians 6 can be interpreted in terms of homoerotic conduct. The chapter deals with Christians' mutual litigation: "Indeed, you already fall below your standard in going to law with one another at all. Why not rather suffer injury? Why not rather let yourself be robbed? So far from this, you actually injure and rob—injure and rob your brothers!" (6:7–8, NEB). This is followed by a list of examples of different ways to exploit and do wrong. Paul probably cites here an older source.[52]

First Timothy, which, according to prevailing scholarly opinion, is later than Paul, provides a list (1:9–10) built from almost entirely different components, apparently drawn from the Decalogue. The list names "the lawless and unruly, the impious and sinful (the first commandment), the irreligious and worldly" (commandments 2 and 3), as well as patricides and matricides (4), murderers (5) and fornicators (6), *arsenokoitai* (6?[53]) , kidnappers (7), liars (8), perjurers (2 and 8). These persons are mentioned as examples of those "all whose behaviour flouts the wholesome teaching which conforms with the gospel entrusted to me, the gospel which tells of the glory of God in his eternal felicity" and because of whom the Law became necessary.

The main concern here is what the terms *malakos* and *arsenokoitēs* signify and whether they relate in any way to homoeroticism. A common assumption is that the terms refer to the partners in a pederastic relationship, *malakos* signifying the passive (*erōmenos*) and *arsenokoitēs* the active partner (*erastēs*).[54] This conception has been recently questioned, and a reevaluation has become necessary. The latter term needs to be examined first, because it appears in both lists and is semantically more crucial than the former.

The word *arsenokoitēs* has an obvious sexual connotation; the second part (*koitē*) refers to "bed," certainly referring to a sexual act. The problem is that the structure does not reveal whether the first part of the word, *arsēn* ("man, male"), should be understood as subject or object. Thus it is difficult to determine whether it means a man who lies (exclusively) with men, ("one who lies with men," with *arsēn* as object), or a male who can lie with both women and men ("a male who lies," with *arsēn* a subject). John Boswell has argued vigorously for the latter alternative.[55] According to his observations, in analogous words with *arseno* in the beginning, the first part of the compound is the subject, whereas in words with *arreno* in the beginning it is the object.[56] The word, according to Boswell, means a male prostitute, whose possible homosexual services the term does not reveal. It adds to the mystery of the term that Paul (or the vice list he cites) seems to be the first to use the word. Greek homoerotic or otherwise erotic literature does not know this word, which is unknown also to Jewish writers.[57] Even the *Didache*, a Christian writing from the second century belonging to the Apostolic Fathers, lists other components of 1 Corinthians 6:9 but fails to mention *malakoi* and *arsenokoitai* (*Did.* 5:1–2). Nor do Clement of Alexandria and John Chrysostom, who discuss homoeroticism more than other church fathers do, use the term even when commenting on these specific biblical texts.[58] Conversely, other sources that use the word do not, says Boswell, associate it clearly with homoeroticism.[59] This all indicates, according to Boswell, that *arsenokoitēs* does not denote the active partner in a homosexual relationship but by and large a male prostitute.

Boswell has been criticized for being too eager to clear *arsenokoitēs* from all traces of homoeroticism. Although the term does not clearly refer to pederasty, this obviously does not mean that it could never have meant that. In some of the sources cited by Boswell, *arsenokoitēs* or its derivative appears in connection with terms that definitely mean pederasty. For instance, the *Apology of Aristides* (9:13), from the second century C.E., relates how Gentiles in their debaucherous ways imitate their gods, who commit a variety of crimes, such as murders, witchcraft, adultery, thefts, and so forth; the list ends with *arsenokoitia*. Earlier (9:8–9), *Ap. Aris.* stated that Gentiles, imitating their gods, commit adultery and are "mad after males" (*arrenomaneis)* and inquired whether a god can be an adulterer or a "corrupter of males" (*androbatēs*). Here and in similar cases[60] the term can be interpreted both ways or to mean exclusively homosexual behavior. Similarly feeble is Boswell's interpretation of the subject/object relation of words that begin with *arseno* and *arreno*; most probably this distinction is one of pronunciation, not a semantic but a dialectic distinction;[61] on this basis, a subject/object distinction seems artificial.[62]

On the other hand, in some words that begin with *arseno* or *arreno*, this term functions as subject: for example, *arsenogenēs* ("male"), *arsenothymos* ("man-minded"), *arsenomorfos* and *arrenofanēs* ("masculine"), and compare *paidomathēs* ("having learned in childhood") and *paidotrōtos* ("wounded by children"). These could be compared with the modern word "nymphomania," which does not denote madness after women but excessive sexual desire on the part of a woman. Although *arsenokoitēs* in many contexts indeed refers to homosexual behavior, its ambiguous structure makes other uses possible also. If the context does not give a clear indication, the meaning of *arsenokoitēs* remains indefinite.[63]

Robin Scroggs has argued for the pederastic interpretation. Scroggs refers to the Rabbinic term *miškab zākûr* (lying with a male), which in the Talmudic interpretation of Lev. 18:22 and 20:13 is used for the active partner in pederasty.[64] The word *arsenokoitēs* is a literal translation of this term.[65] This would explain also why the term is rare and its meaning ambiguous; as a translation it is simply strange and is a poor rendition of the Greek because of its enigmatic structure.

Scroggs's theory can be criticized, because the Rabbinic sources in which *miškab zākûr* appears are considerably later than Paul. However, the Greek expression *lekhos andrōn* ("marriage-bed of men") used in *Pseudo-Phocylides* 192, probably a little earlier than Paul, may be understood as a translation of a similar Hebrew compound.[66] Moreover, the word could have been derived from another source well known to Paul and the whole Hellenistic Jewish community, namely, the Septuagint, which translates Lev. 18:22 and 20:13 as follows:[67]

> Lev. 18:22: *kai meta arsenos ou koimēthēsē koitēn gynaikos*
> Lev. 20:13: *kai hos an koimēthē meta arsenos koitēn gynaikos. . . .*

Especially Lev. 20:13 binds the words *arsēn* and *koite* so closely together that it has been easy for those versed in the Scriptures to create a neologism on the basis of the Septuagint. This explains the rarity and semantic ambiguity of the word in Greek texts.

Following the Septuagint, the male affix of *arsenokoitēs* should be taken as an object: "one who lies with men" (also Jerome translated it in the Vulgate *masculorum concubitores*). Unfortunately, this does not clear the ambiguity or exclude the possibility that the male-affix, regardless of the Septuagint, could have been interpreted as the subject and the word understood to denote a "male who lies with anyone." Thus, the two alternatives to interpret *arsenokoitēs* differ markedly from one another, and neither is thoroughly documented. On the basis of the Septuagint, the homoerotic interpretation seems better grounded than Boswell's argument. Not everyone who has used the term, however, have necessarily taken into consideration the Septuagint or the etymology of the word in general.

The "etymology of a word is its history, not its meaning."[68] It is possible that determining the meaning of the word by combining the meanings of its component parts is semantically misleading. Attempts have been made to understand the word *arsenokoitēs* apart from the same-sex-or-not issue, paying more attention to the contexts in which the word appears.[69]

Whether fully convincing or not, these attempts not only show how difficult it really is to determine the actual meaning of this word in different contexts but also illustrate that our questions do not emerge solely from "objective" philological interest but from ideological needs as well.

The basic meaning of the word *malakos* is "soft," and it is used with its derivatives (*malthakos, malakia*) in various contexts that speak about, for instance, frailty of body or character, illness, sentimentality, or moral weakness. It often has a effeminate nuance, especially when dealing with pederasty.[70] On this basis, it has been assumed that in the vice list Paul cites in 1 Corinthians 6:9, *malakos* would mean the passive partner in a pederastic relationship; Scroggs speaks of an "effeminate call-boy."[71]

In Greek sources the word itself is not used in this sense, although it is sometimes mentioned in the context of pederasty. Hence, although *malakos* can be used to ridicule homosexual behavior, this is not its only meaning and in every context. In a papyrus letter from around 245 B.C.E., Demophon, an Egyptian, asks an official, Ptolemaios, to help with festivities. He asks Ptolemaios to send a musician, Zenobius, whose nickname is *malakos*. According to his reputation, he played his drums and castanets dressed up in fancy clothes, following the wishes especially of the ladies.[72] His nickname may refer to his effeminate appearance, but the text suggests no further sexual associations.

A clearer reference to pederasty comes from an excerpt of Plautus's text, translated from Greek, where a voice that belongs to a beloved boy says about himself: "and when it comes to dancing, there is no lither playboy than I."[73] In Latin the sentence reads, *Tum ad saltandum non cinaedus malacus aequest atque ego.* The word *cinaedus* (Greek, *kinaidos*) certainly means a boy prostitute, but *malacus* (Greek, *malakos*) is not its synonym but an epithet, which in the context of dancing obviously means soft and graceful, perhaps feminine movement.

All in all it seems that the word *malakos* stresses femininity; it appears to correspond to the Latin word *mollis*, which Jerome uses at this point in his translation, the Vulgate.[74] The homosexual connotation may come from effeminacy, because the man who submits to the passive sexual role takes the position of a woman and represents moral values associated with women—mostly in a negative sense.[75]

Some scholars have criticized attempts bluntly to associate homosexual behavior as feminine. This association has no doubt often been made carelessly and without sufficient grounds. Yet the contention that a man's homosexuality does not always appear in his femininity misses the point. Evidently this is the case today,[76] but it is equally clear that in the Greek and especially the Roman cultures at the beginning of the Common Era the passive partner in a homoerotic relationship, the *cinaedus*, was considered expressly girlish and was hence held in contempt.[77] In any case, "effeminacy" in our sources does not refer to the sexual orientation or gender identification of a (male) person of whom it is used but to his moral quality as characterized by the traditional signs of effeminacy—lack of self-control and yielding to pleasures.[78] This certainly motivated Paul to use the word *malakos* in his list of vices.

The question of the exact meaning of the juxtaposition *malakos* and *arsenokoitēs* thus remains obscure. "The evidence is too meager to allow for much more than an educated guess"[79]; this is especially the case regarding the word *arsenokoitēs*. Appearing one after the other, they *can* be interpreted in terms of a pederastic relationship but they *need not* be so interpreted. They do not form a fixed word-pair, because both words stand well also by themselves, yielding different interpretations. The modern concept of "homosexuality" should by no means be read into Paul's text,[80] nor can we assume that Paul's words in 1 Corinthians 6:9 "condemn all homosexual relations" in all times and places and ways.[81] The meanings of the words are too vague to justify this claim, and Paul's words should not be used for generalizations that go beyond his experience and world.

Regardless of the kind of sexuality meant in 1 Corinthians 6:9 and 1 Timothy 1:10, in their current contexts they are examples of the exploitation of persons. This is the hermeneutical horizon for understanding the individual components of the lists of vices. What Paul primarily opposes is the wrong that people do to others. To illustrate his moral advice, he makes use of a list that he thinks best demonstrates various kinds of wrongdoing. Likewise, the writer of 1 Timothy takes "lying with men" as an example of a transgression of the Decalogue.

JESUS AND HOMOSEXUALITY

Did homoeroticism have anything to do with the life and teaching of Jesus of Nazareth? The only sources, the Gospels, do not provide material for far-ranging hypotheses. To the extent that Rabbinic and Hellenistic Jewish literature sheds light on the norms of Jewish society in Jesus' time, it can be assumed that public expressions of homosexuality were regarded as anomalous, idolatrous, and indecent. If they ever should occur, the person in question evidently became *persona non grata*. In an environment that totally rejected homoeroticism, a person with a same-sex orientation would have found it too overwhelming to "come out" and thus probably would choose to deal with the matter in other ways than making this preference public.

According to the Gospels, Jesus did not argue for or against homoeroticism in any form, nor did he give any general advice in the area of sexual ethics. His sympathetic attitude toward the marginalized and the despised—the sick, Samaritans, prostitutes, and women in general—has been noticed, especially in the Gospel of Luke. To what extent this is in accord with the historical figure of Jesus is not certain, but it is noteworthy that this is the way his followers wanted to depict his image a half century later. Jesus' immediate circles and the post-Easter "Jesus movement" apparently were open to various people who might have been rebuffed by others in society. It is not possible to know whether some of these people faced discrimination because of their same-sex preference.

There is hardly anything to learn about Jesus' sexual life. The Christian tradition has subconsciously regarded Jesus as a sexless person, and texts and movies that make innuendoes about Jesus' sexuality often irritate even modern persons. A traditional negative attitude toward sexuality has fostered this stance. Jesus' virgin birth and his alleged freedom from sexual lust have often been taken as the best manifestation of his freedom from sin. The Gospels say almost nothing about Jesus' sexuality and thus leave modern questions unanswered. This has stirred up a variety of speculations, especially the thought that Mary Magdalene was his beloved.[82] The Gnostic *Gospel of Philip* mentions her in the following context (59:6–11).

> There were three (women) who always walked with the Lord: Mary, his mother, and her sister and the Magdalene, the one who was called his companion *(koinōnos)*. For Mary is his sister, his mother and his companion.

Koinōnos, a word taken from the Greek into Coptic, sometimes means also a spouse or a sex partner but, in the context of the *Gospel of Philip,* it is more probably to be interpreted as a spiritual consort whose role is similar to that of Mary Magdalene in the *Gospel of Mary,* another Gnostic text in which Mary is presented as the most beloved disciple of Jesus.[83] This becomes clear from the accounts that introduce her simultaneously as Jesus' sister, mother, and companion, which shows that "she is to be seen as a mythical figure who actually belongs to the transcendent realm but who manifests herself in the women accompanying the earthly Jesus."[84] Hence, even the Gnostic texts reveal nothing historical about Jesus' sex life.

Singleness—an unmarried lifestyle—was exceptional, even suspicious among the Jews, because it was seen as an offense to the divine obligation to procreate (Gen. 1:28).[85] Jesus, however, was apparently single. Attitudes about an adult man staying single in a Jewish society[86] have led to speculation about Jesus' lifestyle, including a possible homosexual tendency.[87] Some have seen homoerotic traits in Jesus' relationship with his disciples, especially with the "beloved disciple" in the Gospel of John. Nevertheless, singleness and celibacy were part of the role of ascetics, prophets, and vagrant preachers, like John the Baptist, and did not up stir any particular speculation.[88] Homoeroticism was never associated with the lifestyle of such figures. Jesus' singleness, too, was a part of his role as an independent preacher. Without being an ascetic in the strict sense of the word—in contrast to John the Baptist, he is depicted as eating and drinking as everyone else (Matt. 11:18–19; Luke 7:33–34)—he did not lead a conventional family life.

In the Gospel of Matthew Jesus comments about the unmarried life in a positive vein (Matt. 19:10–12).[89] He grants this possibility only to those "for whom God has appointed it":

> For while some are incapable of marriage because they were born so, or were made so by men, there are others who have themselves renounced marriage for the sake of the kingdom of Heaven. Let those accept it who can. (Matt. 19:12, NEB)

In the original Greek, those who are "incapable of marriage" are called "eunuchs" (*eunouchoi*). Some are such from their birth, others have been made eunuchs by other people,[90] and the third group consists of those who voluntarily have made themselves eunuchs. Broadly speaking, "eunuch" can mean anybody who finds marital life impossible. People who have voluntarily emasculated themselves, or have been castrated by others, are, of course, eunuchs in a literal sense. We have already seen that in Jesus' world (and especially in Syria, where the Gospel of Matthew originated) there were true eunuchs,[91] and it is not impossible that some of them would have sought entry into early Christian communities (Acts 8:26–40?). This involved deliberate ignoring of the Torah, which excludes eunuchs from the cultic association of Israel (Deut. 23:2). In an expanded sense, the word has been taken as referring to anyone who was physically debilitated, incapable of fathering children, or otherwise unfit and therefore excluded from society.[92]

As discussed above, self-emasculation was a token of total dedication to a specific deity in many cults, and it was a symbolic act people well understood. The symbolism was more important than the physical act of emasculation and makes the statement of Jesus more understandable. A "eunuch" for the sake of the kingdom of heaven was a person who, like a true eunuch, voluntarily devoted himself to the cause of the kingdom by giving up marriage and sexual interaction and whose gender role for that reason was different from conventional standards. In Matthew (as well as in Paul, 1 Cor. 7:32–35) this is not yet a matter of a consistent ascetic ideal but a rare opportunity for those (few?) who in this way devoted themselves to promote the kingdom of God.[93] The early Christian communities probably did not press people to emasculate themselves,[94] but the ascetic way of life that included total sexual abstinence became all the more idealized in time to come.

From a modern point of view, those who had been eunuchs from their mother's womb, that is, people to whom marriage was inherently impossible, might well include homosexuals. It is not apparent whether people in Jesus' time were able to reason in this way, but it is possible to imagine that in that time also there were people who for whatever reason avoided heterosexual sexual activity and were thus considered "eunuchs." Matthew 19:10–12 indicates that the early Christian community did not reject people who by others were considered strange in this respect.

It has been hypothesized that Jesus' startling saying about eunuchs was a response to ridicule and wonderment regarding his own unmarried status.[95] At least Matthew's congregation argued in this way for the unmarried lifestyle of some of its members (and possibly its Lord's). This text does not allow speculation about Jesus' own sexual orientation, but it does enable an interpretation that includes homosexuals in the group of "eunuchs" for whom heterosexual sexual life was not possible. In any event, an essential part of staying unmarried or becoming a "eunuch" was giving up sexual activity. This was regarded as an acceptable lifestyle for those who found it fitting, although it was not promoted as a general ideal for everyone.

Unrelated to the question of the unmarried is whether the relationships between Jesus and his disciples included any aspects of homoeroticism. References to the closeness of Jesus and his disciples have led to speculation on the part of a few scholars whether their interaction might have included intimate physical aspects.[96] Special attention has been paid to the Gospel of John, which frequently speaks of "love" (*agapē*) and of a disciple "whom Jesus loved." This person, who introduces himself as the author of that Gospel (John 21:20–24; cf. 19:35) does not reveal his name; the tradition identifies him as John, the son of Zebedee.

The disciple whom Jesus loved, according to the Gospel of John, was closer to Jesus than were the other disciples. This Gospel highlights particularly the last supper before Jesus' arrest, when that disciple leaned against Jesus' chest and acted as a spokesman for the others (John 13:23–25; 21:20). He also stood by the cross and was assigned the care of Jesus' mother (19:26–27).

The relationship between Jesus and the beloved disciple has been recently considered as a training relationship akin to the ideal in Plato's Athens.[97] Jesus could be seen as the active partner in the relationship, as a teacher and a lover (*erastēs*), and the favorite disciple would be the passive partner, a student and a beloved (*erōmenos*).[98]

Clearly the Gospel of John in particular presupposes a close teacher-student relationship between Jesus and his immediate circle, and in this company the favorite disciple clearly enjoys special status. He is the one whom Jesus quite especially "loved" and who always stood closest to Jesus. Nevertheless, the homoerotic or pederastic dimension of their relationship could be argued only in a strained way from very limited material. Only the scene at the last supper might suggest this direction—and it is questionable evidence at that. The custom of a student resting against his teacher's chest manifests cultural conventions rather than homoeroticism; in this sense the relationship between Jesus and his favorite disciple evinces homosociability that tolerates also physical expressions of mutual attachment. An interesting point of comparison can be seen in Jesus' relationship with Mary Magdalene in the *Gospels of Philip* and *Mary,* mentioned above. Even where the teacher and the student are of different sexes, an erotic relationship is hardly at stake. In the Gospel of John, moreover, the emphasis on the beloved disciple's special relationship with Jesus may be a literary device to underscore the reliability of the writer. A further question is the degree to which the Gospel writers would have been familiar with Greek customs.

Finally, there is the basic question of the historical authenticity of the Gospel of John. Even if this Gospel allows for some homosocial interpretations, this would not necessarily reveal anything about Jesus' actual life.[99] This reservation, of course, applies also to other texts than the Gospel of John; in fact, it applies to all documents treated thus far. Ancient sources portray themselves, their times, and people as they wish. It is difficult to reach the actual world behind them, especially when the questions arise from modern concerns.

7

HOMOEROTICISM IN THE BIBLICAL WORLD AND HOMOSEXUALITY TODAY

HOMOSEXUALITY AND BIBLICAL INTERPRETATION

If we want the Bible and other ancient sources to contribute to today's discussion, the starting point is the sensible hermeneutical principle that there must be a sufficient correlation between the topics discussed today and the ancient sources. The arguments in the Bible and other ancient sources focus on issues and phenomena of their time, from their own premises. Today's questions reflect the world from which they arise, and the motivations for biblical interpretation and argumentation vary. This needs to be remembered especially when biblical arguments are held as normative in today's decisions.[1] The biblical material that relates to same-sex eroticism is sparse, scattered, and ambiguous. What the texts have in common is their negative attitude toward sexual contact between people of the same sex. Is this sufficient to form a clearly defined biblical argument about the modern concept of "homosexuality"? It is true that the Bible has nothing positive to say about sexual relations between people of the same sex. But it is also true that it is the interpreting community of the modern era that unites the texts as a group of biblical references against "homosexuality." The reason for such texts to be gathered together may be sought first and foremost in the needs of the interpreters (many would talk about a heterosexist bias), rather than in the biblical material in its own right.

No single passage in the Bible actually offers a specifically formulated statement about same-sex eroticism. The topic appears as a secondary theme in a variety of contexts, with different texts answering different questions. When the subject emerges, arguments arise spontaneously on the basis of the writer's own tradition and already developed views. If we assume that the biblical authors nonetheless deal with same-sex relations in a universal sense, "homosexuality in general," using examples familiar to their audience, we must realize that there is no such thing as "homosexuality in general." Instead, there are different kinds of same-sex activities and relationships, which always appear in specific cultural conditions—not in timeless space. Gender identities exist only within time and space, and they cannot be simply transferred from one culture to another. The same-sex activities presupposed in the Holiness Code or by Paul inevitably took place under different social circumstances and in cultural contexts other than those of modern discussion. The same is true of the communal interpretation of what happens between the parties involved.

Once again, it is important to remember that "sexuality," with its derivatives "homosexuality" and "heterosexuality," is a modern abstraction with no equivalent in the Bible or other ancient sources.[2] This means that the distinguishing of sexual orientations, with the accompanying rationales and justifications, also is a modern phenomenon with a quite different basis and motivation for argumentation from the way ancient sources deal with same-sex eroticism.

Quite possibly no biblical author approved of homoeroticism in any form they knew. To understand this attitude rightly, it is necessary to examine the way they understood same-sex interaction. The perspective of the biblical texts is clearly centered around physical sexual contacts, the background of which is seen in idolatry or moral corruption and the motivation for which is attributed to excessive lust (Romans 1) or xenophobia (Genesis 19; Judges 19). Love and positive feelings are not mentioned; responsible homosexual partnerships based on love seem to be completely inconceivable. However, the Bible does speak of love in a homosocial sense, in contexts that do not involve sexual acts. Even physical expressions of feelings are not foreign to this kind of "love relationship," as the case of David and Jonathan witnesses.

Paul, for instance, has only negative things to say about same-sex conduct in the way he perceived it. This fact cannot be speculated away. Yet, it would be hazardous to make Paul's text deal with something it does not address. It would not be fair to claim that Paul would condemn all homosexuality everywhere, always, and in every form. Paul's arguments are based on certain Hellenistic Jewish moral codes that are culture-specific and that had their own trajectory of tradition. If these moral codes are regarded as binding in our time, the authority of the Bible might become confused with the authority of the Hellenistic Jewish synagogue.[3]

Paul cannot be held responsible for things he does not appear to know about—such as sexual orientation, which is not a voluntary perversion but an aspect of gender identity that manifests itself in different ways, including love. Although Paul does not speak exclusively of specific forms of homoeroticism, such as pederasty, his arguments should not be considered in a overly theoretical and abstract way. It would be most appropriate to let Paul be Paul—a human being, an educated Jewish theologian converted to faith in Christ who has much to say about justification by faith in his letter to the Romans, who wrote letters and not law books, who has certain values, norms, and prejudices—and who might have needed sexual therapy as much as any of us. Paul might best contribute to today's conversation when understood in this way.[4]

Other biblical authors can be held responsible only for those questions and answers they themselves posed or could have posed. They cannot be expected to give statements about questions for which they were not sufficiently equipped or knowledgeable. Even today, the reasons for or causes of homosexual orientation remain unknown. However, the perspectives of genetics, psychiatry, and sociology, even if partially contradictory, as well as the recent formation of gay and lesbian identities and lifestyles have shed totally new light on same-sex relationships and have thoroughly shaken the whole discussion. All the perspectives of modern scholarship would have been foreign and incomprehensible to the biblical authors. Therefore it is dangerous to assume that the biblical authors would have opposed homosexuality even if they had shared modern ideas about it. We cannot possibly know what they would say today.[5]

An especially dangerous shortcut from the biblical text to modern times is an attempt to define homosexual persons' fate in the hereafter on the basis of lists of vices in the New Testament (1 Cor. 6:9–10; 1 Tim. 1:10). "The biblical teaching" in these matters is not "altogether clear." Arbitrary quoting of chapters and verses often not only ignores the concrete reality behind them but also the textual world to which they belong—not to mention the internalized values and preferences of the one who adduces quotations. "The fact is that we do not simply quote texts. We make decisions on theological and pragmatic grounds about what is applicable and what is not."[6] Using individual and ambiguous biblical passages as a basis for threatening people with eternal damnation leads to a kind of scriptural positivism, which may turn out to be a matter of the cruel abuse of religious power.

Regarding the history of biblical interpretation, if it is a fact that the Christian tradition has "always condemned homosexuality," it is true also that the Christian tradition has in many ways heavily condemned heterosexuality also.[7] The same reasons have been used to condemn both homosexual and heterosexual contacts: sexuality has been considered an expression of lust and thus sinful.

Biblical texts that mention same-sex eroticism, therefore, can make only a limited contribution to modern discussion about what is today called "homosexuality." This can be said without twisting the words. However, this does not mean that the Bible can have no role in solving contemporary issues. It is not necessary to make the biblical authors a laughingstock, even if their questions, approaches, and answers do not always correlate with those of ours. They write on the basis of their own identity, just as people do today, and modern Western people owe a great deal of their identity to them, which should encourage us to try with sensitivity to hear what they want to say. The positive contribution of the Bible to modern discussion can be found by examining and interpreting the biblical passages within their historical framework.

Questions about same-sex relationships are asked very differently today compared with the world in which the Bible was written, and the correlation of these two contexts is often superficial at best. It may well be that unless we totally oppose homosexuality, we have to diverge from the "clear word" of the Bible. But this is true also when one professes that the earth is round and revolves around the sun. Changes in worldview have forced people to adjust even to things and views that appear contrary to the Bible, because all biblical interpretation happens in concrete circumstances. All this forms a hermeneutical circle.

To make the hermeneutical issue more relevant, then, same-sex interaction must be seen as part of a larger whole—a field of problems that covers gender identity as well as citizen-rights issues.

We need to question whether the "biblical view on homosexuality" is thoroughly and finally defined after reading only a few related passages—and only them. Does not the genuinely biblical attitude require that also other biblical texts and comments are carefully sought, for instance, passages that deal with the connection of love and responsibility? Or the texts in which human experience is presented as a meaningful factor in the interpretation of reality?[8]

If in meeting a homosexual person all attention is focused on his or her sexual orientation, then the biblical passages treated in this book play a central role. Then the whole person is characterized, consciously and one-sidedly, by his or her sexual orientation or behavior, and sexual orientation is isolated from other aspects of gender identity. There are other perspectives also. If, for example, homosexual people are seen as a historically oppressed and despised minority yearning for its rights, then quite different texts predominate, other than those that describe sexual orgies and idolatry. Then we are dealing with both social and sexual ethics, as well as with the theology of liberation.[9]

The Deuteronomic Law, which in its humane perspective is seen as standing out from ancient Near Eastern legislation, did not include homosexuals in the group whose rights needed special protection. It lists widows and orphans, Levites and aliens—all underprivileged people without full civil rights. In modern society the list of those discriminated against is different, and modern people themselves need to realize who those people are.

Jesus' attitude toward the marginalized of his time, as it is repeatedly portrayed in the Gospels, is relevant. "Go and sin no more" (John 8:11)[10] was not the only message Jesus had for people who were hated because of the nature of their sexual life. The Gospels depict him as their friend who criticized them less than he criticized their judges. The ethics of the Sermon of the Mount broadens the moral perspective from the actual deeds to the attitudes behind them (Matt. 5:21–47) and forces the judge to look in a mirror. Even Paul applies the same strategy—precisely in his famous text on same-sex relations (Rom. 2:1–6).

Homosexuality is part of morality, just as sexuality as a whole is.[11] Homosexuality itself is neither a moral nor an amoral condition, regardless of a theory of its causes. A moral question is how we can and should live as sexual beings in a gendered society and how we treat fellow human beings with different gender identities. Homoeroticism and heterosexual practice are criticized alike in both Jewish-Christian and Graeco-Roman sources for the faults that could be condemned today also—abuse, frivolousness, violence, dissipation. Suppression, violence, infidelity, and exploitation, on one hand, and love, responsibility, and empathy, on the other, are the criteria for evaluating any sexual practice. Thus questions of sexual ethics enter the realm of the commandment of love[12] that sums up the whole of the Law and the Prophets, according to both Jesus and Paul:

> He who loves his neighbour has satisfied every claim of the law. For the commandments, "Thou shalt not commit adultery, thou shalt not kill, thou shalt not steal, thou shalt not covet," and any other commandment there may be, are all summed up in the one rule, "Love your neighbour as yourself." Love cannot wrong a neighbour; therefore the whole law is summed up in love. (Rom. 13:8–10; cf. Matt. 22:34–40; Gal. 5:14, NEB)

One of the most important theological issues related to homosexuality is that of creation. What is the basis of the claim that homosexual people are or are not created homosexuals? The Greek concept of "nature" (*physis*) that Paul and others used cannot be simply identified with creation. Nor is the problem solved by repeating the point in the creation story according to which God created people male and female and commanded them to procreate (Gen. 1:27–28). Homosexual men and women also are able to procreate. Moreover, it is not only procreation but also companionship that constitutes human sexual activity in Genesis 1–3.[13] Does being created in the image of God, male and female (Gen. 1:27), necessitate a certain (that is, heterosexual) gender identity? The God of the Bible has no sex or gender but is beyond sex and gender. Human beings are images of God as men and women regardless of their gender identity.

Understanding homosexuality from the perspective of creation has sometimes been linked with theories of homosexuality as hereditary or inborn. But the idea of creation does not depend on whether or not there is a gene for homosexuality. Without falling into biological determinism, it is not theologically sound to regard only physiological and hereditary traits as created and to think that social constructions are formed outside of creation. These questions lead us to ponder the correlation between "creation" and "nature" and homosexuality as a problem for the theology of creation. This question, because it is beyond the actual inquiry of this study, will be treated separately, in the appendix.

THE INTERPRETATION OF SAME-SEX RELATIONS THEN AND NOW

The preceding reflection deals primarily with biblical interpretation but is relevant also to other ancient texts. The Bible differs from other ancient sources because it has been a normative guideline of life for thousands of years, and it still is to many. Chapters and verses are still quoted against gay and lesbian people. The Bible has constrained people with different force from other ancient sources—which themselves have also contributed to the formation of Christian culture and views.

The image of homosexuality in the Bible and other ancient sources differs basically from modern images in that no distinction is made in the ancient sources between gender roles (man/woman), sexual orientation (homosexual/bisexual/heterosexual), and sexual practice. In those sources, erotic-sexual interaction on the part of people of the same sex is not considered a question of individual identity but a question of social roles and behavior. "Identity," like "sexuality," is an abstraction that became conceptualized only in modern times (see the introduction, above).

The biblical authors, like other Jews, could obviously not think of homoerotic behavior as arising from any particular identity or orientation. Thus same-sex sexual contacts were regarded as a voluntary perversion. In the cultures of ancient Greece and Rome, it was thought that sexual desire could "naturally" be channeled toward either sex. Had they known the mod-

ern distinction between different sexual orientations, they might have considered a bisexual identity as normal (an assumption that does not justify
categorizing the ancient Greeks as "bisexuals"). Nevertheless, homoeroticism was regulated by socially accepted role restrictions and rules of behavior, and the predominant heterosexual way of life was by no means questioned, let alone threatened. The acceptability of a person's homoerotic
behavior depended on one's social role and status, not on one's personal
identity. From a philosophical-ethical point of view, most important was not
the gender of one's sexual partner but the acceptable role structure of the
relationship, self-control (*enkrateia*), and moderation (*sōphrosynē*)—in
other words, a "proper use of pleasure" (*khrēsis aphrodisiōn*) within the
limits of the socially sanctioned system of gender.[14]

The distinction between active and passive sexual roles has proved to
be central in all descriptions of sexual life in sources from Mesopotamia to
Rome. With few exceptions, it can be said that descriptions of sexual relations were dominated by a hierarchical polarization based on the congru-
ence of social status and sexual hierarchy.[15] This inevitably provoked the
question, "Who's on top?"[16] The fundamental starting point was that men
were the active, enterprising, penetrating partners and the subjects of sexual relationships, whereas women, as passive, receiving partners, were
their objects. The same role distinction was in effect also in same-sex sexual relations, which were not understood as balanced and mutual.
Transgressions of role boundaries, whether by a man or a woman, were
severely condemned in Mesopotamian, Greek, Roman, and Jewish societies—except in cases of socially accepted institutions (Mesopotamian
*assinnu*s and, to some extent, Greek pederasty) where a transgression of
roles was permitted and even favored under certain specific conditions.

The role distinction mirrored social relations and conditions. The relation of the dominant and the receptive partner reflected the relation
between the socially superior and the socially inferior. The legitimate sexual relation, in fact, presupposed the subordinate social status of the passive partner. If there were legitimate forms of homoeroticism, they should
have been carried out between a superior and an inferior. Accordingly, not
only women but in certain cases also other persons in an inferior status, like
boys, slaves, foreigners, and defeated enemies, could be targets of sexual
aggression—of course, within socially sanctioned limits. A sexually superior role on the part of a social inferior, however, was seen as intolerable
and immoral—"contrary to nature," as the Greeks often put it, because the
"natural" order of things would then be turned upside down.

This distinction is clear also in the area of ethics, because the "ethos of
penetration and domination"[17] predominated in a social model that was
hierarchically polarized, rather than principles of mutual respect and

fidelity, important values today. This explains why the feminization or effeminacy of a man was an expressly *moral* issue.

To the extent that ancient sources on homoeroticism allude to transvestism or transsexuality, it happens within the limits of established role thinking. In Greco-Roman cultures feminine dressing manifested a passive sexual role and was in this way connected with homoeroticism. In Mesopotamia and Syria transvestism was part of the role of the cult professionals who had been "changed from men to women." In neither case does dressing in the fashion of the opposite sex correspond to modern understandings of a transvestite need, which is independent of one's sexual orientation.

In the material of this study, the distinction between active and passive partners matches the distinction between male and female roles.[18] In men's homosexual relationships the passive role was that of a socially subjected person. It was virtually identified with a female role and necessitated a feminine appearance and behavior. Same-sex interaction between women, however, was problematic in terms of the patriarchal role distinction but problem-free in other respects. Because of the fundamental asymmetry of gender role structure, it was not regarded as a mere subcategory of the "homosexuality" expressed by male same-sex relationships.[19] The Roman writers especially, from whom the most ancient responses to female homoeroticism come, considered it an outrageous disturbance of established social structures. On the other hand, the scarcity of sources in general may imply that women's mutual eroticism was considered relatively harmless, to the extent that male writers were even aware of it in cultures where men's and women's worlds were segregated. But what disturbed some of these writers was that the traditional role distinction was impossible in lesbian relations. A woman in an active role was found offensive because it was against both reason and morals to have a person without semen or penis assume an active role. However, in the texts of the sole female poet, Sappho, the traditional role distinction is not visible.

Behind the distinction between active male and passive female roles are undoubtedly also ancient ideas about reproduction and woman's role in reproduction. In times when people did not know about the human ovum, people believed that the sperm contained the origin of human life. Woman was considered only as soil for a seed, with no active role in creating new life.[20] The active partner gave the seed and the passive partner received it. Losing it was a harmful waste of life, and woman's menstrual blood was an incomprehensible matter and a taboo. This tremendously influenced the way woman's body and status were understood in relation to man. The structure of modern society and, in principle at least, women's equality in it and proper understanding of woman's biology have caused fundamental changes in this respect, even if this is not always manifest in public attitudes.

It is beyond doubt that in ancient Mesopotamia and Palestine, as well as in Greece and Rome, there were persons whose sexual interest was focused on people of same sex, regardless of existing role structures. Some would call this an appetite rather than an orientation, but I prefer the latter. In ancient Greek and Roman societies a male person of this kind was more free to express his orientation than in ancient Assyria and Israel or, for instance, today's Finland, because a man who preferred the love of boys did not have to feel himself "different" from other men because of this preference as such. To express one's orientation meant, however, accepting the predominant role distinction, and the passive role of an adult man with its feminine characteristics was not respected. It may be that a homosexual man of our times would not have found the ancient homoerotic climate at all comfortable, although he would not need to have hidden his disposition for fear of the hatred of his society, as homosexuals living in Jewish-Christian or Islamic cultures have had to do.

In this respect, modern understanding of the expression of sexual orientation differs from the (male) views and experiences revealed in ancient sources, whether it concerns heterosexual or homosexual relationships. The difference can be illuminated with the help of the four categories of Greenberg (1988): (1) transgenerational homosexuality, involving an older and a younger (male) partner; (2) transgenderal homosexuality, which requires a cross-gender role (i.e., a gender role opposite to one's biological sex) on the part of one of the partners; (3) an egalitarian same-sex relationship; and (4) class-distinguished homosexuality. Today's discussion is obviously and precisely focused on the third category, that of the egalitarian same-sex relationships. That category is virtually nonexistent in ancient sources.[21] The other three categories, all of which are well represented in ancient sources, play hardly any role in modern Western society.

Ancient same-sex interaction and modern notions of homosexual orientation are thus two different things; although they can be compared with each other, they must be kept separate. Ancient sources know no "homosexuality," at least not as modern educated Western people use this word. Persons who were sexually active predominantly or solely with persons of their own sex demonstrably existed and also were recognized and even classified as distinct groups by their contemporaries. Their self-representation, however, was a matter of the blurring of socially sanctioned gender roles rather than of subjective, personal orientation or character. The ancient categorizations of people with an apparently homoerotic preference, characterized by words like *assinnu, galli, mollis, cinaedus, tribas,* and the like, were still far from the fully conceptualized system of sexual orientations with respective psychiatric, psychological, biological, and social factors. In the modern world, scientific attention since the nineteenth century has been devoted especially to individual sexual orientation and its causes. Research on genes, hormones, and the brain has led to biological explanations of homosexuality, psychological sciences have explained its causes on the basis of early childhood experiences, and social sciences have explained it as connected to social learning. Although no single model of explanation is decisive and conclusive, together they have fundamentally influenced the ways modern Western people understand homosexuality and the lifestyles and sexuality of people of the same sex. In this respect, a modern person is far removed from the views and questions of the biblical world. Especially in comprehending the categories of homosexuality and heterosexuality, modern Western citizens have learned their lesson.

This notwithstanding, it may be that I have emphasized the difference between the biblical and the modern worlds too much; after all, the views of modern science on homosexuality have not yet reached the larger audience. In colloquial speech, homosexuality is often linked with different subcultures and their scantily known but often suspected "lewd" customs. Most people have no clear understanding of a homosexual person's sex life, and vulgarisms are used by many to refer to presumed homosexual acts. Caricatures of feminine homosexual men and masculine lesbians still dominate popular notions of homosexuality. Sexual orientation is still confused with gender identification when a homosexual man is thought to consider himself a woman. Few distinguish transsexuality or transvestism from homosexuality.

Moreover, few modern people react to same-sex eroticism calmly and objectively. Hidden role models are at least subconsciously influential, although traditional definitions of femininity and masculinity are in ferment and people's views in flux. The threat of homoeroticism and the homophobia it generates seem, after all, to have more to do with issues of masculinity and femininity than anatomy or psychology. Encounters with homosexual persons and the ensuing positive or negative experiences have a certain effect on people's attitudes and understandings. Therefore, one needs to examine homosexuality as a part of the formation of personal identity in a gendered society, not as an individual trait of individual people.

Many ancient notions are still common. Male and female roles are often understood in a patriarchal fashion, even after the discovery of the human ovum. This is manifest not only in family life and work but also in popular attitudes toward, for instance, prostitution. Female prostitution is recognized as the "oldest profession," which has its social functions and in which the male and female roles are clear. Male prostitution, however—a reality also in Finland—stirs up confusion and disturbs customary role structures.[22]

The label "unnatural" is still generally applied to homosexuality, although today it is understood on the basis of biology and the behavioral sciences rather than from societal standards. In this situation, references are often made to the purpose of the genitals and their appropriate use. On this basis it is possible to say that "life against anatomy is against nature." This would mean that also all heterosexual expressions of sexuality—both intercourse and erotic play—are against nature if they do not aim directly at procreation. Values, however, cannot be derived from anatomy. Could God have created human beings to know sexual pleasure only as a stimulus for procreation?

This question arises, finally, from ancient sources that emphasize mutual erotic pleasure and affectionate love, thus giving us to understand that the dominant male perspective that predominates in the majority of the sources does not tell the whole truth. In the source material there are a few exceptions to the ideology of hierarchical polarization: Sappho's poems, Jesus as depicted in the Gospels, Daphnis and Chloe. Also the biblical representative of the ancient erotic-lyric tradition, the Song of Songs, can be read as a description of the kind of heterosexual love in which patriarchal dominion has faded away. In the Song of Songs, the woman and man are depicted as having a relationship of mutuality in which the patriarchal role structure and social hierarchy plays little if any role. Both lovers in the Song of Songs are subjects of their own eroticism, without either of the partners executing sexual dominance over the other.[23] By and large, the same can be said of Egyptian love poetry, mostly dating to the New Kingdom (second half of the second millennium B.C.E.), which is closely connected to the poetry of the Song of Songs.[24] Also the love of Daphnis and Chloe is mutual—it is difficult to say whether either partner is more active or passive than the other. Their desires are aroused and satisfied reciprocally. The social roles of society are represented by the suitors of Chloe and by Gnathon, who lusts for Daphnis. These men, looking for a wife or a boy-lover, appear as molesting or as threatening the paradisiacal young love.

These rare "alternative" representatives of the ancient erotic-lyric tradition are found in different cultures in different times and thus compel readers to remember that the available sources do not tell the whole truth of the life and reality of ancient people. Our perspective may be distorted by the fact that the sources available to us come from only a few societies and from different times, largely representing the views and ideals of the establishment. This might leave us in the dark about everyday life experience, the records of which are even more random. In any case, it is conceivable that such experiences of life as emotional love—often banal, trivial, and questionable in public images—could at least individually and temporarily shatter established role structures.

What is common to all these examples of the "alternative" view is mutual love, which seems to dissolve conventional gender roles and hierarchical structures. They also show that mutual, emotional love—unlike "sexuality"—is not an invention of modern scholarship, even though marriage was not based on it until the rise of modern Western culture. At the same time these texts reflect difficulties and conflicts created by social pressure. The boundaries set by society are difficult to cross, even by the power of love. This is a matter of the tension between paradise and reality, of which Phyllis Trible has poignantly written, "Yet, somewhere between tragedy and ecstasy lie the struggles of daily life."[25]

APPENDIX

&

CREATION, NATURE,
AND GENDER IDENTITY

Homosexuality as a theological problem is, admittedly, a digression from the theme of this book. Nevertheless, it is relevant to reflect on two theological concepts that are used as hermeneutical keys in the biblical interpretation of same-sex interaction, namely, creation and love.

The authors of the biblical creation stories took heterosexuality for granted: "That is why a man leaves his father and mother and is united to his wife, and the two become one flesh" (Gen. 2:24). In constructing creation theology from the creation stories, one has to solve a number of problems that are not mentioned in these texts; the question of "homosexuality" is one of them. A customary perspective is that the creation stories express the original purpose of creation, which cannot be fully realized after Adam's fall, which caused the corruption of the whole creation. Different "unnatural" phenomena, things "against nature" like same-sex sexual interaction, are thus explained as a perversion that resulted from the fall.

To link "unnatural" with the corruption of creation, however, generates new problems. Notions of the unnatural or things against nature fuse together empirical observations, unconscious taboos, and popular beliefs about the natural sciences and laws of nature. Furthermore, it is risky to transgress time and culture boundaries with this concept, as has become obvious in the study of ancient sources.

There are several creation-related questions regarding sex and gender:

* What in human sexuality is created and what is not? For example, are human biology, anatomy, and inheritable traits created, and roles developed through social processes and their concrete influences outside of creation? In other words, is "sex" created but "gender" not?

- Is same-sex orientation created when it is proved to be genetic in origin and inherited, but not created if its origins are deemed to be psychosocial?
- Is the post-fall corruption to be seen as the cause of the difference in the lives and existence of homosexuals, transsexuals, or people otherwise different with respect to their gender identity? If so, are they responsible for their condition and, if not, for their behavior?
- What is the correlation between creation and gender roles? The traditional strict division between active and passive sexual roles is diminishing today in both heterosexual and homosexual relations. Should the changes in gender roles also be interpreted as a consequence of the post-fall corruption or, rather, as a sign of ongoing creation?

These questions will not be individually examined here; the aim of this appendix is to examine the relevant grounds for answering each of them reasonably. To begin, the concept of "nature" needs to be defined (cf. Pronk 1993, 215–263). In modern language at least three intertwined meanings of this word can be identified: (1) the empirical meaning: the sum of observable facts; (2) the teleological meaning: the function and goal of natural phenomena; and (3) the cultural meaning: a synonym for the word "normal." These different meanings of the word "nature" appear both in everyday language as well as in creation theology and biblical interpretation.

1. In the first case "nature" is understood as the whole of phenomena that can be observed empirically. In scientific discussion there is a tendency to limit "nature" to this meaning, that is, to natural facts. The idea of "unnatural" or "against nature" actually does not belong to this definition at all, because, according to it, all empirically observed things belong to "nature." This concept is thus descriptive rather than normative. However, although deliberate manipulation of natural phenomena can be called "unnatural" or "against nature," values cannot be drawn from observable phenomena, and "nature" in a purely descriptive sense carries with it no moral obligation. Moral questions arise when nature is taken advantage of, when manipulating natural phenomena causes damage to humankind or the environment.

2. Understanding "nature" teleologically is linked with Aristotelian and Thomist notions of "nature" as an actual being with purpose and goal. This way "nature" can be also normative, because natural law orders the purpose and goal of each creature. The natural function of sexuality is seen in procreation. Thomas Aquinas, for example, divided sexual sins on this basis into those that are "against nature," like masturbation and homoeroticism, and those that are "natural," like adultery or prostitution. Even today the Catholic church considers all homosexual acts as "contrary to natural

law" (*The Catholic Catechism* §2357) and thus speaks of "nature" in this normative sense.

A problem in this case is that the normative meaning of "nature" is argued from its empirical meaning. An empirical biological function is taken as a criterion for what is considered natural and moral. When it is said that "homosexuality is against nature because it does not lead to procreation," a moral norm is derived from a biological function, and values are argued from anatomy. But when a conscious decision not to procreate is accepted, not only for single people but also for those who are married (the accepted birth control methods), then the potential to procreate is taken as the moral criterion for proper sexual acts, and the act is justified apart from the purpose of procreation. In this case the intention of the act (for instance, sexual pleasure) and its moral condition (potential to procreate) may be in conflict—and this is often the case in the actual sexual life of people in the West today.

3. The third meaning of "nature" is in many respects a popular derivation of the second meaning. In this, probably the most common meaning of the term in everyday language, "nature" equals common sense and the normal, "straight" condition of things and requires no further argumentation, whereas things that are strange and different, disturb the order of things, and break norms are considered "queer." Not everything of this kind is called "unnatural"—foreigners in Finland, for example, are not called "unnatural." Yet the Finns have prejudices and reactions against foreigners (especially those whose skin color or clothing differs from those of the majority) similar to such feelings against homosexuals. Common factors are cultural disturbance and suspicion of things that are "queer" compared with the majority. The criteria for difference are cultural and often based on unspoken agreements in society. They are also used to create a safe space against external phenomena that are felt to be suspicious or frightening.

The third, cultural meaning of "nature" is more abstract and less sophisticated than the first two. And yet it may be more significant, because cultural "nature" includes the prevalent values and norms and reflects their changes. "Nature" in this meaning is a societal concept, which includes the authority that regulates norms, the internalized taboos, and the inner solidarity of a society. It is not a matter of abstract phenomena but of concrete issues that involve everybody, such as the idea of "straight" and "queer," the sense of "otherness," the distinction between insiders and outsiders, and feelings of safety and insecurity.

These meanings of the term "nature" appear also in theological discourse of creation, orders of creation, and the corruption of creation. A problem here is that creation and "nature" are often confused and merged with social or naturalistic determinism.

Social determinism means that societal structures and roles follow permanent, strictly defined laws. When social determinism blends with cultural "nature," different conventions and taboos easily appear as "orders of creation." "Orders of creation," "the original purpose of creation," or "Christian anthropology" are then equated with the norms of a particular society and become instruments of power.

For instance, the subordination of women, societal discrimination, or the hierarchy of races have in different times and places been considered natural conditions based on the orders of creation and Christian anthropology. The people of sub-Saharan Africa found that they were "negroes" only when white people intruded into their lands. The midwife for "orders of creation" that led to apartheid was colonialism, and its biblical justification was drawn from Gen. 9:18–26, in which Ham's descendants are cursed as slaves of others. Thus a class was created that was defined from the Europeans' perspective. The history of homosexuality follows the same route: a group of people, pathologized by European medicine and psychology, was marginalized in accordance with the alleged orders of creation and on a biblical basis.

To consider creation or nature as a static condition or a series of events according to absolute laws of nature would lead to naturalistic determinism. There is really no such single rule to which all phenomena and creatures could conform. To see "nature" as a machine in which each part serves its own function is reminiscent of the Enlightenment's mechanistic notion of "nature" and easily leads to rigid functionalist definitions.

The determinist or functionalist models do not seem appropriate to creation theology; it is not right to denounce all departures from the ideal as the results of corruption that came with the fall. If creation is not a static condition but constantly being rejuvenating, we can understand that it looks different in different times, in the material world as well as in social communities. A person's gender identity also is evidently variable and does not follow rigid laws. The emergence of people with gay and lesbian identities in this century is an example of this. The fundamental question, then, is the basis from which the variation of a person's gender identity can or cannot be seen as an expression of continuing creation.

As a result of modern development, the question of nature and creation has come to center around sexual orientation and related behavior. This has happened at the expense of other factors of gender identity. The main question has been whether homosexuality is inborn or chosen, and how homosexual behavior might be justified, if at all. It is not only one's sexual orientation and the respective sexual practice that is at stake here, however, but also gender identification and roles. Creation theology cannot ignore gender roles, because people as created beings not only *are* men and women but also *live as* men and women in a gendered society. A further problem for creation theology rises when gender identification in some persons (that is, transsexuals) is evidently in contradiction with their anatomical sex—in other words, a person living in a woman's body feels himself a man, or vice versa. Creation theology thus touches on all the main problems regarding the interpretation of gender. Only a heterosexist bias could make homosexuality a separate issue and exclusively a sexual matter.

Sexual orientation is only one component of gender identity, and its significance varies from person to person. If a person's orientation does not coincide with general expectations, the role of such orientation in a person's identity becomes emphasized—because of society rather than the person himself or herself. This happens when homosexuality is externalized as an exception or curiosity. Homosexual orientation itself may gain a measure of acceptance if it comes to be believed that the person is not responsible for it. However, because there are no generally accepted roles and self-presentation models for homosexual orientation, homosexual people become stigmatized, and their sexual orientation becomes the central characteristic of their personality in the eyes of the heterosexually organized society. One component of gender identity is distinguished from the others and becomes overly significant. This may result in imbalance in a person's individual interpretation of the self, which is projected back to the environment in different unwanted ways. This, then, increases society's need to exclude and externalize—and a vicious circle is in effect.

People create sexual culture together and share the responsibility for it. If love is not the motivation in this situation, fear, unfortunately, can be, and it can easily dominate people's attitudes. In Christian communities, no one denies that love is the preferred and desired attitude toward other human beings. All agree that people must love one another, even if they do not approve of each others' lifestyle. In practice, however, application of the rule of love is problematic. The catchword "love the sinner, hate the sin" has had only meager results.

Love must not be confused with "tolerance," which also is considered an exemplary way to relate to "different" people. Tolerance can be a paternalistic attitude that maintains different processes and systems for externalization and marginalization. The one who tolerates is seen as above the other. The distance and difference between the self and the other remains, because the need to tolerate requires that there is something wrong with the other person. Love, on the other hand, means stepping into another person's shoes, carrying his or her load, suffering together (*sympathein*). Love is not about striving toward an objective good but about putting oneself at risk for another human being. Stepping in the other person's shoes, we can see ourselves in that person and love him or her. This means understanding the other person from his or her own point of view, even when the person's lifestyle or opinions appear strange or wrong.

People do not spontaneously love one another as themselves but need a special command for that. The command to love and its fulfillment is decisive for Christian morality. Specific moral commands and norms are born from the needs of the time and place; the fundamental thing is that love become real and influential in this process.

As mentioned above, love is also the central hermeneutical principle when applying biblical commands, advice, and ideals to the lives of people today. The New Testament emphatically asserts, in the mouths of both Jesus and Paul, that the entire law depends on the commandment of love, that love fulfills the whole Law, and that the one who loves has fulfilled the Law (Matt. 22:34–40; Rom. 13:8–10; Gal. 5:14). This applies also to the passages in the Bible that refer to homoeroticism. Making love a priority in applying these texts in real life does not imply all-accepting "tolerance" or the altering of God's word. To give love priority in biblical interpretation means careful examination of both the Bible and the prevailing reality in which we live with neighbors of flesh and blood.

Love and its fulfillment is the central principle also in discussions about the societal status and civil rights of people of different gender identities—about same-sex partnerships and their public recognition, for example. For love to become a reality, traditional paternalistic, externalizing attitudes must be changed. The question, "Why is this person's sexual orientation something other than purely heterosexual?" may still be relevant. But another question is far more important, a question posed to everybody: "Why is the other person's different gender identity a problem for me and my society?" This question forces us to look into the mirror, which is the first step—a necessary step—in loving the neighbor as oneself.

NOTES

Chapter 1: Introduction

1. The most recent work that studies homosexuality globally is Swidler (ed.) 1993. The scholars in this book approach homosexuality from various religious perspectives (American and African folk religions, Hinduism, Buddhism, Judaism, Catholic and Protestant Christianity, Islam, Japanese and Chinese religions) and bring out a number of social aspects as well.

2. The European countries first to remove homosexuality from the list of punishable crimes were—perhaps surprisingly—Catholic countries: France 1791, Belgium and Luxembourg 1792, Spain 1822, Portugal 1852, and Italy 1889. Other European countries that have removed homosexuality from their legislation are Holland 1811, Denmark 1930, Poland 1932, Switzerland 1937–42, Sweden 1944, Hungary and Czechoslovakia 1961, England and Wales 1967, East Germany and Bulgaria 1968, West Germany 1969, Austria and Finland 1971, Norway 1972, Slovenia, Croatia, and Montenegro 1977, Scotland 1980, Northern Ireland 1982, Ireland, Russia, and Lithuania 1993. Homosexuality was considered as a generally punishable crime in 1993 at least in the following countries: Albany, Bosnia-Herzegovina, Cyprus, Macedonia, Moldova, Romania, Serbia, Belarus. An exhortation ban similar to that of the Finnish criminal law is employed in Austria and Liechtenstein. See Tatchell 1990 and Duda 1993.

3. See the statistics in Heino, Salonen, and Rusama 1997, 15.

4. The latest statistics on the attitudes of the Finns toward gays and lesbians are published by Haavio-Mannila and Kontula 1993, 245–39. According to their results, in 1992, 59% of men younger than 55 and 72% of women considered adult homosexual behavior as a private matter with which officials should in no way interfere; the equivalent numbers in a study from 1971 were 44% and 45%. But only 20% of men and 28% of women supported the official acknowledgment of homosexual relationships; in 1996, however, the numbers were already 49% of men and women combined (Gallup on TV2, April 9, 1996).

5. *Seksuaalirikokset* (Sexual Crimes) 1993, 20.23.

6. The registration of same-sex partnership was achieved by 1996 in Denmark (proposed in 1989), Norway (proposed, 1993), and Sweden (proposed, 1995). On a local level, same-sex partnerships are recognized in one way or the other also in some cities or states of Belgium, France, Spain, and the United States. Pertinent legislation has been discussed, for instance, in Belgium, France, Germany, Italy, The Netherlands, Spain, The Czech Republic, Argentine, and South Africa.

7. *Kasvamaan yhdessä* 1984. This is the view of the majority of the Protestant churches (cf. the statements of the churches, Melton 1991; Siker [ed.] 1994, 195–208). On the discussion within the mainline Protestant churches, see Olyan and Nussbaum (eds.) 1998, 113–68. The Catholic Church today follows the same lines. In the new *Catechism of the Catholic Church,* it is acknowledged that some people are homosexual without their own choice. Their discrimination is forbidden, but because homosex-

ual acts are considered as against natural law, chastity and abstinence from sex are deemed as their call (§§2357–59). Homosexuality itself is not listed among the transgressions of chastity, which include, for instance, masturbation, pornography, prostitution, and violence (§§2351–56). Cardinal Joseph Ratzinger's "Letter to the Bishops of the Catholic Church on the Pastoral Care of Homosexual Persons" from 1986 is a good example how the Congregation for the Doctrine of the Faith in practice interprets this principle (Ratzinger 1994). About the recent discussion in the Catholic Church, see also the contributions in Olyan and Nussbaum (eds.) 1998, 57–109.

8. The whole 1993 discussion in the Finnish Lutheran Church about homosexuality as well as the jurisdictional proceedings connected with it have been documented by Strömsholm 1997 (cf. the English summary, pp. 369–77).

9. On Finnish values and attitudes to the church and religion, see Heino, Salonen, and Rusama 1997.

10. Kinsey, Pomeroy, and Martin 1948, 650–51.

11. Kinsey et al., ii 1953, 499.

12. Rogers and Turner 1991.

13. Haavio-Mannila and Kontula 1993.

14. A similar study of the whole population was made in 1974. Students at the University of Helsinki have been interviewed (1986), as well as youths fifteen to seventeen years old in Helsinki, Uusimaa, and Ostrobothnia (1986). Differences in the studies concerning the whole population were insignificant. Much bigger numbers came from studies concerning young people and students, who much more often identify themselves as predominantly (but not exclusively) interested in the same sex. For a summary of the results of the different studies see Haavio-Mannila and Kontula 1993, 250–52.

15. Haavio-Mannila and Kontula 1993, 254–60.

16. Cf. McClain-Taylor 1996, 78: "The results of scientific work, then, give not just 'hard data,' but ways of interpreting within 'paradigms' that are supported or sometimes altered by communities of flesh-and-blood inquirers."

17. On Freud's theory and its often one-sided interpretations, see Looser 1980, 84–89

18. Cf. also Bieber 1976. For other recent psychoanalytic interpretations of homosexuality see Socarides 1978, Moberly 1983 and van den Aardweg 1986. For psychological explanations of homosexuality and their negative evaluation, see further Pronk 1993, 127–46.

19. R. Green 1987.

20. Carrier 1980.

21. Cf. the summary of Burr 1994.

22. Summary from the 1970s, see Mayer-Bahlburg 1977 and 1979 and Tourney 1980. Since then, Ellis and Ames (1987) have suggested a prenatal hormonal cause of homosexuality. According to them, sexual orientation is largely determined between the second and fifth month of gestation due to fetal exposure to testosterone, its primary metabolite estriadol, and other sex hormones. For criticism of this view, see Money 1987; Halperin 1990, 50–51; Jones and Workman 1994, 99–100.

23. E.g., Bailey and Pillard 1991 and 1993; King and McDonald 1992.

24. E.g., Danneker and Reiche 1974; Bell, Weinberg, and Hammersmith 1981; Masters and Johnson 1979; Grönfors et al. 1984; Rogers and Turner 1991.

25. Boswell's *Same-sex Unions in Premodern Europe* (1994), his last study, eloquently represents this position.

26. Cf. Halperin 1990; Winkler 1990; Halperin, Winkler, and Zeitlin (eds.) 1990.

27. For *scientia sexualis* versus *ars erotica*, cf. Foucault 1978, 53–73.

28. On medicalization, see Greenberg 1988, 397–433; Stålström 1997. The first to use the term is usually thought to have been the Austrian-Hungarian (wrongly thought to have been a doctor) Károly Mária Kertbeny (Benkert), who in 1869 wrote two pamphlets in German (see Herzer 1985). The term was introduced into English in the 1890s by Charles Gilbert Chaddock in his translation of Krafft-Ebing's *Psychopathia sexualis* (second edition of the German original of 1887) from where it found its way into the *Oxford English Dictionary*.

29. *On Acute and on Chronic Diseases* 4:9; see Brooten 1996, 146–62.

30. See Brooten 1996, 115–41.

31. E.g., Daly 1978.

32. Cf. Butler 1990; Heinämaa 1996, 298–99.

33. Graham 1996, 130.

34. On these perspectives, see Graham 1996, 59–98.

35. Foucault 1978, passim; cf. Halperin, Winkler, and Zeitlin, eds., 1990, 5–7.

36. Richlin 1993, Brooten 1996 and Taylor 1997 have challenged the conviction of Halperin and others that the concept of homosexuality has existed only for the past hundred years by demonstrating not only that there were people with a same-sex sexual orientation in antiquity but also that they were recognized as such and, at times, even categorized and medicalized as a group. By careful reading of the sources they show that the concept of homosexuality did not grow out of nothing in the nineteenth century but was based on age-old gendered thinking. I nonetheless think that the modern concept of homosexuality implies more than the recognition and grouping together of people with same-sex orientation. The various psychiatric, biological, sociological, and cultural interpretations of what is called homosexuality as well as twentieth-century gay and lesbian culture have radically changed the epistemological and cultural preconditions of our understanding of same-sex relations suggested by the word "homosexuality."

37. Halperin 1990, 27.

38. Halperin 1990, 28, 43–44.

39. On the problems of the term "gender," see, for example, Heinämaa 1996.

40. Halperin 1990, 24: "Homosexuality presupposes sexuality because the very concept of homosexuality implies that there is a specifically sexual dimension to the human personality, a characterological seat within the individual of sexual acts, desires, and pleasures—a determinate source from which all sexual expression proceeds."

41. This is emphasized by Richlin 1993 and Brooten 1996, partly as a critique of Halperin.

42. On transsexuality, see Bentler 1976.

43. Definition by Dennis M. Dailey quoted by Jung and Smith 1993, 7.

44. See Nanda 1990, 114–16 on the *hijras* of India, and Greenberg 1988, 40–56; Baum 1993, 4–19 on the *berdaches* and *nadles* among Native Americans.

45. On the bearing of this fact on our subject, cf., e.g., Burr 1994, 126–27 and Waetjen 1996, 113–14.

46. On transvestism, see Hirschfeld 1991 (1910), which, because of its documentation, is still an unsurpassable classic; cf. also Brierley 1979.

47. My perspective thus comes close to what in gender studies is called the dialectical or complementary approach; see Graham 1996, 90–98.

48. See Gleason 1995, especially pp. 58–60.

49. Polemo, *Physiognomy* 2,1.192F; I owe this quotation to Gleason 1995, 58.

50. For this development, see the thorough analysis of Allen 1997.

51. See Allen 1997, 48–49.

52. Aristotle, *Generation of Animals*, 727B:34—729A:33. Cf. Cantarella 1992, 65–66; Allen 1997, 98–100.

53. *Generation of Animals*, 728A:27-28.

54. *Generation of Animals*, 729A:10-11.

55. Definition by Dennis M. Dailey, quoted by Jung and Smith 1993, 6.

56. Morgan 1992, 67.

Chapter 2: Mesopotamia

1. 125 A 20, B 27, trans. Wilson 1969, 34, 35. Cf. also Westendorf 1977, 1273; Greenberg 1988, 132–34. The word translated "boy" in B 27 should perhaps be rendered "male lover."

2. There are a few ambiguous sources that may allude to some kind of same-sex interaction (cf. Greenberg 1988, 129–30). The king Neferkare (Pepi II) is said to have made regular secret nocturnal visits to the home of his general, Sisene, who was unmarried. King Akhnaton is depicted naked, stroking his son-in-law, Smenkhare, under the chin. Westendorf (1977, 1273) refers to the fact that close friends of the same sex have even been buried in the same grave in order to make their relationship continue forever. There is also a coffin text with the vow, "I will swallow for myself the phallus of Rē^c. . .," and another in which it is said of the earth god Geb, "His phallus is between the buttocks of his son and heir" (Faulkner 1973/2, 162,264; cf. Greenberg 1988, 129). These texts, referring to sexual contact with a god, give little information about attitudes towards human same-sex interaction.

3. On the battle of Horus and Seth, see Griffiths 1960, 41–46; Assmann 1984, 162–70; Westendorf 1977, 1272; Greenberg 1988, 130–32. The most recent (German) translation of this myth is Junge 1995.

4. Pope (1976, 416) refers in this context to Baal's rage because he was presented with unsatisfactory offerings. To Baal these are "shameless sacrifices (*dbḥ bṯt*), sacrifices of the whores (*dbḥ dnt*) and indecent sacrifices of the maids (*dbḥ tdmmt amht*)" (KTU 1.4 iii 10–22). Nothing indicates that the "indecency of the maids" would mean lesbian behavior; instead it is a matter of Baal considering the offerings below his worth and thus giving them outrageous epithets. Cf. Del Olmo Lete 1981, 123.

5. §§187–200. English translation by Harry A. Hoffner Jr. in Roth 1995, 236–37. See further Hoffner 1973, 82–86,90.

6. Thus, e.g., Vanggaard 1971, 113; Horner 1978, 15–19; Coleman 1980, 53; cf. the more critical Leick 1994, 254–69 and Halperin 1990, 75–87. A number of different versions of the Epic of Gilgameš have remained, and their contents differ considerably. The best manuscript follows the Neo-Assyrian version and originates from the seventh-century library of Assurbanipal. In the present work, the line numbers refer to the newest edition of the Standard Babylonian text (Parpola 1997). The translation is that of Dalley (1989, 50–125).

7. Gilgameš i 78–94 (Parpola 1997a, 72; trans. Dalley 1989, 52–53).

8. The word *šamḫatu* means a prostitute in general, but it is used as a personal name here; see Dalley 1989, 126. On the role of Šamhat as a prostitute and a maternal figure at the same time, cf. Harris 1990, 222–24.

9. Gilgameš i 217–23 (Parpola 1997a, 74; trans. Dalley 1989, 57).

10. Gilgameš i 229–41 (Parpola 1997a, 74; trans. Dalley 1989, 57).

11. Harris 1990, 221: "The all-knowing (*mūdât kalâma*) mother is expert, as are other Mesopotamian women, human and divine, in interpreting dreams."

12. Gilgameš ii 80–153 (Parpola 1997a, 76; cf. Dalley 1989, 60–61).

13. Leick 1994, 258; on Ištar's proposal cf. also Abusch 1986; Harris 1990, 226–28.

14. Cf. Leick 1994, 259–60.

15. Gilgameš viii 41–58 (Parpola 1997a, 99–100; trans. Dalley 1989, 92–93) and x 234–38 (Parpola 1997a, 105–6; trans. Dalley 1989, 106).

16. I prefer the translation "bride" over Dalley's "daughter-in-law."

17. It is commonly assumed that tablet 12 is a later addition to the epic. Parpola nevertheless finds it to be the necessary climax of the whole story, because Gilgameš again meets Enkidu and thus learns about the secret of eternal life (1993, 193–94).

18. As Tropper 1986 has proved, this is not a matter of actual necromancy (calling up dead spirits), with all its ritual practices. Rather, it is a matter of two friends meeting for the last time without any ritualistic purpose.

19. This has been convincingly argued by Leick 1994, 254–69. Cf. also Parpola (1993, 192–96), according to whom the Epic of Gilgameš exhibits the mystical way to perfect divine wisdom. Gilgameš's initial sexual intemperance was not to be imitated as an example. Instead, his love of Enkidu, love that was purified of indecency, lasts until the end of the story. Cf. also Foster 1987 and the following note.

20. According to Foster 1987, 22 "the Nineveh poet portrays sex and love as types of human knowledge. The import of his thematic of sex is that sex belongs to the lowest common level of human knowledge—what everyone must know and experience to become human. Once this knowledge is attained, continued non-productive sex is no longer acquisition of knowledge or affirmation of humanity but characteristic of the street, or, at worst, reversion to the animal state. The import of his thematic on love is that love of another person is the next higher order of knowledge and makes a human into a social being. Knowledge of another leads to unity, which need not be based on sexual union."

21. Held (1983, 134) compares this ideology to Diotima's explication of the nature of love in Plato's *Symposium* (cf. below, p. 59–60); in both works the following two points are made, "1) that love or eros is at the heart of the nature of the laudandus, and 2) that this love or eros is the force which effects the transformation and development of man's nature." Cf. also Parpola 1997a, xcvii, n. 140.

22. Thus one can hardly say that Enkidu is treated by Gilgameš "like a woman and wife" (Harris 1990, 229).

23. See Sergent 1986, 264–73, and, of the homoerotic dimensions of the relationship, also Cantarella 1992, 9–11. Later Greek authors quibbled over who played the active and who played the passive role in the relationship between Achilles and Patroclus (Plato, *Symposium* 180A). This, however, cannot be used as evidence for the idea that this role division would not have been established in classical Greek society (contra Boswell 1994, 57, n. 16)

24. For a comparison of the stories of these three male friendships, cf. Greenberg 1988, 112–15 and, more critically, Halperin 1990, 75–87.

25. KAV 1 ii 82–96; English translation by Roth 1995, 159–60; cf. Borger 1982, 83; Locher 1986, 359–72; Otto 1991, 91–95.

26. The *Middle Assyrian Laws* belonged originally to the library of Tiglath-Pileser I (1243–1207 B.C.E.) but copies found at Nineveh prove that it was known as late as the Neo-Assyrian period, i.e. in the eighth and seventh centuries B.C.E. The preserved

parts of the *Middle Assyrian Laws* concentrate especially on jurisdiction on women and marriage. Its links to the Hebrew Bible, especially to Deuteronomy, are unambiguous; see Otto 1993, 260–62 and *passim*.

27. The exact meaning of the verb *gadāmu* is not clear, but there is no doubt that it denotes some kind of a dishonorable punishment. The action described by this verb may, for example, involve cutting the beard or the hair, or some other way of stigmatizing the offender (cf. CAD G 8; San Nicolò 1938, 403; Locher 1986, 361). It is less probable that castration would be meant here. This is doubtless the case in §§15 and 20, but in these articles castration is expressed in a different way.

28. On connecting the articles, see Otto 1991, 91–93.

29. If a man found his wife in bed with another man, §15 gave him the right to decide about his wife's punishment. If he wanted the death penalty for his wife, that was also ordered for the man; if he wanted to release his wife, then the man was released also. He could also cut off his wife's nose, in which case also the man's face was disfigured, in addition to his being castrated (cf. Otto 1993, 263–64).

30. Locher (1986, 365, 372) finds the principle of talion from §§18 and 19: the punishment of shame equals the shame caused by false accusation.

31. Locher (1986, 356, 369) quite correctly emphasizes that the verb *niāku* does not necessarily have a violent association, unless so stressed (unlike Bottéro and Petschow 1972/75, 462). Also Lambert (1992, 147) notes that *niāku* appears here without further qualification like *emūqāmma* 'by force' in §16. For him, this "seems proof that it was a matter of mutual consent, and so the law is expressing condemnation of homosexuality." This, however, is likely an overinterpretation, because it is difficult to make conclusions about the nature of the sexual contact in §20 on the lexical basis alone, without reference to the gender role system the vocabulary reflects. As Lambert points out, Mesopotamian sexual vocabulary does not include a word for mutual and equal sexual relationships, and this obviously tells something essential about the understanding of sexual relationships in general. It is important to take into account also the implications about roles that are involved with the use of the verb *niāku*: the subject of the verb is also the subject in the sexual act, whereas the other partner is the object. The verb can be applied to the other partner only in the passive voice or reflexively, as is the clear case in §§18–20. The idea that it would be a matter of mutual consent is at odds with this implied role structure.

32. On *tappā'u*, see AHw 1321–22; Bottéro and Petschow 1972/75, 461–62; Olyan 1994, 193.

33. SAA 3 30:1-4,7 (Livingstone 1989, 66). Another text (SAA 3 29) is a warning written for the same person of whom it says: "This is the stele which the prostitute (*ḫarimtu*) set up for the son of Ibâ, the farter, and left for posterity" (lines r.4–5). Several persons with the name Bel-eṭir are known from the Neo-Assyrian period (see M. Dietrich 1970, 32 n. 1). Because SAA 3 29:2-3 mentions the Babylonian rebels ṣallâ (Bab. ṣillaya) and Šamaš-ibni, the person in question may be either Bel-eṭir, the governor of Har, who is connected with ṣillaya in SAA 10 112 r.3,13, or Bel-eṭir, the governor of Uruk (?) who was fired from this office and who escaped to Elam (see M. Dietrich 1970, 57–59).

34. SAA 2 2 v 8-15 (Parpola and Watanabe 1988, 12).

35. Of the distinction between active and passive roles and of the comparison with a woman cf. also Bottéro and Petschow 1972/75, 462; Locher 1986, 369–71; Olyan 1994, 193.

36. Oppenheim 1956, 290–91, 333–34 (K 6705, 6768, 6824) and 1969, 156–57 (K 9169, 13642). The erotic aspect in these texts depends on the sign UM (or DUB/DÍḪ) which may match with the verb *teḫû* meaning sexual intercourse; see Borger 1986, 95.

37. CT 39 (= Gadd 1926) 44–45. The only translated and published edition of *Šumma ālu* (Nötscher 1930) omits the tablets relevant to us (cf. p. 229). The copies preserved to us date from the time of Assurbanipal (668–627 B.C.E.) but the omens themselves must be much older.

38. CT 39 44:13, 45:32,33,34.

39. Akk. *dan-na-tu* DU₈-*su*. The interpretation of the verb is uncertain, because the meaning of DU₈ is not clear here. The translation requires the verb *paṭāru* "to release, free" (so CAD D 88) but its problem is the phonetically wrong personal suffix -*su* (which should be -*šu*).

40. One of the *Šumma ālu* omens refers to this (CT 39 44:17); whether the expression *sinnišūtam epēšu* (CT 39 44:4) means "to play woman," "to take the woman's sexual role," or just sexual intercourse (CAD E 225; AHw 1048) is not quite clear. Cf. BWL 226 i 1–7: "[An A]morite speaks [to] his wife: You be the man, [I] will be the woman" (Lambert 1960, 226,230).

41. See below, pp. 76–77.

42. On the term, see CAD G 95; AHw 285–86. Quite possibly the *gerseqqûs* were eunuchs; so, among others, Meier 1938, 485; Lambert 1992, 147; cf. below, n. 67.

43. So Bottéro and Petschow 1972/75, 461. Thus, should one conclude that the one who acts is thought to belong to the court or to the temple personnel?

44. For *assinnu*, etc., in general, see Oppenheim 1950, 134–46; Bottéro and Petschow 1972/75, 463–66; Groneberg 1986, 33–41; 1997; Maul 1992; Leick 1994, 157–69; Roscoe 1996, 213–17; Parpola 1997b, xcvi–xcvii; CAD A 341–42; CAD K 529, 557–59; also Greenberg 1988, 96–97.

45. Actually "dog-woman," "dog" representing masculinity in a despicable sense. Other cuneiform signs referring to the same group are PI.LI.PI.LI and SAG.UR.SAG. The word *assinnu* appears also in the forms *isinnu, issinnu* and *isinnû.*

46. Sum. GALA; cf. Gordon 1959, 248–49; Renger 1969, 192–94; Gelb 1976, 54–74; Roscoe 1996, 213–14; CAD K 93–94.

47. The Sumerian version is edited and translated by Kramer 1951 (cf. the translation of Römer 1993); the Assyrian version is edited by Borger 1979, I 95–104, II 340–43 and translated by Dalley 1989, 154–62. A good summary of both comes from Leick 1991, 91–93, 98–99. For the role of *assinnu*, etc., in this myth, cf. also Maul 1992, 160–62.

48. *Kalaturru* (GALA.TUR) refers to *kalû*-priest and possibly needs to be read *kalû ṣeḫru* "young *kalû*"; see CAD K 94; AHw 274; Lambert 1992, 151.

49. Kramer 1951, 10 (lines 219–22); Römer 1993, 475–76 (lines 222–25).

50. Borger 1979, 100–101 (lines 92–99); cf. Dalley 1989, 158. The name *Aṣûšunāmir* can be translated as "his departure (from the underworld) is splendid"; Dalley translates it "Good-looks."

51. The waterskin (*ḫalziqqu*) probably means Ištar's body; cf. Dalley 1989, 161; Maul 1992, 161.

52. Farber 1977, 66:36. The prayer is addressed to a manifestation of Ištar called Kilili, i.e., "Ištar looking from the window" (*Kilīli ša apāta ušarru*). The "window" symbolizes the border between this world and beyond. The goddess looking from the window is Ištar, who has risen from the Underworld and is looking for a human being

to go there as her replacement. Thus Maul 1992, 164–65; cf. also Groneberg 1986, 36–37. For *assinnu* in the function of purifying the world of evil (*ramkūtu* "purification priest"), see Groneberg 1997, 293.

53. According to a Neo-Assyrian document, a person taught another person for two years and five months in the art of *kurgarrûtu* (see CAD K 559).

54. In some of the lexical lists they are mentioned in the same group as prophets (*maḫḫû, šāʾilu*) and ecstatics (*zabbu*); see CAD A 341 (*Erimḫuš* iii 170–72); Landsberger and Gurney 1957/58, 84. From Mari we know three prophetic oracles uttered by or connected with an *assinnu* (ARM 26 197, 212 and 213; cf. Durand 1988, 395,424,440–42; Parpola 1997b, ciii, n. 220). From the Neo-Assyrian period no *assinnu* is known as a prophet. Among the identifiable Neo-Assyrian prophets, however, there are two persons who are referred to both as a man and as a woman (see Nissinen 1993, 225, 226; Parpola 1997b, il). This would mean that people with ambiguous gender could act as prophets.

55. The stone that was used for the make-up was called *kurgarrānu*; cf. Maul 1992, 163.

56. Cf., e.g., SAA 3 4 i 10; 8 r.14; 37:29-34; 38:14-15 (Livingstone 1989, 13, 22, 94, 96). Several other examples of the ritual roles and tasks of *assinnu* and *kurgarrû* can be found in CAD A 341; CAD K 558; Römer 1965, 137–38,157–58,160–61,166; Bottéro and Petschow 1972/75, 463 and Maul 1992, 164–65.

57. Lines 45–66; cf. Römer 1965, 130–38; Reisman 1973, 187, 194–95.

58. For *pilaqqu* (GIŠ.BALA), see Römer 1965, 160–61 who, however, translates it "stiletto." On the feminine symbolism of the spindle, see Gordon 1959, 211, 213; Bottéro and Petschow 1972/75, 465; Sjöberg 1975, 224 and cf. the curse in SAA 2 6 §91 (Parpola and Watanabe 1988, 56): "May all the gods who are called by name in this treaty tablet spin you around like a spindle-whorl; may they make you like a woman before your enemy."

59. Cf. the *Hymn of Iddin-Dagan to Inanna*, lines 74–78 (trans. Reisman 1973, 187–88): "The ascending *kurgarra* priests grasped the sword. They walk before the pure Inanna. The one who covers the sword with blood, he sprinkles blood. They walk before the pure Inanna. He pours out blood on the dais of the throne-room."

60. *Kuluʾu* is said to be Ištar's "sweet bed-fellow" (*ṣālilu ṭābu*) and "lover" (*ḫabbubu*); KAR 144:46-47; cf. Oppenheim 1950, 135; Lambert 1992, 152.

61. As to these women, cf. Lambert 1992, 128–45, who does not hesitate to speak of "prostitution" in connection with them, and Leick 1994, 149–53, who pays more attention to problems related to this term; cf. below p. 39.

62. The Ritual Tablet of the so-called "Love Lyrics" from the first millennium B.C.E., published by Lambert 1975, may represent a dramatized ritual against a sexual rival (cf. Edzard 1987; Leick 1994, 240–46). This ritual involves a *kurgarrû* as a chanter and an *assinnu* as a sword-dancer: "He (the *kurgarrû*). . . will depart from the city gate and facing Ḫursagkalamma (the temple of Ištar in Kiš) the *kurgarrû* will kneel and recite prayers and utter his chants. He will arise and sing: 'Let me see great Kiš, let me look on lofty Babylon' . . . 'Battle is my game, warfare is my game,' he will utter and the *assinnu* will go down to battle. . ." (BM 41005 iii 11–14,16–17; Lambert 1975, 104–5).

63. *Erra* iv 52–56 (Cagni 1969, 110–11; Dalley 1989, 305). The *Epic of Erra* is often dated to the eighth century B.C.E., but an earlier date (the reign of Nabû-apla-iddina, tenth century B.C.E.) has also been suggested (Neumann and Parpola 1987, 179–80). The idea of this quotation is expressed already in a Sumerian Inanna-hymn, according to which "to make a man a woman and a woman a man is in your power,

Ištar" (Sjöberg 1975, 190–91), and, furthermore, in the *Inanna and Ebiḫ* hymn in which Ištar says she has changed the *assinnu*'s (PI.LI.PI.LI) sex (Limet 1971, 21). *Kurgarrû*'s and *assinnu*'s sexual character is interpreted best by Groneberg 1986, 33–39 and Leick 1994, 157–69. On the ritual change of one's gender elsewhere, see Delcourt and Hoheisel 1991, 657–58, 665.

64. Probably the text needs to be complemented *i-tak-ka-lu a-*[*sak-ka*]. It is a question of deeds under a taboo, forbidden to ordinary people; see Cagni 1969, 233–34 and cf. the Hebrew *tô'ēbâ* (Lev 18:22; 20:13; cf. below p. 39).

65. Cf. Virolleaud 1908/12, Ištar 8:8-9.

66. Cf., e.g., SAA 3 7:6 (Livingstone 1989, 18) in which the goddess has beard and breasts. On Ištar's gender roles, see Groneberg 1986, who emphasizes that Ištar was in no way imagined as a hermaphrodite but as a female deity to whom also male power and dominance was attributed (p. 44); note, however, the modifications of this view in Groneberg 1997.

67. On this ritual, see Groneberg 1997.

68. Cagni 1969, 111: "per infondere alla gente religioso timore"; Dalley 1989, 305: "to make the people of Ishtar to revere her"; CAD A 341: "to show the people piety"; CAD K 558: "to teach the people religious fear"; unlike Bottéro and Petschow 1972/75, 467, "pour inciter le peuple à une crainte," and Maul 1992, 159.

69. Borger 1956, 99:53-56. The text is written on a monument that praises the victory of the king Esarhaddon over Taharqa, the king of Egypt and Nubia. The monument was erected after the year 671 B.C.E. in Sam'al which is in today's Turkey near the Syrian border.

70. So, e.g., Meier 1938, 485; Bottéro and Petschow 1972/75, 464–65; Pope 1976, 415–16; Lambert 1992, 150–51; unlike, e.g., Renger 1969, 193. Children of an *assinnu* and a *kurgarrû* are sometimes mentioned (see Bottéro and Petschow 1972/75, 464), which seems to speak against this, but it is also possible that adopted children or children conceived before castration are meant. An adopted child is at stake at least in the *Laws of Hammurabi* (§§187,192,193; see Borger 1979, 37; 1982, 67; Roth 1995, 119–20), which prohibit the biological parents from demanding back their child reared by *gerseqqû* (a courtier) and *sekretu* (a woman living in seclusion in a temple or a harem) and the child from returning to their home. Coleman 1980, 54 erroneously interprets *sekretu* (MÍ.ZI.IK.RU.UM) as "man-woman" (*salzikrum*, thus Driver and Miles 1936), thus creating a misleading link to *assinnu*.

71. On their role in the Assyrian society and administration, see Grayson 1995, 91–98.

72. On the seals of the eunuchs, see Watanabe 1992, 362–67; 1993, 304–8.

73. On this designation, the singular of which is *gallos*, see Lane 1996, who refutes the alleged connection of this name with Gauls.

74. On *galli*, see Nock 1988 (1925); Sanders 1972; Pachis 1996; Roscoe 1996, 198–206, and, specifically concerning their appearance in ancient Rome, Taylor 1997, 328–37.

75. Lucian, *De Syria Dea* 50–51; cf. also 15, 22, 27, 43. Lucian speaks of second century C.E. Syria, but there are records of *galli* in anecdotes and epigrams attributed, among others, to Arcesilaus (cf. below, n. 78) and Dioscorides (*Greek Anthology* 6:220 and 11:195), who lived in the third century B.C.E.; cf. Gow and Page 1965, 246–48,266–67; Lane 1996, 118–20.

76. See Roscoe 1996, 195–96.

77. Lucian, *De Syria Dea* 27, 43, 50.

78. Thus the philosopher Arcesilaus (*c.* 318–242 B.C.E.) quoted in the third century C.E. by Diogenes Laertius (4:43). On the permanent role change cf. Nock 1988 (1925), 65 and Pachis 1996, 203–5.

79. Roscoe 1996.

80. For instance, the city of Harran, which lies roughly halfway between central Assyria and the Mediterranean Sea, was an important connecting link between Mesopotamian and Syrian religion, assimilating influences from East and West throughout its long history. Harran was the city of the moon god Sin, whereas the goddess in Harran was represented by many names, including Ištar as Bath Nikkal ("Daughter of Nikkal," who was the consort of Sin) and also Atargatis (Aramaic: Tarʿatha). The functions of the different manifestations of the Divine Feminine overlapped, and the goddesses were thus more or less assimilated with each other. See T. Green 1996, 91–97.

81. Cf. Leick 1994, 168–69.

82. See Groneberg 1986, 37; Maul 1992, 166 and cf. Roscoe 1996, 203–5 on religion and androgyny in general.

83. CT 38 4:76.

84. Borger 1979, 101 (lines 103–7); cf. Dalley 1989, 159.

85. Dalley 1989, 86–87; cf. Lambert 1992, 129–31.

86. The text in question is a ritual to be performed if the eclipse happens in the month of Iyyar (II). Seeing a broken jar was a bad omen from which one recovered by watching a *kurgarrû* (Köcher and Oppenheim 1957/58, 71,76: text B, lines 31–32).

87. Weidner 1935/36, 3: *kuluʾu lā zikāru šū*. So in a letter about a short-term Assyrian king, Ninurta-tukul-Assur (1115 B.C.E.). This man hardly was a real *kuluʾu*; at least he owned a big harem!

88. Gordon 1959, 248–49. Renger (1969, 194) believes this means only the low position of the *kalû* among the priests. However, the cuneiform sign for *kalû*, *uš.ku*, which equals GÌŠ.DÚR, leaves no room for doubt about his sexual character: GÌŠ means penis and DÚR buttocks.

89. Cf. Lambert 1960, 218–19; the tablet including this phrase dates from the Neo-Assyrian period (716 B.C.E.). According to the translation of Lambert, the one who is being addressed is Ištar. Leick (1994, 160) proposes that *anzinnu* means a pimp, and the "rich" who is addressed directly is a female prostitute who, as a real woman, has a better income than a *sinnišānu*. A less probable translation comes from Gruber (1986, 146): "My hire belongs to the proprietor of the brothel. Suppose you take half, and I take half."

90. See Leick 1994 151–53, with textual references.

91. See Maul 1992, 162–63 and 168 n. 35, with textual references.

92. CT 39 44:15: *às-sé-e-ni-iš na-ak zi-ka-ru-ta ḫu-uš-šu-uḫ-šu*; thus Bottéro and Petschow 1972/75, 464. Otherwise CAD Z 117: "Like that of a eunuch, the potency to mate is taken away from him" and, accordingly, Lambert 1992, 151 and Leick 1994, 160: "like an *assinnu*, fails to achieve a sexual climax during intercourse." Cf. the discussion in Lambert 1992, 156 n. 30.

93. Virolleaud 1908/12, Adad 12:12-14. Cf. Bottéro and Petschow 1972/75, 465–66; Groneberg 1986, 36.

94. I think Greenberg (1988, 106) is right here, even though I am not convinced of his psychological explanations that lead to this conclusion (p. 103: "The castrated,

effeminate, dying son-consort represents the male child who identifies with his mother, loves her, and is punished for it").

95. On the word-plays in the *Epic of Gilgameš* cf. Kilmer 1982.

96. CAD claims that, based on the available evidence, they cannot be considered homosexuals but rather transvestites who went through a role change (A 341–42; K 558–59; cf. also Renger 1969, 193). This claim is justified insofar as the modern concept of an inherent homosexuality is being discussed, but it must be qualified to the extent that this role change may have been manifested also in concrete sexual acts— which CAD seems to be reluctant to admit.

97. Cf. the speculation of Taylor 1997, 337 concerning the emasculated Roman *galli*: "That they sacrifice their genitals is remarkable evidence of the lengths to which some homosexually oriented men will go to seek acceptance of and outlet for their sexuality."

98. That hermaphrodites (persons with physical characteristics of both sexes) were known in ancient Mesopotamia is clear from both astrological omens (e.g., SAA 8 241; see Hunger 1992, 131) and mythology. In the *Enki and Hinmah* myth Ninmah creates human beings with genital deformities. One of them is "a person on whose body was neither a penis nor a vulva" (Jacobsen 1987, 161; cf. Leick 1991, 42–43; 1994, 159). Lambert 1992, 148, however, considers this to refer to eunuchs.

99. Kilmer 1972, 171–72 discusses chastity, celibacy, and methods of sexual intercourse that would avoid pregnancy as a means to control overpopulation. In this connection, she mentions certain classes of "clergywomen" (*nadītum* etc.), but not the *assinnu*.

100. According to Simo Parpola, the role of the *assinnu* and self-castration manifested the culmination of a long process during which a person renounced his carnal desires and devoted himself to the goddess; castration thus was the result more of a spiritual process than a physical (1997b, xxxiv).

101. For these attempts, see Maul 1992, 163–64; cf. also Greenberg 1988, 101.

102. Definition by Nanda 1990, xv. For comparison with *assinnu*, cf. Leick 1994, 158–59, and with *galli*, cf. Roscoe 1996, 208–9.

103. Cf. Nanda 1990, 13–23; Roscoe 1996, 206–13.

104. Nanda 1990, 29–31.

105. See Roscoe 1996, 211–12.

106. Nanda 1990, 1–6.

107. Nanda 1990, 52–70.

108. This ritual includes an operation in which the penis and testicles are removed surgically, but the vagina is not constructed. The operation is called 'nirvan' by the hijras themselves. See Nanda 1990, 26–29.

109. Like "Salima," one of the informants of Nanda (1990, 97–112).

110. BRM 4 20:5-7 (Ungnad 1944, 258; cf. Lambert 1992, 146).

111. On these, see Brooten 1996, 115–41.

112. TCS 4 24:33 (cf. Leichty 1970, 194): "If one (male) dog mounts another, women will copulate (sal.meš *igarrušā*)."

113. Bottéro and Petschow (1972/75, 468) propose that the possible lesbian affairs were "affaire de femmes," an autonomous world where men had no authority.

114. Bottéro and Petschow (1972/75, 461,467) argue, on the basis of the carefully examined source material, that the Mesopotamians' attitude toward homosexuality was neutral and uncensored, as it was not regarded as immoral. The extreme sparse-

ness of the material as well as a firm negative attitude of a part of it, however, compel to rethink this argument.

Chapter 3: The Hebrew Bible

1. On the Holiness Code and its dating, see, e.g., Smend (1984, 38–40), who places the Holiness Code between Deuteronomy and the Priestly Code, close to the tradition of Ezekiel. Gerstenberger (1993, 6–9) agrees with this dating, although he disputes the existence of the Holiness Code as a literary entity (pp. 16–17), recognizing its links to Deuteronomistic thinking (e.g., p. 267).

2. Cf. Melcher 1996, 91–92.

3. The comparison to a catechism is made by Gerstenberger (1993, 138–242), who believes that the law has been read in worship rather than in legal proceedings. He compares the death penalty to Christian sermons in which people are threatened with hell (p. 277).

4. See Gerstenberger 1993, 262–63; unlike Coleman 1980, 47–48, and the authorities he cites, who see the correlation in the opposite way, based on the assumption that death penalty would have been practiced only before the exile.

5. According to the redaction-critical observations of Olyan 1994, 186–88, in an earlier stage of the development of the prohibition, only the partner who takes the active role in the sexual act was considered guilty, whereas in the final version (the present context), the receptive partner is also declared culpable. Olyan takes the grammatically suspicious change from singular (If a man. . .) to plural (they both. . .) in 20:13 as evidence of a later expansion.

6. On tôʿēbâ, see Humbert 1960 and, e.g., Olyan 1994, 180, 199. The term occurs especially often in the book of Ezekiel, which is in several respects close to the ideology of the Holiness Code; cf. especially Ez. 6:9, 11; 7:20; 8:4-18 (6x); 14:6; 16:36, 43, 44-58 (5x); 18:12-13; 20:7; 22:2.

7. This has been emphasized by, e.g., Boswell 1980, 100–101; Coleman 1980, 49; G. R. Edwards 1984, 52–54.

8. On the diffusion of the phenomena related to "sacred prostitution" in the Mediterranean, see Yamauchi 1973.

9. Thus Arnaud 1973; cf. Fisher 1976; Wacker 1992. The "Golden Bough" school, characterized by its tendency to connect all sources that include erotic connotations with the rite of "sacred marriage," derives its name from the epoch-making monograph of the same name by Sir James Frazer (cf. Renger 1972/75, 251–52).

10. This is the view of an increasing number of scholars, e.g., Lerner 1986; Bird 1989; 1997, 38–43; Westenholz 1989; Wacker 1992. Cf. also Nissinen 1998, 596–97, 624–27.

11. On this problem, cf., e.g., Westenholz 1989, 260–63; Leick 1994, 150–51.

12. As possibly was the case in the rite of the "sacred marriage" of the god Dumuzi and the goddess Inanna, in which the roles of Dumuzi and Inanna were played by human parties. Sources indicate that this ritual really belonged to the Sumerian royal cult, although on a smaller scale than has been assumed. Besides, this cult had hardly anything to do with promoting fertility; it was rather a matter of "determining the destiny" (NAM.TAR) of the king, i.e., establishing his rule. See the critical and source-oriented survey of the issue by Renger 1972/75 and Leick 1994, 130–38.

13. According to van der Toorn 1989, for example, prostitution—cultic or profane—was a means of last resort for women to pay vows.

14. Cf. van der Toorn 1994, 100.

15. The question whether the word *qĕdēšâ* and the duty it describes originally had any sexual aspects is nonetheless interesting. According to Bird (1989, 87), *qĕdēšâ* was a female cult functionary without any specific sexual role that has been attached to her person only through the polemic and secondary pairing of *zônâ* with *qĕdēšâ*. Gruber (1986) argues that *qĕdēšâ* means a regular prostitute, who had nothing to do with any cult, whereas the Akkadian word *qadištu* signifies a female cult professional, who was not a prostitute. A male *qādēš*, like the term *keleb*, "dog," means, according to Gruber, a Canaanite cult official, but not a prostitute. Gruber's solution is forced and breaks the inherent logic of the verses in Deut. 23:18-19 (cf. Westenholz 1989, 248). Besides, the immediate context of Hos. 4:14, makes it clear that the text indeed speaks of sex associated with cultic practices—real or imagined; cf. Nissinen 1991, 213–15. The Septuagint does not translate these terms with words that would imply cult prostitution (Gruber 1986, 135–36). The reason may be that the translators wanted to assert that no such thing ever happened in Israel; cf. chapter 5, note 22.

16. It is not quite clear whether the plural *qĕdēšîm* includes both male and female persons; so Würthwein 1985, 182–83, but see Bird 1997, 55–56.

17. Cf. Würthwein 1984, 264, 457 and, in particular, Bird 1997.

18. Bird 1997.

19. Gruber (1986, 138–46) and Westenholz (1989, 250–60) deny that *qadištu* would have been a prostitute, arguing that the sources do not stress the sexual role of *qadištu*, but present her as a wet nurse, midwife, and singer. The evidence has been interpreted also in terms of the *qadištu*'s sexual duties (cf. Renger 1967, 183–84; Yamauchi 1973, 214; Wilhelm 1990; Lambert 1992, 139–45). The *qadištu*'s place in relation to other classes of women with sacerdotal and/or sexual roles remains to be examined, and we need to consider whether "prostitution" is a correct designation even in the cases where concrete sexual activities are evident. Another important question is the *qadištu*'s role in relation to the cult of Ištar; the roles of a wet nurse and midwife may refer to the roles of this goddess. On Ištar as a midwife and a wet nurse, see Nissinen 1991, 280–90; 1993, 242–47.

20. Cf. von Soden 1970 and van der Toorn 1994, 106, who reckon with the sexual role, and Gruber 1986, 147–48; and Westenholz 1989, 249–50; and Del Olmo Lete and Sanmartín 1998, 179–81, who refute it. This designation occurs in a ritual text as an epithet of a singer (KTU 1.112) and in the staff lists (KTU 4.29:3; 4.38:2; 4.68:73; 4.47:1; 4.126:7), which do not reveal the different tasks of different personnel; it appears regularly after "priests," and it is followed by, e.g., "merchants," "silver-smiths," and "sculptors." That the task was permanent is illustrated by the term *qadšūtu*, which means a permanent condition from which a person is released by royal decree (PRU 3 140–41:2-8; see Huehnergard 1987, 173).

21. Lucian, *De Syria Dea* 43,50; cf. above pp. 31–32.

22. KAI 37 B 10 (trans. Donner and Röllig 1973: 'Tempelpäderast'); see Delcor 1979, 161–63. Mentioned earlier are the 'maidens' (*ʿlmt*) and later the 'young men' (*nʿrm*), even though their tasks are not explained; Delcor (1979, 162–63) associates them also with prostitution.

23. On the other hand, van der Toorn 1994, 106, assumes on the basis of Job 36:14 that their case was not a life-long dedication, but that the role of *qādēš* was restricted to the young. It is, however, very difficult to know the extent to which a text as late as the speech of Elihu in Job 32–37 can inform us about the concrete historical status of *qādēš*.

24. For instance, it has been assumed that infertile women would have sought a remedy with the help of male prostitutes (e.g., Bailey 1955, 52), but it is unclear how

a homosexual act could have been thought to advance fertility (Scroggs 1983, 71). This problem, however, is only apparent, the result of applying the ideas of "sacred prostitution" and "fertility cult" to sources in an anachronistic way.

25. In the context of the proscriptions of Leviticus, this is emphasized by, e.g., Gerstenberger (1993, 271–72).

26. See Olyan's criticism of attempts to interpret the prohibitions of Lev. 18:22 and 20:13 primarily in terms of procreation (1994, 199–202).

27. See Satlow 1994b, who dates this concern to the redactors of the *Babylonian Talmud*, but cf. also Philo's concern about nonprocreative sex in *Laws* 3:32-36. Cf. below, chapter 5, note 55.

28. See the argument to this effect in Douglas 1966, 54–72.

29. Cf. Gerstenberger 1993, 15,235,277; Petuchowski 1982, 146.

30. This reservation reflects the fact that, according to the Bible, Israelite priests wore a mixed garment, mules existed in Israel, and different seeds were planted in the same field (Isa 28:25), as if there were no rules prohibiting such things. Carmichael (1995) has recently pointed to this problem. His solution is to suggest that rules about forbidden mixtures include allusions to the story of Joseph in Genesis, with encoded historical messages about the problems of the Israelites' identity in the past; thus the Israelites would not express any kind of taboo but make the implied readers perceive their contemporary (exilic) struggle for identity.

31. Cf. Gerstenberger 1993, 249.

32. It may be true, also, that assuming the role of the opposite sex was confusing the divine order of creation, according to which all human beings are created as male *or* female (Gen. 1:27); cf. Waetjen 1996, 105. It should not be taken for granted, however, that this theology of the Priestly account of creation would have emerged independently from the postexilic identity strategy of the Israelites.

33. Thus Greenberg 1988, 19; Gerstenberger 1993, 271; cf. Brooten 1996, 62, and see Biale 1984, 196, on the Rabbinic sources.

34. Cf. Jung and Smith 1993, 74, referring to an unpublished paper by David M. Gunn; Stone 1995, 98–99.

35. These exceptions are Gen. 19:32-35, where the daughters of Lot make their drunken father lay with them, thus virtually take the active role, and 2 Sam. 13:11 where Amnon says to her sister Tamar: "Sleep with me, my sister!" (*šikbî ʿimmî ʾaḥôtî*); in this case there is no doubt which of the two plays the active role. These exceptions show that it is not a linguistic necessity to have the male party as the subject of the verb. However, the fact that this is the case in the vast majority of the occurrences makes the role structure crystal clear. See Brenner 1997, 24–26.

36. See the linguistic analysis of Olyan 1994, 183–85.

37. See also Olyan 1994, 183–86; Boyarin 1994, 340–48; Stone 1995, 96–98; Brenner 1997, 140.

38. See Olyan 1994, 195.

39. I owe this observation to Boyarin 1994, 347.

40. Pace Waetjen 1996, 105.

41. E.g., the story of Filemon and Baukis in Ovid's *Metamorphoses* (8:616-724); Bömer 1977, 190–232; cf. McNeill 1976, 55–56; Boswell 1980, 96–97.

42. Thus Levin (1993, 159–64), whose theory of the origins and history of the passage seems plausible. Loader (1990, 15–48) takes the text as a unified creation of one author, but also he assumes that the author has used older sources. Loader does not name the Yahwist as the author.

43. Levin (1993, 430–34) assumes that the Yahwist is later than the basic layer of Deuteronomy but earlier than the Deuteronomistic writers or Deutero-Isaiah—in other words, from the beginning of the sixth century, the time of the exile. Loader (1990, 46) dates the work about a hundred years earlier.

44. The King James Version translates with this word the Hebrew term *qādēš*, which has been interpreted to mean a male temple prostitute (Deut. 23:17-18; 1 Kings 14:22-24; 15:12; 22:46; 2 Kings 23:7; Joel 3:3). Of the modern Bible translations, the New Revised Standard Version, for example, uses the word "sodomites" in 1 Cor. 6:9 and 1 Tim. 1:10 to translate the Greek word *arsenokoitēs*, on which see below, pp. 114–17.

45. In addition to the mentioned passages of the Yahwist, cf. Gen. 38:26; Num. 31:17, 18; Judg. 11:39; 21:11; 1 Sam. 1:19; 1 Kings 1:4.

46. Bailey 1955, 1–28. The aspect of "knowledge" has also been highlighted by Brenner 1997, 138, without, however, denying that the verb *yādaʿ* is used of concrete sexual action: "The 'knowing' agent aspires to establish power and control over other male newcomers, experienced as potential usurpers of male knowledge and power."

47. Bailey's view is shared by, among others, Boswell 1980, 94 and McNeill 1976, 54–55.

48. A corresponding verb *ginōskō* is used in the New Testament about Mary, who "knows nothing of a man" (Lk. 1:34; cf. Mt. 1:25).

49. Bailey 1955, 6; cf. Boswell 1980, 95.

50. Cf. Levin 1993, 160.

51. Deut. 29:23; 32:32; Isa. 1:9.10; 3:9; 13:19; Jer. 23:14; 49:18; 50:40; Ez. 16:46-48; Amos 4:11; Zeph. 2:9; Lam. 4:6; indirectly also Hos. 11:8. See Loader's (1990, 49–74) thorough survey.

52. In Ez. 22:10-11, where several sexual crimes mentioned in Leviticus 18 and 20 are listed, male-to-male copulation is missing: "In you, men have exposed their fathers' nakedness [cf. Lev. 18:7-8; 20:11]; they have violated women during their periods [cf. Lev. 18:19; 20:18]; they have committed an outrage with their neighbours' wives [cf. Lev. 18:20; 20:10] and have lewdly defiled their daughters-in-law [cf. Lev. 18:15; 20:12]; they have ravished their sisters, their own father's daughters [cf. Lev. 18:9; 20:17]" (NEB).

53. Boyarin 1994, 350.

54. Sir. 16:7-10; Wis. 10:6-9; 3 Macc. 2:5; see Loader 1990, 76–80. De Young (1990, 438–46), reading between the lines and from other contexts, finds homosexual associations in these passages.

55. The word *hyperēfania* means "arrogant pride." Coleman 1980, 62 finds a reference to Sodom also in Sir. 39:23: "But the doom he assigns the heathen is his wrath, as when he turned a watered plain into a salt desert." The wording, however, is obviously derived from Ps. 107:33-34.

56. Cf. Mk. 6:11; Mt. 10:15; 11:23-24; Lk. 10:12; 17:29; Rom. 9:29 (Isa. 1:9); Heb. 13:2; Rev. 11:8; see Loader 1990, 118–27.

57. See Uro (1987, 83–85), who points out that the wording in Luke is closer to the original text of Q.

58. Sura 26:165-166: "How can you lust for males, of all creatures in the world, and leave those whom God has created for you as your mates? You are really going beyond all limits." Cf. sura 15:73-74. In Islamic tradition homosexual men are, somewhat illogically, called "Lot's folk" (*qaum luṭ* or *luṭī*); see Duran 1993, 181–82; Wehr and Cowan 1976, 883.

59. Cf. Loader 1990, 36–37. This was well understood still in the early Christian literature, as 1 Clem. 10:7—11:1 shows: "Because of his faith and hospitality, he [Abraham] was granted a boy even in his old days. . . . Because of his hospitality and righteousness Lot was rescued from Sodom, when the whole surroundings were doomed to be destroyed in fire and brimstone."

60. G. R. Edwards 1984, 46; cf. also Vanggaard 1971, 100; Fehling 1988 (1974), 298–99.

61. Cf., e.g., Jung and Smith 1993, 69; Brenner 1997, 138.

62. Cf. Duran's (1993, 187–89) examples of Islamic countries (the phenomenon, however, is no more prevalent there than anywhere else).

63. See Vanggaard 1971, 98–109; Fehling 1988 (1974), 282–96.

64. Schauenburg 1975, plate 25; cf. Dover 1978, 105; Fehling 1988, 322. Thucydides 1:100.1 relates the battle itself.

65. *Eurymedōn eimi kybade hesteka.* On the translation, see Schauenburg 1975, 103–4.

66. Dover (1978, 105) comments on the picture as follows: "This expresses the exultation of the 'manly' Athenians at their victory over the 'womanish' Persians at the river Eurymedon in the early 460s; it proclaims, 'We've buggered the Persians!'"

67. On Priapus, see Herter 1954; Fehling 1988 (1974), 285–89; Lilja 1990, 78–79.

68. On the Priapic poetry in general, see Richlin 1983.

69. Cf. Richlin 1983, 59.

70. This was the interpretation of Josephus, *Ant.* 1:200; accordingly Gunkel 1910, 208 and a number of younger scholars following him.

71. Frankfurter and Ulmer (1991, 51) comment sharply: "Had Lot considered the people of his city as homosexuals, he would have most certainly not offered them his virgin daughters but his son-in-laws and sons!" Cf. also Boyarin 1994, 349.

72. The Hebrew word *pīlegeš* is usually translated "concubine"; see, however, the criticism of Exum (1993, 177), who considers this translation to give the impression that "she is less valued, and probably more expendable than a legitimate wife."

73. Cf. G. R. Edwards's (1984, 35–38) convenient synopsis.

74. The wording is almost identical: *ʾal-nāʾ ʾaḥay tārēʿû* (Gen. 19:7) and *ʾal-ʾaḥay ʾal-tārēʿû nāʾ* (Judges 19:23).

75. The reason may be an unwillingness to impute to Israelites (Benjaminites) a sin similar to that of the Sodomites (cf. G. R. Edwards 1984, 40–41). Perhaps the translator of the Septuagint had the same thought when translating the verb *yādaʿ* with a common verb, *ginōskō*, which means "to know." The translator of Genesis chose in 19:5 a synonym, *synginomai*, which has a clear sexual meaning.

76. Pseudo-Philo 45:2; see Harrington 1985, 359.

77. If we accept the traditional preexilic dating of the Yahwist and agree with most commentators that Judges 17–21 is a postexilic addition to the Deuteronomistic history (see, e.g., Smend 1984, 117,127–28), then the case is clear; but if the work of the Yahwist dates as late as the exilic or postexilic period (so, e.g., Levin 1993, 430–34) and Judges 17–21 stems from the editorial work of the first Deuteronomistic historian (Veijola 1977, 15–29), the difference of the date between the stories is not large, and the literary primacy is more difficult to determine.

78. Niditch 1982, 375–78, represents the contrary opinion, arguing that Judges 19, unlike Gen. 19:1-11, is an integral part of its literary framework, constituting a complex and realistic narrative, whereas Gen. 19:1-11 is, theologically as well as narratologically, more simple and straightforward. However, if her use of the *lectio difficilior*

rule (the more complex, the earlier) is not acceptable, these arguments are not compelling; cf. the criticism of Brettler 1989, 411 n. 91.

79. Cf. Boyarin 1994, 352.

80. Exum (1993, 170–201) notes the contrast between the active position of the Levite's wife in the beginning of the story, where it is told that she left her husband on her own initiative, and her total passiveness in the remaining story. According to Exum, she is not only raped by the men of Gibeah in the narrative but also by the narrator's pen when the rape becomes a "narrative punishment" for her sexual independence expressed in v. 2.

81. For the interrelation of gender, power, homoeroticism and hospitality in Judges 19, see Stone 1995.

82. On the portrait and status of the Levite's wife in Judges 19, see Niditch 1982, 369–71; Trible 1984, 65–91, and Exum 1993, 176–84.

83. Thus Stone 1995, 100.

84. See Veijola 1977, 27–29. Brettler 1989 also reckons with a pro-Davidic redaction.

85. Cf. Bassett 1971, 233–34; Gerstenberger 1993, 273; Levin 1993, 119.

86. So, e.g., McNeill 1976, 69; Levin 1993, 119; Brenner 1997, 108–9. Less likely is Bassett's (1971, 235–36) assumption that Ham was joined with Noah's wife, his mother. Bassett refers to the statements in the Holiness Code where "revealing a woman's nakedness" meant disgrace for her husband; the literal translation of Lev. 18:8 is, "Do not reveal the nakedness of the wife of your father, because that is your father's nakedness," in other words, do not humiliate your father by sleeping with his wife (cf. 18:14,16; 20:11, 20, 21). This theory would well explain why Noah does not curse Ham but Canaan, who would be a child born from incest. The homosexual aspect would disappear altogether. However, this theory is hard to match with the wording of the story, according to which Noah, drunk, lay naked (literally, "revealed himself," *gālâ* hitp.). It was *Noah's* nudity that Ham saw and his brothers veiled.

87. Cf. Melcher 1996, 94–95.

88. If Gen. 9:20-27 is from the time of the exile, this approach would be particularly apt; cf. Levin 1993, 119.

89. For a recent survey of different opinions regarding the origins and redaction of this story, see W. Dietrich 1997, 213–20.

90. Verses 12–17 appear to be later than the basic layer of the story; apparently the Deuteronomistic historian wanted to expand the union between David and Jonathan (18:3) to include both families; the editor may have thought of the pardoning of the crippled son of Jonathan, Mephibosheth (2 Samuel 9). The same editor may have added the ending of David's and Jonathan's farewells (20:42b). See Veijola 1975, 82–90.

91. The farewell scene contradicts the earlier story about the shooting of arrows. The men had agreed to use sign language for the reason that Jonathan could not meet David face to face. This would have been unnecessary if their meeting was as easy to arrange as the farewell scene implies. The farewell scene thus has been considered a later addition (see Veijola 1975, 83, note 18). But some problems remain with this solution: Why would the editor have wanted to create this obvious contradiction?

92. This scene also is added by the Deuteronomistic historian (Veijola 1975, 88–90).

93. Cf., e.g., Horner 1978, 26–39; Terrien 1985, 169; Schroer and Staubli 1996; more carefully Gerstenberger 1993, 271.

94. The Septuagint here has a substantive, *metokhos*, which means a partner—not necessarily in an intimate sense, however, as Horner (1978, 32) reads it.

95. Many researchers have been careful not to overemphasize the homoerotic interpretation; cf., e.g., Bailey 1955, 56–57; Räisänen 1975, 270–71; Pope 1976, 416. Some general presentations (McNeill 1976; Boswell 1980, G. R. Edwards 1984) do not discuss David's and Jonathan's relationship at all.

96. Seebaß (1973, 572) interprets Saul's reaction in terms of David's aspirations to power: as a rival for the kingship he would have included Jonathan's mother in his harem.

97. Bailey 1955, 57.

98. Because the history of David's rise to power was augmented by the Deuteronomists from the time of the exile, it is unnecessary to assume that the story of David and Jonathan would exhibit an essentially older culture with more positive attitudes towards homoeroticism than the Holiness Code (so Terrien 1985, 169; Gerstenberger 1993, 271). Greenberg (1988, 114) states correctly that "an explicit homosexual relationship between David and Jonathan could easily have been deleted by priestly editors." There is, however, no indication that this ever happened.

99. Cf. W. Dietrich 1997, 291–92.

100. On this concept, see Morgan 1992, 67, and cf. above, p. 17.

101. For comparison, see Halperin 1990, 75–87.

Chapter 4: Classical Antiquity

1. Cf. Cantarella 1992, 8–16 on Homeric poems and the lyric poetry from the Archaic Period.

2. On Sparta, see Cartledge 1988 (1981). On Crete, see Patzer 1982, 71–84; Sergent 1986, 34–47.

3. Plato, *Symposium* 182A-B.

4. E.g., Dover 1978, 196–203. Devereux (1988 [1968], 214–19) explains pederasty as an artificial prolongation of diffused puberty. "It was a *by-product* of the unfortunate *manner* in which the Greeks implemented a psycho-social constellation" (p. 207; emphasis in the original). Devereux's starting point is the same as that of traditional psychiatry, which has explained modern homosexuality by means of the concepts of perversion and neurosis. Devereux is criticized, among others, by Scroggs 1983, 146–49, Sergent 1986, 62, and Cantarella 1992, 81.

5. Especially Sergent (1986, 56, 62), who views Greek homosexuality not as an exceptional local-historical "accident" or distortion but "as a local variation of a social interpretation of sexuality." This view finds sound support from recent cross-cultural studies of homoeroticism (e.g., Greenberg 1988; cf. also Baum 1993).

6. The initiation theory was inaugurated already by Erich Bethe 1907 (=1988) in his article "Die dorische Knabenliebe." He argues that anal intercourse was a matter of transmitting virtues and heroism (*aretē*), which supposedly lived in the sperm, to boys. While many of the article's ideas have been subsequently rejected, the idea of initiation is still widely supported. Cf. Vanggaard 1971, 62–63; Bremmer 1980; Cartledge 1988 (1981), 398–405; Sergent 1986, 48–62; Greenberg 1988, 108–10. A modern counterpart to this type of initiation can be found in a Sambia tribe in New Guinea, where boys' upbringing includes a period of living together with unmarried men. This training involves, among other things, oral sex, because "feeding" with sperm is regarded as necessary for raising a man. Once matured, boys themselves then assume the role of a sperm giver and, eventually, when old enough to marry, switch to exclusively heterosexual sex life; see Stoller and Herdt 1985; Greenberg 1988, 27–29.

7. Cf. Koch-Harnack 1983, 237–38.

8. If not earlier, at least in Plato's time the relationship of Zeus and Ganymedes was seen as sexual. The Athenian in Plato's *Laws* (1:636C-D) claims that the Cretans had invented this myth to justify their own conduct. see Sergent 1986, 220–28.

9. Plutarch, *Dialogue on Love* 761D; see Sergent 1986, 155–64.

10. On the idea of initiation, see Patzer 1982, 67–125; Sergent 1986, 57–62; Cantarella 1992, 3–8.

11. So Plato in *Protagoras* 325–26E; cf. Koch-Harnack 1983, 34. According to Patzer (1982, 104–5), this "klassische Knabenliebe," which applied only to the upper class and required a democratic polis-society, represents a development younger than the "dorische Knabenliebe," which was prevalent, for instance, in Crete and Sparta.

12. Plato, *Symposium* 179A-B: this claim pertains to women also.

13. According to Xenophon, this was the practice of the Thebans and Eleans, but not the Spartans (*Symposium* 8:35). Plutarch (*Pelopidas* 18) tells of Gorgidas, who arranged his Theban elite troops on the basis of this principle. On this ideology, see Koch-Harnack 1983, 43–48; Greenberg 1988, 110–16; Boswell 1994, 62–64.

14. Even if Boswell 1994, 57 declares this role disctinction to be a "cultural myth" that the historian should view critically, he does not, in my judgment, prove that it would not have really functioned. Even in homoerotic relationships in which both partners were adults (thus not pederastic) this role division appears to be the rule.

15. See Cartledge 1988 (1981), 395. Devereux (1988 [1968], 207.216) character-izes this foster-fatherhood with the term "inadequate fathering."

16. Plato, *Symposium* 192A; *Laws* 7:804D.

17. Plato, *Symposium* 178E.

18. Plato, *Symposium* 184DE (trans. A. Nehamas and P. Woodruff). Cf. *Symposium* 185B etc. It should be noted that "in doing anything" does not include improper deeds.

19. Cf. Wender 1984 (1973), 217–18.

20. Plato, *Symposium* 209C.

21. Plato, *Symposium* 211B; Cf. Xenophon, *Symposium* 8:23.

22. Plato, *Phaedrus* 204E.

23. Plato, *Symposium* 211B-C (transl. A. Nehamas and P. Woodruff). Lilja (1990, 83) identifies this quote as the philosophical core of the *Symposium*. Held (1983) compares the gradual ascending from the lower forms of love to the higher to the ideology of the *Epic of Gilgameš*; cf. above p. 24 with n. 21.

24. Plato naturally knows that "his [the boy's] desires are similar to his lover's, but weaker: to see, touch, kiss and lie down with him; and indeed, as one might expect, soon afterwards he does just that. So as they lie together, the lover's licentious horse has something to suggest to the charioteer, and claims a little enjoyment as recompense for much hardship; while its counterpart in the beloved has nothing to say, but swelling with confused passion it embraces the lover and kisses him, welcoming him as someone full of goodwill, and whenever they lie down together, it is ready not to refuse to do its own part in granting favours to the lover. . ." *Phaedrus* 255E–265A (trans. C.J. Rowe).

25. Cf. Dover 1980, 3.

26. Plato, *Phaedrus* 253C–256D.

27. Plato, *Symposium* 218C–219E. In the same fashion Xenophon praises his friend Agesilaos II and his chastity and continence (*enkrateia*) in his homoerotic relations; see Cartledge 1988 (1981), 389.

28. Cf. Cantarella 1992, 23–24.

29. Plato, *Phaedrus* 233A–234B.

30. Henderson 1975, 206: "Homosexual gratification became, with marriage, at best a marginal luxury, and its distinctly secondary role did not usually become the focus of intense and lasting emotions of the kind we find exalted by Plato."

31. Halperin 1990, 32: "To assimilate both the senior and the junior partner in a paederastic relationship to the same '(homo)sexuality,' for example, would have struck a classical Athenian as no less bizarre than to classify a burglar as an 'active criminal,' his victim as a 'passive criminal,' and the two of them alike as partners in crime."

32. Foucault 1985, 190: "People did not have the notion of two distinct appetites allotted to different individuals or at odds with each other in the same soul; rather, they saw two ways of enjoying one's pleasure, one of which was more suited to certain individuals or certain periods of existence."

33. There is no scholarly consensus about using the term "homosexuality" of antiquity; regarding different definitions see, e.g., Dover 1978, 1; Lilja 1983, 8–11. Cf. also Patzer's (1982, 43–67) extensive criticism of Dover's use of the concept, its total rejection with regard to antiquity by Halperin 1990, and its partial rehabilitation by Richlin 1993. Devereux (1988 [1968]) talks about "pseudo-homosexuality," but this term has the same ambiguity as the term "homosexuality."

34. E.g., Aeschines, *Timarchus* 138 (yet just the opposite in 185); Plutarch, *Dialogue on Love* 767A, etc. On "nature" and pederasty, see also Dover 1978, 60–68.

35. Plato, *Symposium* 189D–193A (quotation 191D–192B; trans. A. Nehamas and P. Woodruff).

36. Cf. Halperin 1990, 19–21 against Boswell 1980, 94–101.

37. See Allen 1997, 64.

38. Cf. Foucault 1985, 38–93.

39. Plato, *Symposium* 196E–197A. Of the virtues of a citizen, this list omits only piety (*eusebeia*), because, of course, Eros is a god.

40. See Dover 1974, 205–6.

41. On adultery, see Pomeroy 1975, 87–88; Cantarella 1990, 43–46; on legislation in particular, see Cole 1984, 100–108; Cohen 1991, 98–132.

42. According to Plutarch (*Solon* 23:1), Solon "permitted an adulterer (*moichos*) caught in the act to be killed; but if a man committed rape upon a free woman, he was merely to be fined a hundred drachmas" (trans. B. Perrin; cf. Cole 1984, 101). Cf. the oration of Lysias (1:32-33), according to which also rapists of free women and children may deserve the death penalty (cf. Cohen 1991, 105–6).

43. Dover 1974, 207.

44. E.g., Plato, *Phaedrus* 238A-C; Aeschines, *Timarchus* 42, 75; cf. Dover 1974, 179, 208–9.

45. So speaks Antisthenes in Xenophon's *Symposium* (4:38). The Cynic Diogenes is known for being even more ascetic; he masturbated publicly only if he inadvertently had an erection (Plutarch, *On Stoic Self-Contradictions* 1044B).

46. See Dover 1974, 95–98.209–10; 1988 (1973), 267–69; Pomeroy 1975, 79–84.

47. Xenophon, *Oeconomicus* 7:30.

48. Cf. Keuls 1985, 210–15.

49. Cf. Cohen 1991, 84–88, 150–54.

50. Pomeroy (1975, 35–42) explains Spartan women's more independent status as due to the fact that Spartan men (like the Romans) spent longer periods in military service, whereas the Athenian men's absences were shorter (pp. 39, 119). Cartledge

(1988 [1981], 407) remarks that, in spite of their women's freer status, the atmosphere in Sparta was even more exclusively masculine than that of the other Greek cities.

51. On women in the Hellenistic and Roman worlds, see Pomeroy 1975, 120–48.

52. See Dover 1974, 179, 210; Pomeroy 1975, 90–91.

53. Demosthenes 59 (*Against Neaera*):122 (trans. A. T. Murray, who, however, translates "persons" instead of "bodies" for *tou sōmatos*). This schematic statement should not be overgeneralized, but it does give an idea of the male philosophers' attitudes toward women. The statement is quoted already by Athenaeus (*Deipnosophistae* 13:573B); cf. Dover 1974, 14; Mossé 1990a, 28.

54. For an illustrated presentation of heterosexual prostitution in Athens, see Reinsberg 1989, 80–162.

55. See Mossé 1990a, 34.

56. Demosthenes 59: *Against Neaera*.

57. Plato, *Menexenos* 235E; cf. Xenophon, *Oeconomicus* 3:14-15.

58. See Herter 1960, 83–84; Pomeroy 1975, 89.91–92.139–41; Dover 1978, 20–21; Keuls 1985, 187–203. Cf. Reinsberg (1989, 84ff), who concludes that the appellation *hetaira* signifies a prostitute in general, not just a particularly cultured or rich courtesan (which, of course, also existed). This euphemism, however, is mainly used of well-to-do prostitutes, whereas *pornē* has a pejorative tone and is used of all prostitutes.

59. Of this difference in status, see Keuls 1985, 204–28; Cantarella 1990, 49–51 et passim.

60. See Pomeroy's (1975, 91–119) review and cf. Dover 1974, 99–101; on the Hellenistic period, see Alganza Roldán 1990.

61. On Plato's view of women, see Pomeroy 1975, 115–19; Mossé 1990b; Allen 1997, 57–75.

62. Wender (1984 [1973], 213–20) has gathered representative examples of both attitudes.

63. See Pomeroy 1994, 39 (cf. her remarks on feminism and Xenophon's *Oeconomicus*, p. 87–90); Allen 1997, 53–57.

64. Cf. Carson 1990, 137–45 on women's "wetness" and wantonness; Cohen 1991, 144.

65. Xenophon, *Oeconomicus* 10:1 (trans. S. B. Pomeroy); for further references to Xenophon, cf. Wender 1984 (1973), 224–25.

66. Cf. Cohen 1991, 144–70.

67. Cf., e.g., Xenophon, *Oeconomicus* 7–9, and the commentary of Pomeroy 1994, 274–303; cf. also Reinsberg 1989, 34–45.

68. See Reinsberg 1989, 76–79.

69. On the exceptions, see, e.g., Xenophon, *Symposium* 8:3: "Nay, Niceratus too, so I am told, is in love with his wife and finds his love reciprocated" (trans. O. J. Todd).

70. The militaristic nature of homoeroticism has traditionally been emphasized, and its origins have been explained on the basis of the barrack context; so, e.g., Marrou (1965, 62–63) in his influential work on ancient upbringing; for a different view, cf., e.g., Sergent 1986, 57–59.

71. Cf., e.g., Aeschines, *Timarchus* 138; Plutarch, *Solon* 1:3; see also Lilja 1983, 103–5.

72. The best example may be Plato's *Charmides* (154A-C).

73. Dover 1978, 66.

74. E.g., Athenaeus, *Deipnosophistae* 13:565F-566A; see Koch-Harnack 1983, 37.

75. Cf., e.g., Aeschines, *Timarchus* 156–57.

76. On this development, see Dover 1978, 67–73, 79–81.

77. See Dover 1978, 88–91; Koch-Harnack 1983, 50–54. An interesting point of comparison can be found in some contemporary Muslim societies and their premarital homoeroticism, which arises from the segregation of the sexes; see Duran 1993, 185.

78. On the etiquette of pederastic courtship, cf. Dover 1978, 87–97; Cantarella 1992, 17–22.

79. Plato, *Symposium* 183C.

80. Aeschines, *Timarchus* 12. The Law of Beroea also contains a list of those who may not enter the gymnasium; cf. Cantarella 1993, 28–29.

81. Aeschines, *Timarchus* 11.

82. On the age structure of the pederastic relationship, see Reinsberg 1989, 165–70; Cantarella 1992, 36–42.

83. Of this tells Plutarch, *Lycurgus* 16–17; Cartledge 1988 (1981) 393–94.

84. For this reason Devereux (1988 [1968], 210–11) speaks of social prolongation of the undifferentiated pubertal sexuality to adulthood. "Diffuse pubertal sexuality is 'normal' *for that age only*, it must be outgrown eventually. The Greeks postponed the outgrowing of this 'developmental neurosis' by cultural means" (emphasis in the original). This, according to Devereux, separates pederasty from true homosexuality, because the roots of a genuine "perversion" lie in the early childhood.

85. *Greek Anthology* 12:4 (trans. W. R. Paton).

86. Cf. Dover 1978, 86; Cantarella 1992, 37–39.

87. Strato in *Greek Anthology* 12:186 (trans. W. E. Paton). The growth of body hair was sometimes used as an argument for loving women; so Erastosthenes in *Greek Anthology* 5:277. "There is no beauty in youths at the age of puberty; I hate the unkind hair that begins to grow too soon."

88. This was the case with, e.g., Charmides's lovers, according to Plato (*Charmides* 154A).

89. Xenophon (*Symposium* 8:2) gives an example of this: "Critobulus, though even yet the object of love, is already beginning to feel this passion for others" (trans. O. J. Todd).

90. Even Patzer (1982, 55) acknowledges this, although he thinks that nonpederastic homosexual relations between adult men exist only in comedies and even then only as comic exaggerations with no basis in reality. His argument, however, is unconvincing; cf. Scroggs 1983, 130–39.

91. Xenophon (*Anabasis* 2:6:28) was horrified by Menon, who, while still beardless, had the already bearded Tharypas as his beloved.

92. Aeschines accuses Timarchus for his pubertal prostitution and does not deny "that jealousies and quarrels that commonly arise from the practice" have happened to him also (Aeschines, *Timarchus* 136). Aeschines himself was forty-five years old at this point.

93. E.g., Plato, *Laws* 7:823B.

94. Koch-Harnack 1983, 242. Koch-Harnack treats extensively these picture themes, which actually disappeared already after the Persian Wars in the 5th century.

95. Of pederasty as a part of cultural competition, see Cartledge 1988 (1981), 409–10.

96. Plenty of examples come from Dover 1978, Koch-Harnack 1983, Keuls 1985; 277–96, and Reinsberg 1989, 163ff.

97. Of these pictures, see Dover 1978, 92–99.

98. On the nature of a pederastic sexual contact and the differences between anal intercourse and intercrural contact, see Dover 1978, 100–103; Reinsberg 1989, 189–99. Cantarella (1992, 24–27), however, does not regard anal intercourse as oppressive, as Dover does. In the homoerotic poetry of the *Greek Anthology*, the buttocks is seen as an extremely erotic area, and the descriptions of anal intercourse lack the ridicule that color Aristophanes' words.

99. Cf. also Xenophon, *Memorabilia* 1:6:13; Aeschines, *Timarchus* 137; cf. Koch-Harnack 1983, 48.

100. Cf. Xenophon, *Symposium* 8:21: "For a youth does not share in the pleasure of the intercourse as a woman does, but looks on, sober, at another in love's intoxication" (trans. O. J. Todd).

101. Cf. Dover 1978, 96, 103.

102. See, e.g., Xenophon, *Memorabilia* 1:6:13; Aeschines, *Timarchus* 137; cf. Koch-Harnack 1983, 48.

103. On this term, the opposite of which is rationality (*sōphrosynē*), see Dover 1978, 34–39; Cohen 1991, 177–80.

104. Cf. Winkler 1990, 46–54.

105. Aeschines, *Timarchus* 21, 29-32; cf. Dover 1978, 19–34; Winkler 1990, 56–64; Cantarella 1992, 48–53.

106. Cf. Aeschines, *Timarchus* 74, 119–20, 123, 188. This tax was called *pornikon telos*.

107. On male prostitution in Athens, see Reinsberg 1989, 201–12.

108. Dover 1978, 29.

109. Cf. Cohen 1991, 187–88; Cantarella 1992, 50–51.

110. Aeschines, *Timarchus* 136.

111. Plato, *Symposium* 182A-C. So Cartledge 1988 (1981), 392; cf. Dover 1978, 81–83.190–91; Cantarella 1992, 20. Cohen (1987, 5–9; 1991, 175–77) treats extensively the norms regulating homoerotic behavior. Based on these norms it is hardly possible to conclude that Athenian society would have condemned homoeroticism in principle; but Cohen's contribution is important in reminding that Plato's and Xenophon's idealistic views do not tell the whole truth about homoerotic practice in the concrete life of the Athenians.

112. Cf. Foucault 1985, 191.

113. See below p. 84.

114. Cf. Wilkinson 1978, 140–41; Boswell 1980, 84–85.

115. Boswell 1980, 61, quotes Edward Gibbon's argument from 1789. This impression is based on Suetonius's descriptions of the sexual lives of the emperors; see Cantarella 1992, 156–64; Richlin 1993, 531–32, 538–40.

116. Thus Lilja, who discusses these poets extensively (1983, 51–87); unlike, e.g., Wilkinson (1978, 138), who doubts that the poems would reveal much about the writers' dispositions. But Catullus, Virgil, and Horace never married, although they did write verses also in praise of women.

117. Lilja does not agree with the view that the homoeroticism of Plautus's plays, for example, would have been borrowed from Greek sources; Plautus surely uses Greek texts as his sources but then adds to them homosexual scenes that were unknown in the original Greek models (1983, 105, 129).

118. Richlin 1993, 569–71 argues that the law was against passive homosexual behavior by free men and that its purpose was perceived as preventing an adult male from having sex with another adult male.

119. Thus Boswell (1980, 65–69), Lilja (1983, 112–21, 132–33, 137) and Cantarella (1992, 106–14); cf. Hoheisel 1992, 313–14. Unlike, e.g., Kroll 1988 (1930), 91–92, and Wilkinson 1978, 136, 140, who believes this law was a "dead letter" at least in the third century C.E. It has been presumed that *Lex Scantinia* got its name from Scantinius Capitolinus, who around 226 B.C.E. got involved sexually with the son of a citizen named Claudius Marcellus (Valerius Maximus 6:1:7); Lilja 1983, 113, and Cantarella 1992, 109 have doubts about this view.

120. Valerius Maximus 6:1:6-12; in one case (6:1:10) an accused even admits openly to having been in a homosexual relation and emphasizes that no crime was committed there.

121. Cicero, *De domo sua* 139: *imperitus adolescens. . .qui contra fas et inter viros saepe mulier et inter mulieres vir fuisset*; cf. Lilja 1983, 92.96.

122. *Tusculan Disputations* 4:33:70. Cicero quotes Ennius, according to whom *flagiti principium est nudare inter civis corpora* ("Shame's beginning is the stripping of men's bodies openly"; trans. J. E. King).

123. See Herter 1960, 71–75, 85–88; Boswell 1980, 77–79; Taylor 1997, 358–60.

124. *Corpus inscriptionum Latinarum* I, 2, p. 317. The day off for female prostitutes was the day before; see Boswell 1980, 70; Lilja 1983, 114.

125. This becomes apparent throughout the sources Lilja has analyzed (see Lilja 1983, 39, 46, 103–4, 106–12, 122). See also Vertstraete 1980; Cantarella 1992, 98–99, 101–4.

126. On this institution, see Taylor 1997, 360–70.

127. Lilja 1983, 112. According to Greenberg (1988), it could be maintained that the transgenerational type of homoeroticism was in Rome replaced by a class-distinguished one.

128. Cf. Lilja 1983, 85.

129. As to *Carmina Priapea*, see Richlin 1983, passim and cf. above p. 48–49.

130. The Elder Seneca 4, pref. 10 (trans. M. Winterbottom). The word translated "losing one's virtue" is *impudicitia*, which means sexual passivity and penetrability. The words are a quotation from the orator Haterius, not Seneca's own.

131. Catullus 61:134-141 (trans. Guy Lee).

132. Richlin 1993, 535.

133. Cf. Martial 11:43; 12:97; Juvenal 6:268-272.

134. See Richlin 1993, 555–61 and, on blaming the victim, also 563–65.

135. Lilja (1983, 106–12) discusses the offenses Valerius Maximus mentions; cf. also Cantarella 1992, 104–6.

136. Boswell (1980, 76) tries in vain to invalidate the feminine dimension of the word, which in its use and meaning is very close to the Greek word *malakos*.

137. Cf. Boswell 1980, 74; Lilja 1983, 86.

138. See the evidence in Richlin 1993, 537–38.

139. This word, derived from the Greek *kinaidos* (see above, pp. 68), has a plethora of synonyms in Latin; Richlin 1993, 531 gives the following equivalents: *pathicus, exoletus, concubinus, spintria, puer* (boy), *pullus* (chick), *pusio, delicatus, mollis* (soft), *tener* (dainty), *debilis* (weak), *effeminatus, discinctus* (loose-belted), *morbosus* (sick).

140. On *cinaedi*, see Richlin 1993; Gleason 1995, 64–65; Taylor 1997, 338–60.

141. Taylor 1997, 349–57 documents reciprocal relationships in which the *cinaedus* takes the active role; cf. Seneca 47:7 (see below, p. 84). On the involvement of *cinaedi* in heterosexual relationships, see Richlin 1983, 91–93.

142. E.g., Apuleius, *Metamorphoses* 8:26; cf. also the mockery of Martial 3:81,1: "What is a woman's crevasse to you, Baetius, you *gallus*?" On *galli* in Rome, see Taylor 1997, 328–37, and cf. above, pp. 31–32.

143. On Juvenal, see Richlin 1983, 195–209; 1993, 543–54; Cantarella 1992, 156–64.

144. See especially Juvenal 2 (the "homophobia" of which, according to Richlin 1993, 544, is undeniable); cf. 6:40-138.

145. For a Roman typology of an effeminate man, see Richlin 1993, 541–42; Gleason 1995, 62–67.

146. Martial's attitude to *pueri* was ambivalent. He himself wanted a boy "with a cheek smooth with youth, not with pumice, for whose sake no maid would please me" (14:205). On the other hand, there is no lack in his works of invective against the passive sexual role of males (cf. Richlin 1983, 135–39; Cantarella 1992, 148–52). The poems of Martial were obviously literally inspired by the contemporary Greek epigrams now collected in book 12 of the *Greek Anthology* (see Richlin 1983, 39–44).

147. See Cantarella 1992, 128–34, and, further, on Propertius, Lucretius, Virgil, Horace, and Ovid, ibid. pp. 134–41. According to Cantarella's final conclusion "the *Lex Scatinia* had been forgotten, and the crime it had defined as *stuprum cum puero* now become in practice an absolutely normal relationship, socially accepted, engaged in with total freedom, and celebrated by the poets." But if these relationships are celebrated only by poets, one could ask whether their verses reflect only the somewhat freer and more liberal moral code adopted by the poets than was the rule of society.

148. Poems 24, 48, 81, and 99 certainly describe his relationship to Juventius, and several other poems indicate the same; see Lilja 1983, 51–62; Cantarella 1992, 121–28.

149. So Lilja (1983, 51), who refutes Boswell's (1980, 79) view that Juventius was a prostitute.

150. Catullus 16:1-6 (trans. Guy Lee).

151. On the graffiti of Pompeii, which date from the time after the earthquake of 62 B.C.E.; see Lilja 1983, 97–102, 131. Also Kroll 1988 (1930), 89–90, gives text examples, but their illustrative power suffers from the fact that offensive words are not translated: "Jarinus hat hier mit Athetus gev–."

152. On Sappho see Page 1955, 140–46; Dover 1978, 173–84; Pomeroy 1975, 53–56; Cantarella 1992, 78–86; Brooten 1996, 29–41. Pomeroy and Cantarella give 612 B.C.E. as the year of Sappho's birth.

153. See Plutarch, *Lycurgus* 18:9, who says that similar *thiasoi* are known to have existed also elsewhere in Greece, especially in Sparta.

154. Sappho, fragm. 31 (trans. Rayor 1991, 57; cf. p. 1955, 19–20, and the LCL edition of David A. Campbell, pp. 79–80). On the discussion of this text see, e.g., Devereux 1970, who analyzes the psycho-physiological symptoms of an anxiety attack; and Winkler 1990, 178–80, who reads the poem of Sappho as a re-reading of Odysseus's speech to Nausikaa (*Odyssey* 6:158-161) finding that Sappho identifies herself with the roles of both persons: "Sappho sees herself both as Odysseus admiring the nymph-like maiden and as Nausikaa cherishing her own complex emotions" (p. 180).

155. The Greek and Latin literature from the beginning of the Common Era to the Byzantine period includes several mentions, on which see Dover 1978, 174, 179; Brooten 1996, 31–39. E.g., Plutarch (*Dialogue on Love* 763A) tells of Sappho's homoerotic feelings and calls her partners *erōmenē*, which is a feminine form of the word *erōmenos*.

156. Thus *Suda* (Σ 107), a lexicon compiled in the late tenth century C.E. (see the LCL edition of Campbell, pp. 5–6). The presumed husband of Sappho has a satirical name: *kerkos* means tail but is also a euphemism for penis, while *andros* stands for "man" (Henderson 1975, 128; Brooten 1996, 39).

157. Winkler 1990, 187.

158. Winkler 1990, 187. The intimate friendship between Sappho and her apprentices has never been denied, though its erotic dimensions have been questioned, especially in the older scholarship; according to the judgment of Winkler (1990, 162–63). Lobel and Page, the publishers of Sappho's lyrics, "assumed the validity of Victorian no-no's" and were therefore "deaf to much of what Sappho was saying, tone-deaf to her deeper melodies."

159. Sappho, fragm. 94:21-23.

160. Cf. also fragm. 94:1-20.

161. Especially Alcman, fragm. 3:61-81; see Dover 1978, 179–81; Pomeroy 1975, 55; Cantarella 1992, 81–82. On Alcman's poems in general, see Calame 1977.

162. Plutarch, *Lycurgus* 18:4.

163. Calame 1977, 94–97; Bremmer 1980, 292–93. Of the correlations and differences of the girls' initiation and the boys' pederastic type, see Cantarella 1992, 83–84.

164. So Pomeroy 1975, 55–56.

165. So Dover 1978, 172–73, 182. There are six plays called Sappho that were created in the classical age; see the list in Brooten 1996, 34, n. 21.

166. See Henderson 1975, 183; cf. Dover 1978, 182; Pomeroy 1975, 54; Cantarella 1992, 87.

167. Cf. Halperin 1990, 104.

168. See Brooten 1996, 29–41 who argues that what might have contributed to the loss of Sappho's writings was the discrediting of her intellectual achievements by attacks on her sexual life on the part of the second century C.E. Christian writer Tatian (*Address to the Greeks* 33).

169. Dover 1978, 177; cf. Cantarella 1992, 80: "If one puts aside all preconceived notions, it is difficult to deny that what we have here is true love, in the fullest sense of the term."

170. See Allen 1997, 16–17.

171. As to this text, cf. Price 1990 and, especially with regard to sexual dreams, Foucault 1986, 4–36; Winkler 1990, 23–44; Brooten 1996, 175–86.

172. Translation of these chapters can be found in Winkler 1990, 210–16.

173. I.e., not only penetrating a social inferior such as wife, another man's wife, a prostitute, an unknown streetwalker, a slave (male or female), but also being penetrated by another man and masturbating. The social significance of penetration presented by Artemidorus resembles very much the way penetration is seen in the Mesopotamian omen series *Šumma ālu* (cf. above pp. 27–28): "If a man penetrates his peer's behind, he wins the leading position among his brothers and comrades" (CT 39 44:13). Cf. Artemidorus 1:78: "To penetrate one's brother, whether elder or younger, is good for the dreamer; for he will be above his brother and will look down on him."

174. Cf. Foucault 1986, 24–25; Winkler 1990, 36–40; Brooten 1996, 183–86.

175. Cantarella 1992, 167.

176. *Hic ubi vir non est, ut sit adulterium* ("Where no man is involved, adultery takes place"; trans. Howell 1980, 76). So Martial (1:90; cf. 7:35, 67, 70), who thinks that a woman in this case imitates a man; likewise the Elder Seneca (1:2:23), according to whom, when women copulate, one of them pretends to be a man: "But I looked at the man first, to see whether he was natural or artificial" (trans. Michael Winterbottom); see Hallett 1989, 212–13; Brooten 1996, 43–44.

177. Thus Hallett 1989.

178. Seneca 95:20, 2: *virorum licentiam aequaverint. . .pati natae*; see Hallett 1989, 214–15; Brooten 1996, 44–45. Seneca, in fact, does not refer to female homoeroticism but the masculinization of women who enter men.

179. Cf. Howell 1980, 297–99; Brooten 1985a, 67–68; 1996, 46–47; Hallett 1989, 215–17.

180. Bömer 1977, 469–73; see also Hallett 1989, 213–14; Brooten 1996, 44.

181. *Nec vaccam vaccae, nec equas amor urit equarum. . .Femina femineo correpta cupidine nulla est. (Metamorphoses* 9:731-734); cf. Boswell 1980, 83. 152; Lilja 1983, 80.

182. Lucian, *Dialogue of the Courtesans* 5:4; on this dialogue, see Brooten 1996, 51–53.

183. *Dialogue of the Courtesans* 5:1. The word *allokotos* does not mean "unnatural," as translated by MacLeod in the LCL (also Cosby 1984, 162; Cantarella 1992, 92), at least not in the sense of "contrary to nature."

184. Pseudo-Lucian, *Affairs of the Heart* 28. On this text, the ideology of which is comparable with the *Dialogue on Love* of Plutarch, see Foucault 1986, 211–27; Brooten 1996, 54–56.

185. Pseudo-Lucian, *Affairs of the Heart* 28 (trans. M. D. MacLeod).

186. Cf. illustrations nos. 5 and 43 in Reinsberg 1989, 44, 97, and see Brooten 1996, 57–60 with figures 1–5 for artistic representations of love between women in general.

187. Cf. Dover 1978, 102.132.

188. Cf. Howell 1980, 298.

189. Cf. Brooten 1996, 49, according to whom the male writer's "focus on penetration as the principal sexual image led to a simplistic view of female erotic behavior and a complex view of the erotic choices of free men."

190. Cf. Gleason 1995, 59, 159.

191. Brown 1989, 30.

192. Cf. Henderson 1975, 208–22; Dover 1978, 135–53; Cantarella 1992, 44–48.

193. The word refers to those whose hind parts (*prōktoi*) "have been widened by constant buggery and who are on that account depraved or evil" (Henderson 1975, 210). Alcibiades, among others, is ridiculed with this name in Aristophanes, *Acharnians* 716.

194. Aristophanes, *Clouds* 1083ff.

195. Aristophanes, *Plutus* 152–59.

196. This kind of self-presentation conformed to the typical paradigm of the effeminate male also in Rome; see Gleason 1995, 62–67.

197. Aristophanes, *Thesmophoriazusae* 146–51, 204, 214–31, etc.; cf. Henderson 1975, 88–89, 219–20 and Taaffe 1993, 74–102, who examines men with a feminine role in the play *Thesmophoriazusae*. According to Taaffe, Agathon's feminine appearance is calculated to be looked at, just like women whose appearances are designed

for being viewed by men. "Agathon knows this, not only because of his method of composition but also because of his own personal life. He dresses, as a woman does, to be an object of vision and desire" (p. 83). It is difficult to know the extent to which Aristophanes' satire corresponds with Agathon's real appearance. However, Patzer's (1982, 52–58) claim that the caricature of a sexually passive man in comedies was only a comic exaggeration with no real basis cannot be proved.

198. Aeschines, *Timarchus* 131.

199. Athenaeus, *Deipnosophistae* 13:565B-C; this kind of man on a horse Diogenes calls *hippopornos*. Notice that *hippos* was often used in the meaning of "lecherous woman" (Henderson 1975, 127).

200. Athenaeus, *Deipnosophistae* 13:605D.

201. According to Effe 1987, 102, the reason for this may be that these works deliberately emulate the genre of the archaic epics, which rarely include homoeroticism.

202. Longus, *Daphnis and Chloe* 4, 11ff.; cf. Effe 1987, 101.

203. This and the following translation by Winkler 1990, 112. Thornley and Edmonds in the LCL translate the bawdy expressions only in Latin or not at all.

204. Even if both Daphnis and Chloe take erotic initiative, it is Daphnis's sexual desire that finally grows so fervent that he tries to do to Chloe "what rams do to sheep and he-goats do to she-goats." This was, however, without success until Lykainion, the young and beautiful wife of a neighbor, makes it clear to Daphnis that the deeds of love are not "just kissing and embracing and not what rams and he-goats do, but something quite different and much more delightful," and demonstrates concretely what this means (3:14-20). Thus, even if Daphnis is more enterprising than Chloe in trying to cope with sexual intercourse, he is rather helpless and receives instructions from an adult woman who assumes a remarkably active role in her teaching.

205. Aristotle, *Nicomachean Ethics* 7:6:1148b (trans. H. Rackham, with the exception that "love of men" is translated by him "sexual perversion").

206. Plato, *Phaedrus* 239C (trans. C. J. Rowe).

207. Plato, *Phaedrus* 240D-E (trans. C. J. Rowe).

208. Plato, *Laws* 1:636C (trans. R. G. Bury).

209. *Laws* 1:635C-D; cf. *Laws* 8:837A: "It is necessary to discern the real nature of friendship and desire and love (so-called) (*tēn tēs philias te kai epithymias hama kai tōn legomenōn erōtōn physin idein anagkaion*), if we are to determine them rightly; for what causes the utmost confusion and obscurity is the fact that this single term embraces these two things, and also a third kind compounded of them both" (trans. R. G. Bury).

210. Cf. Cantarella 1992, 61–62; Allen 1997, 64–65.

211. On the Roman idea of the symbolic language of masculinity, see Gleason 1995, passim.

212. Thus, e.g., Cicero, *Philippicae* 3:12.

213. Cf. Richlin 1983, 83–104.

214. *Philippicae* 2:44-45; cf. Lilja 1983, 93–94. Also Josephus knew this accusation (*Ant.* 15:23-30); see below, p. 94.

215. See Lilja 1983, 91–92, 124–27.

216. "No more of that, pray, for it is well known what he gave you, and what you gave him in turn." In the same context, what the soldiers sang during the triumph that followed Julius Caesar's conquest of Gallia is told: *Gallias Caesar subegit, Nicomedes Caesarem. Ecce Caesar nunc triumphat, qui subegit Gallias. Nicomedes non triumphat, qui subegit Caesarem* ("All the Gauls did Caesar vanquish, Nicomedes

vanquished him; Lo! now Caesar rides in triumph, victor over all the Gauls, Nicomedes does not triumph, who subdued the conqueror") (Suetonius, *Divus Iulius* 49–50, trans. J. C. Rolfe). The point is that Caesar was only nineteen when he held his first post in Bithynia—almost too old to play the part of a *puer*.

217. Seneca 47:7. This is an interesting reference to the reversal of active and passive roles which, even if generally shunned, doubtless took place; see Taylor 1997, 324–28,349–57.

218. Suetonius (*Nero* 28) tells about this. Cf. also Dio Chrysostom (*Disc.* 21:6-8), who mentions also other castrated slaves (*Disc.* 21:4; 77/78: 36).

219. On this text and its ideology, cf. Foucault 1986, 193–210.

220. Plutarch, *Dialogue on Love* 750C.

221. *Dialogue on Love* 751C-E., trans. W. C. Helmbold.

222. *Dialogue on Love* 752A.

223. *Dialogue on Love* 770B-C: The lovers are like nomads who arrive during the flourishing spring and then leave as from the land of an enemy.

224. Plato, *Phaedrus* 231A-C; 240E–241A.

225. Aeschines, *Timarchus* 136.

226. See Allen 1997, 195–98.

227. Cf. *Dialogue on Love* 766D-767E; *Bravery of Women* 142F and see Cantarella 1992, 72; Allen 1997, 198–201.

228. Cf. Foucault 1986, 206–9.

229. *Dialogue on Love* 769A.

230. *Lycurgus* 18:1-4.

231. On Plutarch and pederasty in Sparta, see Cartledge 1988, 388, 393–94. Plutarch's view of the ancient Sparta is clearly largely fictitious and somewhat dependent on Xenophon's partial presentation.

232. Dio Chrysostom, *Disc.* 7:133.

233. *Disc.* 7:135-136.

234. *Disc.* 7:151-152.

235. *Disc.* 77/78:36 (trans. H. Lamar Crosby): *genos. . .asthenesteron tou gynaikeiou kai thēlyteron.*

236. Epictetus, *Disc.* 3:1:27-37.

237. *Disc.* 3:1:42-44 (trans. W. A. Oldfather). Epictetus uses the expression *mē genoito* to refute a thought he deems impossible, an expression used also by Paul (Rom. 6:1-2, 14; 7:7).

238. Cf. Foucault 1986, 209–10.

239. *eran en gamō tou erasthai meizon agathon esti;* Plutarch, *Dialogue on Love* 769D.

240. See Scroggs 1983, 48–49.

Chapter 5: Judaism

1. The Apocrypha, nevertheless, have deutero-canonical status in many Christian churches (e.g., Roman Catholic and Greek Orthodox) since they are included in the Septuagint and the Vulgate and thus form an original part of the Christian Bible.

2. Trans. Shutt 1985, 23.

3. The *Book of Jubilees* is a paraphrase composed in the second century B.C.E. on the parts of Genesis and Exodus, and its perspective on the biblical text is a strict interpretation of the Torah; see Wintermute 1985, 35–50; Collins 1998, 79–84. On these particular passages, see De Young 1990, 448–50.

4. On Sodom in the Apocrypha and Pseudepigrapha, see Loader 1990, 76–86.

5. Cf. Coleman 1980, 64; Countryman 1988, 63; also De Young 1990, 443–44, who on the basis of the passages in Wisdom wants to see here a reference to Sodom; more cautiously so Scroggs 1983, 92. A similar and equally obscure expression appears in the *Psalms of Solomon* (2:13), where it is said that the daughters of Jerusalem have (literally) "tainted themselves in the confusion of uniting" (*emiaiōsan autas en fyrmō anameixeōs*). This also has been translated as "unnatural intercourse" (e.g., Coleman 1980, 70), but the text says nothing about "nature" in this context. It is doubtless a sexual expression but does not particularly refer to homosexuality.

6. Aquila was a Jewish proselyte who in 130 C.E. created an extremely literal Greek translation of the Hebrew Bible. Its purpose may have been to replace the Septuagint, which had come to be favored by the Christians.

7. Räisänen 1975, 280–81 corrects here Liddell and Scott's (1940, 559) translation, "sodomite."

8. The *Testament of Naphtali*, like the earlier quoted *Testament of Benjamin* and *Testament of Levi*, is a part of the *Testaments of the Twelve Patriarchs*, a Hellenistic Jewish document of the first century B.C.E., later interpolated by Christians; see Kee 1983, 775–828; Collins 1986, 154–62; 1998, 133–43.

9. Trans. Kee 1983, 812.

10. So, e.g., Loader 1990, 82.

11. Gen. 6:1-8, although brief, is a confusing and heterogeneous text. According to Levin (1993, 103–17), the basic layer of the text consists of verses 1-2, 5a, 6-8, which come from the Yahwist, whereas verses 3, 4, 5b are later explanatory additions. Later interpreters, of course, read the text as a unity.

12. 1QapGen ii (trans. García Martínez 1994, 230–31). Parts of *Genesis Apocryphon*, written in Aramaic, have survived among the texts of Qumran. The manuscript comes from the beginning of the Common Era, but the actual work is probably from the second century B.C.E. Its connections to the *Book of Jubilees* are obvious, but their mutual dependence is yet to be clarified.

13. The book of *1 Enoch* is named after the seventh son of Adam and Eve, whom God "took away" (Gen. 5:24). This collection of apocalyptic writings was written over a long period and probably reached its final form only at the beginning of the Common Era; cf. Isaac 1983, 5–12; Collins 1998, 43–84.

14. So Levin 1993, 104.160; cf. p. 46 above.

15. Trans. Wintermute 1985, 94.

16. On the dependence of 2 Peter on Jude, see, e.g., Paulsen 1992, 97–100.

17. Furnish 1994, 20; cf. Loader 1990, 123–24; Hoheisel 1992, 341; Paulsen 1992, 64.

18. On Josephus's and Philo's arguments, see Furnish 1979, 64–65; Coleman 1980, 79–85; Scroggs 1983, 88–91, 94–96; Edwards 1984, 34–35, 39–42, 79–80; Cosby 1984, 150–54; Loader 1990, 86–104; Satlow 1994a, 7–9.

19. Especially in Philo, *physis* (like *nomos physeōs*, "law of nature") is a key concept, which at times is used almost as a synonym for God; see Sandmel 1979, 120–22; Bockmuehl 1995, 39–42.

20. *Ant.* 1.195 is sometimes translated to the effect that the Sodomites "hated strangers and abused themselves with Sodomitical practices" (so Bailey 1955, 23; McNeill 1976, 84–85). This mistranslation is based on an old English version of the Greek text *einai te misoxenoi kai tas pros allous homilias ektrepesthai*. The word *homilia*, which led to this translation, can mean sexual intercourse, but in this context

it means interaction only, without sexual association. Josephus's pederastic interpretation becomes clear later.

21. Trans. H. St. J. Thackeray.

22. So G. R. Edwards 1984, 40–42, who presents also other reasons for Josephus's silence. He remarks that Sodom was punished with fire and brimstone, and that the Benjaminites should have shared the same fate for the same sin. Also, Edwards traces in Josephus some of the same modesty found in the books of Chronicles and the Septuagint with regard to *qĕdēšâ* and *qādēš* (Deut. 23:18, etc.). Chronicles makes no mention of them, and the Septuagint's double translation uses ordinary words that mean prostitution, *pornē/telesforos* and *pornos/teliskomenos*—not *hierodoulē* and *hierodoulos*, which would correspond better to the Hebrew terms.

23. Trans. H. St. J. Thackeray, except that I translate *tēn de pros arrenas arrenōn* by "the sexual connection of a man with another man," instead of Thackeray's "sodomy."

24. Cf. Koch-Harnack 1983, 237–38.

25. Cf. Furnish 1979, 65; Edwards 1984, 79–80.

26. Trans. F. H. Colson.

27. Or: "the natural way of mounting and being mounted"; in the original text *andres ontes arresin epibainontes, tēn koimēn pros tous paskhontas hoi drōntes physin ouk aidoumenoi*. A distinction between active and passive partners is at stake here, and Philo sees it natural only when the passive partner is a woman.

28. Cf. also *On the Contemplative Life* 62.

29. Elsewhere Philo calls also eunuchs *androgynous* and opines that they have changed themselves into women (*Laws* 1.325). Also Josephus (*War* 4.560-563) describes men who "from mere satiety unscrupulously indulged in effeminate practices, plaiting their hair and attiring themselves in women's apparel, drenching themselves with perfumes and painting their eyelids to enhance their beauty" (trans. H. St. J. Thackeray). These men, according to Josephus, wallow in the city "as in a brothel," imitating women but also engaging in activities as masculine as bloodshed; for Josephus this was utterly confusing and outrageous.

30. On the date and general overview, see van der Horst 1985, 565–73; cf. also Collins 1986, 143–48.

31. *Ps. Phoc.* 187; trans. van der Horst 1985, 581.

32. *Ps. Phoc.* 3 (*mēte gamoklopeein mēt' arsena Kyprin orinein*); trans. van der Horst 1985, 574. "Homosexual passion" is rendered from a Greek expression that means rousing Cypris, i.e., erotic passion toward a male person (Cypris was the Aphrodite of the island of Cyprus).

33. *Ps. Phoc.* 190–91; trans. van der Horst 1985, 581.

34. *Ps. Phoc.* 213–14; trans. van der Horst 1985, 581.

35. *Ps. Phoc.* 192 (*mēde ti thēlyterai lekhos andrōn mimēsainto*); trans. van der Horst 1985, 581; cf. Brooten 1985a, 63–64; 1996, 63–64. The expression *lekhos andrōn*, literally, "the marriage bed of men," comes close to the Hebrew expression *miškab zākûr*, which indicates male-male sexual contact. By analogy it could be assumed that the Greek expression would refer to female imitation of a male homoeroticism.

36. *Ps. Phoc.* 210–12; Trans. van der Horst 1985, 581; cf. also Philo, *Laws* 3.37 and 1 Cor. 11:14.

37. Collins 1986, 143.

38. Cf. Sandmel (1979, 122) on Philo: "There are two sides in Philo's accomplishment. One is his Hellenization of Judaism in that he presents Scriptural matters in Grecian categories. But the other side is possibly even more important: Philo also Judaizes Grecian ideas." The same could be said, in a way, of Paul; cf. below, p. 104–5.

39. See Satlow 1994a and Boyarin 1994, whose contributions complement the picture given by earlier contributions, e.g., Scroggs 1983, 77–84; Eron 1993, 108–21, and Frankfurter and Ulmer 1991.

40. E.g. b. *Sanhedrin* 109a; b. *Ketuboth* 103a; b. *Baba Bathra* 12b; 59a; 168a; b. *Erubin* 49a.

41. *Lev. Rabba* 23:9; *Gen. Rabba* 26:5; 50:5,7; cf. Frankfurter and Ulmer 1991, 51.

42. This interpretation may be quite close to the truth; cf. above, pp. 52–53 and see Brenner 1997, 108. The rabbis quibbled over whether Ham castrated or just raped his father.

43. E.g., *Gen. Rabba* 2:16; t. *Abodah Zarah* 8:4; b. *Sanhedrin* 58a; see Coleman 1980, 77–78; Eron 1993, 114.

44. See above, p. 44 and Olyan 1994, 183–86.

45. E.g., b. *Shabbath* 17b (Jewish youths are warned of *miškab zākûr*); b. *Sukkah* 29a (*miškab zākûr* as a reason of solar eclipse); b. *Sanhedrin* 82a (*miškab zākûr* as the abomination of Israel and Jerusalem according to Jer 3:20); y. *Berakoth* 9:50,13c; cf. Scroggs 1983, 83; Eron 1993, 112. On the meaning of this expression in interpreting the word *arsenokoitēs* (1 Cor. 6:9; 1 Tim. 1:10), see below, p. 116.

46. See Satlow 1994a, 9–15.

47. This is discernible from b. *Niddah* 13b, where intercrural intercourse (*derek ᵓebārîm*), common in Greek pederasty (see above, pp. 67–68), is classified as a lesser offense than an anal one (*miškab zākûr*), perhaps comparable to masturbation; see Boyarin 1994, 336–39.

48. Elsewhere (m. *Keritoth* 1:1-2) the same sexual offenses are listed, with only an exclusion from the community as punishment, not the death penalty. Later in the same tractate (2:6) the other partner in a sexual offense is declared innocent if he is a minor or asleep. If he has fallen into a crime by mistake, a sacrifice for his sin is satisfactory as punishment.

49. If both partners are adults, the death penalty applies to both. If one is adult and the other a boy of 9–13 years old, the adult will be sentenced to death and the younger whipped. If the boy is younger, he is free from any punishment, but the adult may be whipped, depending on the judgment of the rabbis.

50. See Frankfurter and Ulmer 1991, 55; Satlow 1994a, 11–21. Already *Targum Neophyti* translates this: "There must not dwell among the daughters of Israel a woman who is a prostitute (*ᵓyth npqt*), neither should there be a prostitute among the sons of Israel (*gbr npk*)." The terms used refer to ordinary prostitution, unassociated with cultic practices. A similar translation can be found in the Septuagint; cf. note 22 above.

51. Cf. Boyarin 1994, 340–48; Satlow 1994a, 14–15.

52. See Satlow 1994a, 18–23. The association of homoeroticism with bestiality is made many times in rabbinic catalogues of vice, e.g., t. *Abodah Zarah* 2:1; 3:2.

53. Cf. Boyarin 1994, 347–48.

54. Cf. Eron 1993, 106–8.

55. Cf. Frankfurter and Ulmer 1991, 59. The wasting of male seed is also highlighted by Cantarella 1992, 202 who, however, overemphasizes "the sense of horror over the wastage of semen" by deriving it from Torah; Satlow 1994ab has shown that

the concept that the nonprocreative emission of semen should be condemned as such is developed only by the redactors of the Babylonian Talmud (cf., however, the concern of Philo about nonprocreative sex, above, pp. 95–96). There might be some truth in Cantarella's assertion that "Jewish aversion to homosexuality, then, derives from a perception of the need. . .to concentrate their efforts on procreation," especially in the light of the writings of Philo (cf. above), but this motif is insufficient to explain the Jewish attitude toward homosexual practices as a whole. Actually, the Hebrew Bible does not contain a single assertion that sex was meant for procreation only, and there are plenty of examples of the contrary (for example, the eroticism of the Song of Songs has nothing to do with procreation). The two examples mentioned by Cantarella miss the point. Lev. 15:16-18 is about the emission of semen in heterosexual intercourse and not at all about wasting semen. Gen. 38:8-10, on the other hand, condemns the *coitus interruptus* of Onan because he failed to fulfill the duty of Levirate marriage. The way he evaded this rule is of secondary importance in the narrative.

56. "Leaving" in this context does not mean leaving mother and father but incestuous relationships with them.

57. This may be compared with the tendency of Roman writers to consider female homoeroticism as a Greek vice not inherent or even real in Roman society; see Hallett 1989, 223.

58. Earlier a story is told in which a pious man meets two men having sex with a dog. But when the case was taken to the court, the two men testified that the pious man himself had been the one to commit the illegal act, and they won, because there were two of them (Frankfurter and Ulmer 1991, 56).

59. Trans. Neusner 1988, 498.

60. This probably refers to a married man whose wife is not with him, for one reason or another; cf. Danby's (1933, 329) translation: "Even a man that has no wife [with him] may not be a teacher of children."

61. Cf. Biale 1984, 192–97; Satlow 1994a, 15–17; Boyarin 1994, 339–40.

62. So Biale 1984, 196; cf. Gerstenberger's (1993, 271) similar take on the Holiness Code and its sentences.

63. Cf. Boyarin 1994, 339–40.

64. *Sifra Ahare* 9:8; see Boyarin 1994, 16–17; Brooten 1996, 64–65. Marriage between two women is listed together with marriage between two men, between a man and a woman and her daughter, and between a woman and two men.

65. Cf. Biale 1984, 193–94; Eron 1993, 119–21; Brooten 1996, 66–68.

66. The term *pĕrīṣût* obviously means frivolousness for which there is no punishment. But *zĕnût*, which in the Hebrew Bible means "adultery," is expanded in the Rabbinic texts to involve all punishable sexual crimes.

67. See Satlow 1994a, 16.

68. Cf. Coleman 1980, 76; Satlow 1994a, 17–18.

69. This explanation is part of the printed editions of the Mishnah, but it did not originally belong to it; it is a later addition, with textual variants; see Danby 1933, 98, who has translated the longest version. Neusner 1988 omits this enlargement.

70. m. *Bikkurim* 4:1; trans. Danby 1933, 98.

71. m. *Bikkurim* 4:5; trans. Danby 1933, 98.

72. Literally, "eunuch of the sun," meaning a person who is a eunuch from the time of seeing the sun; whatever this means in concrete terms remains somewhat obscure. According to the Talmud this means a person who "has never seen a moment of fitness" (sexual potency) and who, while urinating, does not form a bow (this refers to

deformities of sexual organs). Moreover, those who are eunuchs from birth are claimed to have neither pubic hair nor beard, a voice that is neither male nor female, and so on (b. *Yebamoth* 80ab). Cf. p. 120 and n. 90 below.

Chapter 6: The New Testament

1. See Brooten 1996, who has a detailed commentary on Rom. 1:18-32 (pp. 215–66) as well as a survey of the intertextual echoes in it (pp. 267–302) and an annotated bibliography (pp. 363–72).

2. Cf. Brooten 1996, 217–19.

3. In the Septuagint, *askhēmosynē* translates the Hebrew *'erwâ*, "nakedness," referring to female genitals (see above, p. 52); it is used frequently in connection with incest in Leviticus 18 and 20, where also the prohibition of male-male intercourse is to be found. The words *akatharsia/akathartos* "impurity/impure" translate derivatives of the Hebrew root *ṭm'*, which denotes ritual impurity. In the Septuagint of the book of Proverbs (3:32; 6:16; 16:5; 17:15; 20:10; 24:9) *akatharsia* also renders *tō'ēbâ*, "abomination," used of male-male intercourse in Lev. 18:22 and 20:13.

4. A good, albeit late, example of Stoic usage of these expressions is Diogenes Laertius, who writes about Zeno of Kition, founder of the Stoic school in the third century C.E. (7:1-160; see esp. 108-13). On passions in Stoic philosophy, see also Sandbach 1975, 59-67; on *ta kathēkonta*, ibid., p. 45–48 and White 1978.

5. On the different aspects of Paul's concept "against nature," see the (partially contradictory) contributions of Boswell 1980, 110–14; Scroggs 1983, 115; Hays 1986, 192–95,196–99; Countryman 1988, 113–14; Pronk 1993, 276–78; Wischmeier 1996; Brooten 1996, 271–80.

6. On the concept of "nature" and its use in ancient and modern discourse, cf. e.g., Pronk 1993, 219–31. Winkler 1990, 17, recommends a basic rule for studying ancient texts: For "nature," read "culture."

7. On the Stoic concept of *physis* and the life according to it, see Sandbach 1975, 31–38. On Philo's "unwritten law of nature," which combines the originally antithetical concepts of *physis* and *nomos*, see Sandmel 1979, 119–22; Bockmuehl 1995, 39–42.

8. Seneca 122:7-8; cf. Winkler 1990, 21.

9. *Pseudo-Phocylides* 212: "Long hair is not fit for boys, but for voluptuous women." Cf. also Philo, *Laws* 3:37 and see Gleason 1995, 69 on the Stoic perception of hair as a gender signifier.

10. Cf. Dover 1973, 66; Sergent 1986, 56. The force of the word *physis* as "widespread social usage" does not fall flat even in our context, as Countryman 1988, 114 thinks.

11. Differently Cantarella (1992, 193): "In Paul, the expressions *kata physin* and *para physin*, unlike the situation in previous times, signaled the imperative and inescapable rule of heterosexuality, and the abnormality of any practice which moves away from it. Paul's preaching, then, lays the foundations for a new sexual ethic, which Christian writers in the following centuries were to repeat with decisive constancy, without any concession or hesitation." But, as noted above, contrary to the contention of Cantarella (1992, 221), it was definitely not Christianity—neither Paul nor any other early Christian—who introduced the idea of "naturalness" into discussions of sexual morality.

12. So in particular Schmithals 1988, 76–78,82.

13. Brooten 1996 282–83 lists the following: (1) the texts use similar terminology (LXX: *akatharsia*, *askhemōsynē*), (2) both texts contain a general condemnation of

sexual relations between men, and (3) both describe those engaging in such relations as worthy of death. Cf. ibid., p. 288–94, for further echoes of Leviticus in Paul's writings.

14. See above p. 90. On the relation between Wisdom and Romans 1–2, see, e.g., Furnish 1979, 74–78; Brooten 1996, 294–98.

15. The Septuagint of Psalm 106:20 is evident in the background of Rom. 1:23:

Ps 106:20	*Rom 1:23*
kai ēllaxanto	*kai ēllaxan*
tēn doxan autōn	*tēn doxan tou aphthartou theou*
en homoiōmati moskhou. . .	*en homoiōmati eikonos. . .*

16. On "natural law" in Second Temple Judaism, see Bockmuehl 1995.

17. On *physis* and *ktisis*, see Wischmeier 1996.

18. See Wischmeier 1996, 361–64; Brooten 1996, 267–71. The concept of the law of nature is important for Philo (see n. 7 above), and Paul also uses the related expression *physei ta tou nomou* (Rom. 2:14) with a similar meaning.

19. Thus, with Scroggs 1983, 114–15; Countryman 1988, 114–15 (note 20), Pronk 1993, 277–78, and Furnish 1994, 30, and contra, e.g., Hays 1986, 194. I agree with Mauser 1996a, 10–12; 1996b, 46, that the sequence "human being, birds, four-footed animals and reptiles" in Rom. 1:23 may be an echo—even though not necessarily a quotation—of Gen. 1:26, but this again underlines the difference between Creator (who should be worshiped) and creation (which should not be worshiped) and thus is linked with the preceding rather than with the following text in Romans 1.

20. Bockmuehl 1995, 43: "The law of nature is in keeping with the Law of God. . . . Creation, rightly perceived (i.e., according to revelation and common convention), manifests the purposes of the Creator. And to the extent that a moral law is suggested by the order of the creation, this law is therefore identical with the Law of God. This means not that any given phenomenon by itself is thought to constitute a law. . ., but that by rightly observing the regular *patterns* of creation one can discern both order and purpose as intended by the Creator."

21. Cf. Brooten 1996, 241 and Rom. 7:2, where a married woman is referred to as *hypandros*, "under a man." Contrary to the implications of the NEB translation, the text does speak of "their women" but not of "their men."

22. Cf. Wright 1989, 295.

23. Cf. Brooten 1985a, 75–78; 1996, 238, and, on the issue of honor and shame, especially Moxnes 1988. Mauser (1996a, 8–9; 1996b, 43–45) thinks that Paul here responds to a situation in which some Christian women wanted to abrogate the differentiation of the sexes altogether; logia 22 and 114 of the *Gospel of Thomas*, in which this genderless ideal is expressed, are presented as evidence to support this view. This is a tempting idea, but comparable ideas play no explicit role in Paul's argument in 1 Corinthians 11, and it is difficult to trace them even between the lines.

24. Cf. Brooten 1996, 264–65.

25. On the aspect of impurity in Paul's writings, see Countryman 1988, 109–23; Brooten 1996, 233–37, 288–93.

26. Cf. Rom. 6:19; 2. Cor. 12:21; Gal. 5:19; 1. Thess. 2:3; 4:7. On the question whether impurity should be equated with "sin," see the negative assessment of Countryman 1988 and the critique of Brooten 1996, 235–36, n. 57. Countryman does not discuss Rom. 6:15–23, where Paul parallels "the service of impurity and lawlessness" (6:19) with servitude to sin (6:16).

27. Note that a woman's active sexual role is explicitly repudiated in *Pseudo-Phocylides* 192. Cf. Greenberg 1988, 214–15; Carmody and Carmody 1993, 137; Brooten 1996, 241.

28. So Kuss 1963, 50; cf. above, pp. 78–79, on Pseudo-Lucian's criticism, in which women's homoeroticism was seen as even stranger and more objectionable than that of men (*Affairs of the Heart* 28).

29. Theologians of the early church already found it particularly difficult to understand Paul's comments about women "changing" their sexual behavior. Many, Augustine for instance, interpreted it as a distorted form of heterosexual sex life (see Brooten 1985a, 63, 80). For modern interpretations, which include anal or oral heterosexual intercourse, see Brooten 1996, 246–52.

30. Pace Scroggs 1983; cf. Brooten 1996, 256–57.

31. Not much can be discerned from the fact that the word *aschēmosynē*, "shameless acts," used by Paul of male-male intercourse (1:27), has no less than thirty-two occurrences in the Septuagint of Lev. 18 and 20 (an observation of Brooten's 1996, 257). The Hebrew word translated *askhēmosynē* is ʿ*erwâ*. The use of this word may have reminded a Jewish reader of Lev. 18:22 and 20:13 and thereby of forbidden sexual relations.

32. I agree here with the analysis of Countryman 1988, 115–16; cf. also Scroggs 1983, 115–16; Brooten 1996, 221. The grammatical structure indicates that what is at stake is not a threatening future punishment but rather an existing condition. That men "have flared in lust for one another" is expressed in the aorist tense (*exekau-thēsan*), which describes an act already completed. The existing results of this act are described by present participles: men "exercise (*katergazomenoi*) among themselves immodesty" and—at the same time—receive (*apolambanontes*) their due recompense.

33. Many scholars have been satisfied with this answer, among others, McNeill 1976, 66; Boswell 1980, 109; G. R. Edwards 1984, 98.

34. So, among others, Hays 1986, 199–202; 1994, 9; Pronk 1993, 273. Brooten 1996, 242, referring to astrological and medical sources from the Roman period, calls attention to the fact that in some learned circles congenital sexual orientations (or inclinations to mostly unconventional forms of sexual life) were indeed conceptualized and classified. However, as Brooten herself notices, these classifications do not correspond to the modern distinction between homosexuality and heterosexuality; in addition, it is not clear to what extent Paul was aware of such classifications on the part of his contemporaries.

35. Cf. Hays 1986, 189; 1994, 8; Schmithals 1988, 80; Countryman 1988, 110–11.

36. This fully concurs with Wis. 13:8-9: "Yet even so they do not deserve to be excused, for with enough understanding to speculate about the universe, why did they no sooner discover the lord and master of it all?" On the question of natural theology in Paul, see Brooten 1996, 222–28.

37. Cf. Räisänen 1972, 85–86.

38. The relation between the concepts *chrēsis* and *physis* is clear in Ignatius *Trall.* 1:1, where the words appear similarly side by side, but in a positive sense: "I have heard that your way of thinking is irreproachable and your fortitude solid, not only in terms of your behavior but your nature also (*ou kata chrēsin alla kata physin*)."

39. Countryman 1988, 117.

40. Hoheisel (1992, 338) does not want to restrict Paul's perspective to pederasty but concludes that Paul means all sexual acts that do not take place between a man and a woman; also Wright 1989, 295, 298–99; Brooten 1996, 256–57.

41. *Disc.* 3.1:27-44. Brooten 1996, 261 gives attention to the destination as well: Paul may have known Rome as the contemporary center of discussion about same-sex interaction.

42. This rational possibility is proposed by Koskenniemi 1994, 81.

43. Cf. Strecker 1982, 133.

44. In *Epistolam ad Romanos*, 4 on Rom. 1:26-27.

45. Cf. Hays 1986, 195; Schmithals 1988, 77.

46. Cf. Hays 1986, 189; 1994, 8–9; Furnish 1994, 29.

47. In an open letter to the Finnish Archbishop signed by a group of theologians, it is stated that the approval of homosexual relations "closes for these people the road to repentance and saving faith" (Stenbäck 1993, appendix 2, p. 39).

48. Of lists of virtues and vices, see, e.g., Conzelmann 1987, 321–22.

49. Cf. Strecker 1982, 135; Conzelmann 1987, 322.

50. *On the Sacrifices of Abel and Cain* 32.

51. Scroggs 1983, 103–4.

52. Conzelmann (1987, 322) considers the list in 1 Cor. 6:9-10 to derive from Christians before Paul; this is indicated, among other ways, by a saying untypical of Paul, "to inherit the kingdom of God."

53. Cf. below, n. 69.

54. Thus the standard dictionaries, among others, Bauer, according to whom *arsenokoitēs* is "jemand, der mit Männer und Knaben Unzucht treibt, der Knabenschänder, der Päderast" and the word *malakos* is used "besonders von Lustknaben, Männern und Jünglingen, die sich mißbrauchen ließen" (Bauer, Aland, and Aland 1988, 220, 991). According to Liddell and Scott (1940, 246) *arsenokoitēs* is a "sodomite."

55. Boswell 1980, 336–53; also McNeill 1976, 64, whose main source seems to be Boswell's work, at that point yet unpublished (cf. p. 214).

56. Boswell 1980, 342–43.

57. Cf. Filon's concepts *erastēs*, *paiderastēs*, *erōmenos*, and *androgynos*, mentioned above (p. 95). A vice list in the *Testament of Levi* (17:11) calls the active partner in pederasty a *paidophthoros*, "corrupter of boys"; cf. also *Did.* 2:2; *Barn.* 19:4.

58. Boswell 1980, 346–48.

59. Boswell 1980, 350–52.

60. Plenty of further evidence from Wright 1984, 132–40.

61. Koskenniemi 1994, 82.

62. Wright 1984, 131

63. Cf. Hoheisel 1992, 340.

64. Scroggs 1983, 83; cf. also Jastrow 1903, 398, 854. The compound appears, e.g., in the following Talmudic passages: b. S*habbath* 17b; b. *Sukkoth* 29a; b. *Sanhedrin* 82a; y. *Berakoth* 9.50.13c.

65. Scroggs 1983, 107–8. Likewise, e.g., Hays 1994, 7; Furnish 1994, 24, and many others.

66. See above, chapter 5, note 35.

67. Cf. Wright 1984, 126, 129; 1989, 297.

68. Thus Martin 1996, 119, referring to the classic work of James Barr, *The Semantics of Biblical Language* (1961).

69. Countryman (1988, 128) sees *arsenokoitai* as a link between adultery (*pornoi*) and theft (*andrapodistai*), referring to "legacy hunters who used sexual attraction as a bait." This interpretation is based on the Decalogue-pattern of 1 Tim. 1:10. Martin

(1996, 118–23), on the basis of the contexts in which the word occurs in *Sibylline Oracles* 2:70-77 and *Acts of John* 36, concludes that the word refers to some kind of exploitation by means of sex—perhaps, but not necessarily homosexual sex.

70. E.g., Socrates (Plato, *Phaedrus* 239C) castigates those men who, to appease their desire, look for a beloved who is "sissy" (*malthakos*) and used to a nonmasculine life (*anandros*); cf. above, pp. 81–82.

71. Scroggs 1983, 62–65.106. Malick (1993, 487–90) denies this, but only in terms of the passive partner in pederasty. He, too, believes that *malakos* and *arsenokoitēs* mean the passive and active partners, respectively, in a homosexual relationship, but he does not want to restrict their use to pederasty alone. Cantarella (1992, 192–93) mentions that the feminine tone of the word *malakos* excludes every possibility that it could mean a young boy: "How could a boy who was not yet a man become effeminate, despising his manliness?"

72. *Papyrus Hibeh* i 54,11; see Edwards 1984, 83–84; Malick 1993, 488–89.

73. Plautus, *Mil.* 668.

74. On this word, see above, p. 72.

75. Cf. the well-documented appraisal to this effect by Martin 1996, 124–28.

76. According to Halperin 1990, 9 the concept of the formation of sexual orientation independent of relative degrees of masculinity and femininity does not take place until the latter part of the nineteenth century. "Its highest expression is the 'straight-acting and appearing gay male,' a man distinct from other men in absolutely no other respect besides that of his 'sexuality.' "

77. See Lilja 1983, 74, 96; Richlin 1993; Taylor 1997.

78. Cf., e.g., Plutarch, *Dialogue on Love* 768D, and see Foucault 1985, 85.

79. Countryman 1988, 119; cf. Hoheisel (1992, 340), who concludes that it is impossible to define an exact subject for "lying with men" in this context.

80. Cf. Petersen 1986; Countryman 1988, 118.

81. Cantarella 1992, 193 and Malick 1993, 492, among others, fall into this generalization.

82. See, e.g., Horner 1978, 113–16; Phipps 1996, 122–42.

83. See Marjanen 1996, 149–60.

84. Marjanen 1996, 161.

85. A rabbinic text (t. *Yebamoth* 8:4) makes a firm case: "Who refuses from marriage, breaks the order for the humankind to procreate. That person must be considered a murderer, who diminishes the number of people created in the image of God." Also among Hellenistic Jews getting married and procreating a family was everybody's responsibility: "Do not remain unmarried, lest you die nameless. Give nature her due, beget in your turn as you were begotten" (*Pseudo-Phocylides* 175–76; trans. P. W. van der Horst 1985, 580).

86. Ben-Chorin (1983, 92) believes Jesus was married. He considers it almost impossible that an adult Jewish man of Jesus' age would have been single. It is true that a Jewish man, in normal cases, was always married, and that many passages from the rabbinic literature (b. *Yebamoth* 63ab; b. *Qiddushin* 29b; t. *Yebamoth* 8:4 etc.) even require it. However, Jesus' lifestyle did not correspond with the life of an ordinary man in many other respects either. Also, it can be asked why his wife was not at the cross and the tomb with the other women. For other arguments used in the debate about the celibacy of Jesus, see Phipps 1996, 44–109.

87. So in 1967 Canon Hugh Montefiore, an Anglican clergyman, whose thoughts are recapped by Horner 1978, 117. On this discussion, see also Phipps 1996, 69–72.

88. Cf. Brown 1989, 40–41.

89. The text follows the prohibition of divorce (Mt. 19:1-9 cf. Mk. 10:1-12) and can be found only in the Gospel of Matthew. A number of scholars (e.g., Moloney 1989; Schweizer 1989, 249–50; Aejmelaeus 1991, 22–23) think that the words are originally from Jesus himself, particularly because they are strange and problematic. Even the members of the "Jesus Seminar" rank this passage, although without the clause, "Let those accept it who can," among the sayings printed in pink, indicating that Jesus himself "probably" said something like this; see Funk et al., eds., 1993, 220–21.

90. These two categories are known also in rabbinic writings (m. *Yebamoth* 8:1-6; cf. above p. 102), even if it is difficult to determine exactly what the rabbis had in mind when they talked about "eunuchs by birth" (*sārîs ḥammâ*). According to Rabbi Eliezer, unlike those castrated by humans, they can be "healed" (m. *Yebamoth* 8:4). Does this refer to male persons whose gender identity is not characterized by genital deformities but who, for other reasons, are incapable of conventional sexual practice?

91. The Gospel of Matthew most probably originated in Syria, where eunuchs (*galli*) were an essential part of the cult of the Syrian mother goddess; see above pp. 31–32. Also, one must take into consideration emasculated slaves and officials (cf. Acts 8:26-40).

92. Thus Schweizer 1989, 250.

93. Cf. Brown 1988, 67–68. The Catholic church even today argues for celibacy of the clergy on the basis of this biblical passage (*The Catholic Catechism* 1992, §1579; cf. §922, §1618).

94. The church father Origen, however, is said to have taken this passage so literally that he emasculated himself. Eusebius, who related this in his *Ecclesiastical History* (6:8), regarded the act as immature but nonetheless a sign of solid faith and a desire to fulfill Jesus' words. Eusebius thought that Origen by this act prevented the occasion for "shameful accusations that the pagans could raise against him, a young Christian teacher." Whether or not this is the case, by this act he demonstrated the view that the life "lived in a body endowed with sexual characteristics, was but the last dark hour of a long night that would vanish with the dawn" (Brown 1988, 168). He himself was "a walking lesson in the basic indeterminacy of the body" (Brown 1988, 169).

95. Thus, e.g., Moloney 1979, 52.

96. Morton Smith (1973) found a text, interesting in this context but dubious as evidence because of its questionable authenticity. A copy of a letter of Clement of Alexandria discovered in 1958 borrows from the so-called *Secret Gospel of Mark*, that is, a longer version of Mark that was intended only for those initiated into the great mysteries. This excerpt tells how Jesus raised a young man from death and escorted him out of his tomb. "The young man looked at him and loved him and intended to invite him to his house. . . .After six days Jesus told him what to do. In the evening the young man came to him, dressed in a cotton cloth that covered his naked body, and stayed with Jesus that night, as Jesus taught him about the secret of the kingdom of God" (iii 4–10). This is an initiation, most probably baptism, in which the disciple "united with" Jesus; Smith speculates that this uniting might have happened also physically (1973, 251).

97. van Tilborg 1993, 77–110. According to him, Jesus himself had gained his instruction from John the Baptist (pp. 59–77). On the basis of Freud's and Bieber's psychoanalytical explanations, van Tilborg explains Jesus' readiness for a kind of

pederastic relationship on the basis of his family relationships. They are characterized by an absent father (who is replaced by the heavenly Father), an intrusively close mother, and sisters with whom Jesus had tense relations (pp. 3–57, 247–48).

98. van Tilborg separates homosexuality from pederasty, which he deems as initiation that symbolizes God's love: "But in the code, contemporary to the story as told, such imaginary homosexual behaviour is not an expression of homosexuality. It is an expression of *paiderastia*, the love for a *pais* as the perfect entrance into the knowledge of God's love for his son and consequently of God's love for the cosmos" (1993, 248). "In contrast with modern discourse regarding homosexuality such behaviour strengthens the masculine code in ancient discourse on love" (1993, 2).

99. van Tilborg 1993, 246, stresses that a narrative, not historical reality is at stake here: he agrees that the pederastic model is the result of the imagination of the author who wrote the Gospel of John. "It is a narrative reality which comes closest to what moderns would call male homosexual behavior: the love of an older man for a younger one."

Chapter 7: Homoeroticism in the Biblical World and Homosexuality Today

1. For related hermeneutical principles regarding homosexuality, cf. Scroggs 1983, 125–26; Furnish 1994, 31–32; Nelson 1994, 78–82; Long 1996, 68–72.

2. Foucault (1985, 187): "As a matter of fact, the notion of homosexuality is plainly inadequate as a means of referring to an experience, forms of valuation, and a system of categorization so different from ours."

3. Cf. the reflections of Blount 1996, 36–37 to this effect.

4. Cf. the attempt of E. G. Edwards (1996) to understand different aspects of Paul's sexuality and its background. While not quite convinced about Edwards's idea of Paul's unconscious association of "flesh" (*sarx*) with male genitalia, I certainly agree with the statement that "Paul was not writing a sort of inspired, 'objective' account of theology, revealed to him apart from his own sexuality. He spoke not only out of his patriarchal context, but out of his own personhood, his maleness included" (p. 76).

5. Jung and Smith 1993, 83, however, venture to speculate about what Paul might have argued if he had known what we know today about human sexual orientations: "Any sexual orientation, whether heterosexual, homosexual, or somewhere between, is God's gracious gift. . . .However, all of our particular desires and behaviors are inevitably disordered by sin and fall short of expressing God's original intentions and blessings for us. Desires and behaviors that run counter to one's natural, God-given orientation, whether gay or straight, are vividly expressive of the bondage of concupiscence."

6. Seow 1996a, 19.

7. Cf. Carroll 1991, 80.

8. Cf. the examples of "theology from below" in the Wisdom literature of the Hebrew Bible in Seow 1996a, 27–30; 1996b, 19–24.

9. Cf. G. R. Edwards 1984, 7–23.

10. John 8:1-11 is missing from the best New Testament manuscripts and cannot be regarded as a historical account of an eyewitness. The same reservation applies, however, to many other texts of the Gospel of John as well. What is at issue here is not historical facticity but the figure of Jesus as perceived by the early Christians behind this literary product.

11. On moral positions regarding homosexuality, cf. Jung and Smith 1993, 21–31.

12. Cf. the reflections of Miller 1996, 58–60 on the importance of the "rule of love" alongside of the "rule of faith" in the interpretation of the Bible.

13. Cf. Whitaker 1996 on different aspects of human sexuality in Genesis 1–3.

14. Foucault (1985, 92) claims that "classical antiquity's moral reflection concerning pleasures was not directed toward a codification of acts, nor toward a hermeneutics of a subject, but toward a stylization of attitudes and an aesthetics of existence." This may be somewhat philosophical and abstract, especially when it comes to the codification of sexual acts, which, indeed, existed in classical Athens; cf. Cohen 1991.

15. Cf. Halperin 1990, 29–38 (on classical Athens) and Foucault 1985, 215.

16. Winkler's words, 1990, 37.

17. So Halperin 1990, 35, with the clarification: "a socio-sexual discourse structured by the presence or absence of its central term: the phallus," whereby "phallus" is understood not just as the male organ but as "a culturally structured signifier of social power" (p. 166, n. 83).

18. It is certainly not the case that Christianity "replaced the old contrast between activity and passivity with a new, fundamental dichotomy between heterosexuality and homosexuality," as Cantarella 1992, 193, asserts. In early Christian communities, active and passive (sexual) roles—the male and female gender roles, respectively— hardly deviated in any remarkable degree from their cultural environment. On the other hand, the condemnation of homosexual practices as they knew them by early Christian writers neither constitutes any "fundamental dichotomy" between homosexuality and heterosexuality nor represents a "new morality" created by the Christians. Cantarella is right in her assertion that the Christian condemnation of homosexual practices had its roots in Jewish tradition (1992, 194–202; cf., however, my criticism, above, pp. 172–73, n. 55), but she totally overlooks the demonstrable impact of Hellenistic philosophy on both Jewish and Christian authors.

19. Cf. Brooten 1996, 359–62.

20. Cf. above, pp. 15–16.

21. Pace Boswell 1994, 53–107. Also in the study of Greenberg (1988, 66–73) the proportion of this kind of relationship is rather meager. According to him (p. 71), "where they exist, they are usually not recognized publicly, but are carried on on an individual and often temporary, sometimes covert basis, and commonly do not exclude heterosexual relationships or marriage." Some of them could be understood in terms of homosociability, a concept not used by Greenberg.

22. Cf. D. Green 1996 on young men selling sex in London. When the Helsinki Counselling Center for Prostitutes (the first project ever run in Finland in this area) started its work in 1990, it came as a public shock that male prostitution existed at all in that country; most of the first clients were men selling sex for women or men.

23. On this aspect of the Song of Songs, cf., e.g., Trible 1978, 161–62.

24. On the relationship between Egyptian love poetry and the Song of Songs, see Fox 1985; the newest English translation of the Egyptian poems is Fowler 1994.

25. Trible 1978, 162.

ABBREVIATIONS

AHw	W. von Soden, *Akkadisches Handwörterbuch*. 3 vols. Wiesbaden 1985²/1972/1981.
ARM	Archives Royales du Mari
BRM	Babylonian Records in the Library of J. Pierpont Morgan
BWL	W. G. Lambert, *Babylonian Wisdom Literature*. Oxford 1960.
CAD	The Assyrian Dictionary of the Oriental Institute of Chicago. Chicago 1956—.
CT	Cuneiform Texts from Babylonian Tablets in the British Museum, London.
KAI	H. Donner and W. Röllig, *Kanaanäische und aramäische Inschriften*. 3 vols. Wiesbaden 1979⁴/1973³/1976³.
KAR	E. Ebeling, *Keilschrifttexte aus Assur religiösen Inhalts*. Leipzig and Berlin 1919–1923.
KAV	O. Schroeder, *Keilschrifttexte aus Assur verschiedenen Inhalts*. Leipzig and Berlin 1920.
KTU	M. Dietrich, O. Loretz, and J. Sanmartín, *Die keilalphabetischen Texte aus Ugarit*. Kevelaer and Neukirchen-Vluyn 1976.
LCL	The Loeb Classical Library
NEB	The New English Bible
PRU	Palais Royal d'Ugarit
RSV	The Revised Standard Version
SAA	State Archives of Assyria
TCS	Texts from Cuneiform Sources. Locust Valley, New York.

BIBLIOGRAPHY

Abusch, Tzvi. 1986. "Ishtar's Proposal and Gilgamesh's Refusal: An Interpretation of the *Gilgamesh Epic*, Tablet 6, lines 1–79." *History of Religions* 26, 143–87.

Abusch, Tzvi; Huehnergard, John; and Steinkeller, Piotr; eds. 1990. *Lingering over Words: Studies in Ancient Near Eastern Literature in Honor of William C. Moran.* Atlanta.

Aejmelaeus, Lars. 1991. "Taivasten valtakunnan eunukit (Matt. 19:12)" [The Eunuchs of the Kingdom of Heaven]. *Teologinen Aikakauskirja* 96, 18–27.

Aeschines. *The Speeches of Aeschines.* Trans. Charles Darwin Adams. LCL (1919).

Alcman. *Greek Lyric. Vol. 2: Anacreon, Anacreontea: Choral Lyric from Olympus to Alcman.* Trans. David A. Campbell. LCL (1988).

Alganza Roldán, Minerva. 1990. "La mujer en la historiografía griega helenística: Polibio, mujeres e historia viril." In López, Martínez, and Pociña eds., 1990, 53–72.

Allen, Laura S. and Gorski, Roger A. 1992. "Sexual Orientation and the Size of the Anterior Commissure in the Human Brain." *Proceedings of the National Academy of Sciences USA* 89, 7199–7202.

Allen, Prudence. 1997. *The Concept of Woman: The Aristotelian Revolution, 750 B.C.–A.D. 1250.* Grand Rapids, Mich., and Cambridge, U. K.

Apuleius. *Apuleius, Metamorphoses 2: Books 7–11.* Trans. J. Arthur Hanson. LCL (1989).

Aristophanes. *Aristophanes, Vol. 3: The Lysistrata, The Thesmophoriazusae, The Ecclesiazusae, The Plutus.* Trans. Benjamin Bickley Rogers. LCL (1924).

———. *Acharnians.* Trans. Alan H. Sommerstein. In *The Comedies of Aristophanes*, Vol. 1. Warminster (1980).

———. *Clouds.* Ed. Alan H. Sommerstein. In *The Comedies of Aristophanes*, Vol. 3. Warminster (1982).

Aristotle. *Generation of Animals.* Trans. A. L. Peck. LCL (1943).

———. *The Nicomachean Ethics.* Trans. H. Rackham. LCL (1934).

Arnaud, R. 1973. "La prostitution sacrée en Mésopotamie, un mythe historio-graphique?" *Revue d'histoire de religion* 183, 111–15.

Artemidorus. *Artemidorii Daldiani Onirocriticon Libri V.* Recognovit Roger A. Pack. Bibliotheca Teubneriana. Lipsiae (1963).

Assmann, Jan. 1984. *Ägypten: Theologie und Frömmigkeit einer frühen Hochkultur.* Urban-Taschenbücher 366. Stuttgart et al.

Athenaeus. *The Deipnosophists, Vols. 1–7.* Trans. Charles Burton Gulick. LCL (1927–41).

Bailey, D. Sherwin. 1955. *Homosexuality and the Western Christian Tradition.* London.

Bailey, J. Michael and Pillard, Richard C. 1991. "A Genetic Study of Male Sexual Orientation." *Archives of General Psychiatry* 48, 1089–96.

———. 1993. "Heritable Factors Influence Sexual Orientation in Women." *Archives of General Psychiatry* 50, 217–23.

Bassett, Frederick W. 1971. "Noah's Nakedness and the Curse of Canaan: A Case of Incest?" *Vetus Testamentum* 21, 232–37.

Bauer, Walter; Aland, Kurt; and Aland, Barbara. 1988. *Griechisch-deutsches Wörterbuch zu den Schriften des Neuen Testaments und der frühchristlichen Literatur.* 6th ed. Berlin and New York.

Baum, Robert M. 1993. "Homosexuality in the Traditional Religions of the Americas and Africa." In Swidler, ed., 1993, 1–46.

Bell, Alan P. and Weinberg, Martin S. 1978. *Homosexualities: A Study of Diversity among Men and Women.* New York.

Bell, Alan P.; Weinberg, Martin S.; and Hammersmith, Sue Kiefer. 1981. *Sexual Preference: Its Development in Men and Women.* Bloomington, Indiana.

Ben-Chorin, Schalom. 1983[2]. *Mutter Mirjam: Maria in jüdischer Sicht.* Munich.

Bentler, P. M. 1976. "A Typology of Transvestism: Gender Identity Theory and Data." *Archives of Sexual Behavior* 5, 567–84.

Bethe, Erich. 1988. "Die dorische Knabenliebe: Ihre Ethik und ihre Idee." In Siems, ed., 1988, 17–57 (= *Rheinisches Museum für Philologie* 62, 1907, 438–75).

Biale, Rachel. 1984. *Women and Jewish Law: An Exploration of Women's Issues in Halachic Sources.* New York.

Bieber, Irwing. 1962. *Homosexuality: A Psychoanalytic Study of Male Homosexuals.* New York.

_____. 1976. "A Discussion of Homosexuality: The Ethical Challenge." *Journal of Consulting and Clinical Psychology* 44, 163–66.

Bird, Phyllis A. 1989. "'To Play the Harlot': An Inquiry into an Old Testament Metaphor." In Peggy L. Day, ed., *Gender and Difference in Ancient Israel.* Minneapolis, 75–94.

_____. 1997. "The End of the Male Cult Prostitute: A Literary-Historical and Sociological Analysis of Hebrew *qādēš-qĕdēšîm*." In J. A. Emerton, ed., *Congress Volume Cambridge 1995.* Supplements to *Vetus Testamentum* 66. Leiden, New York and Cologne, 37–80.

Blount, Brian K. 1996. "Reading and Understanding the New Testament on Homosexuality." In Seow, ed., 1996, 28–38.

Bockmuehl, Markus. 1995. "Natural Law in Second Temple Judaism." *VT* 45, 17–44.

Börner, Franz. 1977. *P. Ovidius Naso, Metamorphosen, Buch VIII–IX.* Heidelberg.

Borger, Rykle. 1956. *Die Inschriften Asarhaddons, Königs von Assyrien.* Archiv für Orientforschung, Beiheft 9. Graz.

_____, 1979. *Babylonisch-Assyrische Lesestücke I–II.* 2. Auflage. Analecta Orientalia 54. Rome.

_____. 1982. *Akkadische Rechtsbücher.* Texte aus der Umwelt des Alten Testaments I/1, 32–95.

_____. 1986[3]. *Assyrisch-babylonische Zeichenliste.* Alter Orient und Altes Testament 33/33A. Kevelaer and Neukirchen-Vluyn.

Boswell, John. 1980. *Christianity, Social Tolerance, and Homosexuality: Gay People in Western Europe from the Beginning of the Christian Era to the Fourteenth Century.* Chicago and London.

_____. 1994. *Same-Sex Unions in Premodern Europe.* New York.

Bottéro, J. & Petschow, H. 1972/75. "Homosexualität." *Reallexikon der Assyriologie* 4, 459–468.

Boyarin, Daniel. 1994. "Are There Any Jews in 'The History of Sexuality'?" *Journal of the History of Sexuality* 5, 333–55.

Brawley, Robert L., ed. 1996. *Biblical Ethics and Homosexuality: Listening to Scripture.* Louisville, Kentucky.

Bremmer, Jan. 1980. "An Enigmatic Indo-European Rite: Paederasty." *Arethusa* 13, 279–98.

Brenner, Athalya. 1997. *The Intercourse of Knowledge: On Gendering Desire and 'Sexuality' in the Hebrew Bible*. Biblical Interpretation Series 26. Leiden, New York, and Cologne.

Brettler, Marc. 1989. "The Book of Judges: Literature as Politics." *Journal of Biblical Literature* 108, 395–418.

Brierley, H. 1979. *Transvestism: A Handbook with Case Studies for Psychologists, Psychiatrists and Counsellors*. Oxford.

Brooten, Bernadette. 1985a. "Paul's View on the Nature of Women and Female Homoeroticism." In Clarissa W. Atkinson, Constance H. Buchanan and Margaret R. Miles, eds., *Immaculate and Powerful: The Female in Sacred Image and Social Reality*. The Harvard Women's Studies in Religion Series. Boston, 61–87.

____. 1985b. "Patristic Interpretations of Romans 1:26." *Studia patristica* 18,1, 287–91.

____. 1996. *Love between Women: Early Christian Responses to Female Homoeroticism*. Chicago and London.

Brown, Peter. 1989. *The Body and Society: Men, Women and Sexual Renunciation in Early Christianity*. London and Boston.

Burr, Chandler. 1994. "Homosexuality and Biology." In Siker, ed., 1994, 116–34.

Butler, Judith. 1990. *Gender Trouble: Feminism and the Subversion of Identity*. New York and London.

Cagni, Luigi. 1969. *L'Epopea di Erra*. Studi Semitici 34. Rome.

Calame, C. 1977. *Les Chœurs de jeunes filles en Grèce archaïque, II: Alcman*. Rome.

Cantarella, Eva. 1990. "Donne di casa e donne sole in Grecia: sedotte e seduttrici." In López, Martínez, and Pociña, eds., 1990, 35–51.

____. 1992. *Bisexuality in the Ancient World*. Trans. Cormac Ó Cuilleanáin. New Haven and London.

Carmichael, Calum M. 1995. "Forbidden Mixtures in Deuteronomy xxii 9–11 and Leviticus xix 19." *Vetus Testamentum* 45, 433–48.

Carmody, Denise and Carmody, John. 1993. "Homosexuality and Roman Catholicism." In Swidler, ed., 1993, 135–48.

Carrier, J. 1980. "Homosexual Behavior in Cross-Cultural Perspective." In Marmor, ed., 1980, 100–122.

Carroll, Robert P. 1991. *Wolf in the Sheepfold: The Bible as a Problem for Christianity*. London.

Carson, Anne. 1990. "Putting Her in Her Place: Woman, Dirt, and Desire." In Halperin, Winkler, and Zeitlin, eds., 1990, 135–69.

Cartledge, Paul. 1988. "The Politics of Spartan Pederasty." In Siems, ed., 1988, 385–415 (= *Proceedings of the Cambridge Philological Society* 207, 1981, 17–36).

Catechism of the Catholic Church. 1994. Mahwah, New Jersey.

Catullus: see Lee 1990

Charlesworth, James H., ed. 1983. *The Old Testament Pseudepigrapha 1: Apocalyptic Literature and Testaments*. New York.

____. 1985. *The Old Testament Pseudepigrapha 2: Expansions of the "Old Testament" and Legends, Wisdom and Philosophical Literature, Prayers, Psalms and Odes, Fragments of Lost Judeo-Hellenistic Works*. New York.

Cicero. *Tusculan Disputations*. Trans. J. E. King. LCL (1927).

____. *The Speeches of Cicero: Pro Archia Poeta, Post Reditum in Senatu, Post Reditum ad Quirites, De Domo Sua, De Haruspicum, Responsis, Pro Plancio*. Trans. N. H. Watts. LCL (1923).

_____. *Philippics*. Ed. and trans. D. R. Shackleton Bailey. Chapel Hill and London 1986.

Cohen, David. 1987. "Laws, Society and Homosexuality in Classical Athens." *Past and Present* 117, 3–21.

_____. 1991. *Law, Sexuality, and Society: The Enforcement of Morals in Classical Athens*. Cambridge.

Cole, Susanne Guettel. 1984. "Greek Sanctions against Sexual Assault." *Classical Philology* 79, 97–113.

Coleman, E. 1985. "Developmental Stages of the Coming Out Process." In J. C. Gonsiorek, ed., *A Guide to Psychotherapy with Gay and Lesbian Clients*. New York.

Coleman, Peter. 1980. *Christian Attitudes to Homosexuality*. London.

Collins, John J. 1986. *Between Athens and Jerusalem: Jewish Identity in the Hellenistic Diaspora*. New York.

_____. 1998. *The Apocalyptic Imagination: An Introduction to Jewish Apocalyptic Literature*. Second Edition. Grand Rapids, Mich.

Conzelmann, Hans. 1987[4]. *Grundriß der Theologie des Neuen Testaments*. Uni-Taschenbücher 1446. Tübingen.

Cosby, Michael R. 1984. *Sex in the Bible: An Introduction to What the Scriptures Teach Us about Sexuality*. Englewood Cliffs, New Jersey.

Countryman, L. William. 1988. *Dirt, Greed, and Sex: Sexual Ethics in the New Testament and Their Implications for Today*. Philadephia.

Dallas, Joe. 1994. "Another Option: Christianity and Ego-Dystonic Homosexuality." In Siker, ed., 1994, 137–44.

Dalley, Stephanie. 1989. *Myths from Mesopotamia: Creation, The Flood, Gilgamesh and others*. Oxford.

Daly, Mary. 1978. *Gyn/Ecology: The Metaethics of Radical Feminism*. Boston.

Danby, Herbert, trans. and ed. 1933. *The Mishnah*. Oxford and London.

Danneker, Martin and Reiche, Reimut. 1974. *Der gewöhnliche Homosexuelle*. Frankfurt a. M.

Delcor, M. 1979. "Le personnel du temple d'Astarté à Kition d'après une tablette phénicienne (CIS 86 A et B)." *Ugarit-Forschungen* 11, 147–64.

Delcourt, Marie and Hoheisel, Karl. 1991. "Hermaphrodit." *Reallexikon für Antike und Christentum* 15, 649–82.

Del Olmo Lete, Gregorio. 1981. *Mitos y leyendas de Canaan según la tradición de Ugarit*. Valencia and Madrid.

Del Olmo Lete, G. and Sanmartín, J. 1998. "Kultisches in den keilalphabetischen Verwaltungs- und Wirtschaftstexten aus Ugarit." In Dietrich and Kottsieper, eds., 1998, 175–97.

Demosthenes. *Private Orations L–LVIII. In Neaeram LIX*. Trans. A. T. Murray. LCL (1939).

Devereux, George. 1970. "The Nature of Sappho's Seizure in fr 31 LP as Evidence of Her Inversion." *Classical Quarterly* 20, 17–31.

_____. 1988. "Greek Pseudo-Homosexuality and the 'Greek Miracle'." In Siems, ed., 1988, 206–31 (= *Symbolae Osloensis* 42, 1968, 69–92).

De Young, James B. 1990. "A Critique of Prohomosexual Interpretations of the Old Testament Apocrypha and Pseudepigrapha." *Bibliotheca Sacra* 147, 437–54.

Dietrich, Manfried. 1970. *Die Aramäer Südbabyloniens in der Sargonidenzeit (700–648)*. Alter Orient und Altes Testament 7. Kevelar and Neukirchen-Vluyn.

Dietrich, Manfried and Kottsieper, Ingo, eds. 1998. *"Und Mose schrieb dieses Lied auf": Studien zum Alten Testament und zum Alten Orient. Festschrift für Oswald Loretz*. Alter Orient und Altes Testament 250. Münster.

Dietrich, Manfried and Loretz, Oswald, eds. 1993. *Mesopotamica–Ugaritica–Biblica: Festschrift für Kurt Bergerhof.* Alter Orient und Altes Testament 232. Kevelaer and Neukirchen-Vluyn.

Dietrich, Walter. 1997. *Die frühe Königszeit in Israel: 10. Jahrhundert v. Chr.* Biblische Enzyklopädie 3. Stuttgart, Berlin, and Cologne.

Dio Chrysostom. *Dio Chrysostom. Vol. 1: Discourses I–XI.* Trans. J. W. Cohoon. LCL (1932).

———. *Dio Chrysostom. Vol. 2: Discourses XII–XXX.* Trans. J. W. Cohoon. LCL (1939).

———. *Dio Chrysostom. Vol. 5: Discourses LXI–LXXX.* Trans. H. Lamar Crosby. LCL (1951).

Diogenes Laertius. *Lives of Eminent Philosophers,* Vols. 1–2. Trans. R. D. Hicks. LCL (1925).

Donner, H. and Röllig, W. 1973³. *Kanaanäische und aramäische Inschriften II.* Wiesbaden.

Douglas, Mary. 1966. *Purity and Danger: An Analysis of the Concepts of Pollution and Taboo.* London.

Dover, Kenneth J. 1974. *Greek Popular Morality in the Time of Plato and Aristotle.* Oxford.

———. 1978. *Greek Homosexuality.* Cambridge, Mass.

———. 1980. *Plato, Symposium.* Cambridge, Mass.

———. 1988. "Classical Attitudes to Sexual Behaviour." In Siems, ed., 1988, 264–81 (= *Arethusa* 6, 1973, 59–73).

Driver, G. R. and Miles, J. C. 1936. "The SAL-ZIKRUM Woman in Old Babylonian Texts." *Iraq* 6, 66–70.

Duda, Alexandra. 1993. *Comparative Survey of the Legal and Societal Situation of Homosexuals in Europe.* Cologne. Unpublished report.

Duran, Khalid. 1993. "Homosexuality and Islam." In Swidler, ed., 1993, 181–97.

Durand, Jean-Marie. 1988. *Archives épistolaires de Mari I/1.* Archives Royales de Mari 26. Paris.

Edwards, Elizabeth Gordon. 1996. "Exploring the Implications of Paul's Use of *Sarx* (Flesh)." In Brawley, ed., 1996, 69–86.

Edwards, George R. 1984. *Gay/Lesbian Liberation. A Biblical Perspective.* New York.

Edzard, Dietz Otto. 1987. "Zur Ritualtafel der sog. 'Love Lyrics'." In F. Rochberg-Halton, ed., *Language, Literature and History: Philological and Historical Studies Presented to Erica Reiner.* American Oriental Series 67. New Haven, 57–69.

Effe, Bernd. 1987. "Der Griechische Liebesroman und die Homoerotik: Ursprung und Entwicklung einer epischen Gattungskonvention." *Philologus* 131, 95–108.

Ellis, Lee and Ames, M. Ashley. 1987. "Neurohormonal Functioning and Sexual Orientation: A Theory of Homosexuality-Heterosexuality." *Psychological Bulletin* 101, 233–58.

Epictetus. *The Discourses as Reported by Arrian: The Manual, and Fragments.* Vol. 2. Trans. W. A. Oldfather. LCL (1928).

Eron, Lewis John. 1993. "Homosexuality and Judaism." In Swidler, ed., 1993, 103–34.

Eusebius. *The Ecclesiastical History and the Martyrs of Palestine.* Trans. H. J. Lawlor and J. E. L. Oulton. London (1927).

Exum, J. Cheryl. 1993. *Fragmented Women: Feminist (Sub)versions of Biblical Narratives.* Valley Forge, Pennsylvania.

Farber, Walter. 1977. *Beschwörungsrituale an Ištar und Dumuzi. Attī Ištar ša ḫarmaša Dumuzi.* Akademie der Wissenschaften und der Literatur. Veröffentlichungen der orientalischen Kommission 30. Wiesbaden.

Faulkner, Raymond O. 1973. *The Ancient Egyptian Coffin Texts.* Warminster.

Fehling, Detlev. 1988. "Phallische Demonstration." In Siems, ed., 1988, 282–323 (= *Ethnologische Überlegungen auf dem Gebiet der Altertumskunde.* Munich 1974, 7–38).

Fisher, E. J. 1976. "Cultic Prostitution in the Ancient Near East? A Reassessment." *Biblical Theology Bulletin* 6, 225–36.

Foster, Benjamin. 1987. "Gilgamesh, Sex, Love and the Ascent of Knowledge." In J. H. Marks and R. M. Good, eds., *Love and Death in the Ancient Near East: Essays in Honor of Marvin H. Pope.* Guilford, Connecticut, 21–42.

Foucault, Michel. 1978. *The History of Sexuality, Vol. 1: An Introduction.* Trans. Robert Hurley. New York.

———. 1985. *The History of Sexuality, Vol. 2: The Use of Pleasure.* Trans. Robert Hurley. New York.

———. 1986. *The History of Sexuality, Vol. 3: The Care of the Self.* Trans. Robert Hurley. New York.

Fowler, Barbara Hughes. 1994. *Love Lyrics from Ancient Egypt.* Chapel Hill and London.

Fox, Michael V. 1985. *The Song of Songs and the Ancient Egyptian Love Songs.* Madison, Wisconsin.

Frankfurter, Gershom and Ulmer, Rivka. 1991. "Eine Anfrage über Homosexualität im jüdischen Gesetz." *Zeitschrift für Religions- und Geistesgeschichte* 43, 49–68.

Funk, Robert W.; Hoover, Roy W.; and the Jesus Seminar, eds. 1993. *The Five Gospels: The Search for the Authentic Words of Jesus.* New York.

Furnish, Victor Paul. 1979. *The Moral Teaching of Paul.* Nashville.

———. 1994. "The Bible and Homosexuality: Reading the Texts in Context." In Siker, ed., 1994, 18–35.

Gadd, C. J., ed. 1926. *Cuneiform Texts from Babylonian Tablets* 39. London.

García Martínez, Florentino, ed. 1994. *The Dead Sea Scrolls Translated: The Qumran Texts in English.* Trans. W. G. E. Watson. Leiden et al.

Gelb, I. J. 1976. "Homo ludens in Early Mesopotamia." *Studia Orientalia* 46, 43–76.

Gerstenberger, Erhard S. 1993. *Das 3. Buch Mose. Leviticus.* Das Alte Testament Deutsch 6. Göttingen.

Gleason, Maud W. 1995. *Making Men: Sophists and Self-Presentation in Ancient Rome.* Princeton, New Jersey.

Gordon, Edmund I. 1959. *Sumerian Proverbs: Glimpses of Everyday Life in Ancient Mesopotamia.* Philadelphia.

Gow, A. S. F. and Page, D. L. 1965. *The Greek Anthology: Hellenistic Epigrams. Vol I–II.* Cambridge.

Graham, Elaine. 1996. *Making the Difference: Gender, Personhood and Theology.* Minneapolis.

Grayson, A. Kirk. 1995. "Eunuchs in Power: Their Role in the Assyrian Bureaucracy." In M. Dietrich and O. Loretz, eds., *Vom Alten Orient zum Alten Testament: Festschrift für Wolfram Freiherrn von Soden.* Alter Orient und Altes Testament 240. Kevelaer and Neukirchen-Vluyn, 85–98.

The Greek Anthology, Vols. I–V. Trans. W. R. Paton. LCL (1916–1918). (See also Gow and Page 1965.)

Green, Doug. 1996. "Young Men Selling Sex: Where Do They Come from?" In M. Jyrkinen, ed., *Changing Faces of Prostitution. Conference Book Helsinki 3–5 May, 1995.* Helsinki, 97–103.

Green, R. 1987. *The "Sissy Boy" Syndrome and the Development of Homosexuality.* New Haven.

Green, Tamara. 1996. "The Presence of the Goddess in Harran." In Lane, ed., 1996, 87–100.

Greenberg, David F. 1988. *The Construction of Homosexuality*. Chicago and London.

Griffiths, J. Gwynn. 1960. *The Conflict of Horus and Seth*. Liverpool.

Groneberg, Brigitte. 1986. "Die sumerisch-akkadische Inanna/Ištar: Hermaphroditos?" *Die Welt des Orients* 17, 25–46.

———. 1997. "Ein Ritual an Ištar." *MARI* 8, 291–303.

Grönfors, M.; Haavio-Mannila, E.; Mustola, K.; and Stålström, O. 1984. "Esitietoja homo- ja biseksuaalisten ihmisten elämäntavasta ja syrjinnästä" [Preliminary Information on the Lifestyle and Discrimination of Homo- and Bisexual Persons]. In Sievers and Grönfors, eds., 1984, 132–60.

Gruber, Mayer I. 1986. "Hebrew *qĕdēšāh* and Her Canaanite and Akkadian Cognates." *Ugarit-Forschungen* 18, 133–48.

Gunkel, Hermann. 1910³. *Genesis*. Göttinger Handkommentar I/1. Göttingen.

Haas, Volkert. ed. 1992. *Außenseiter und Randgruppen: Beiträge zu einer Sozialgeschichte des Alten Orients*. Xenia. Konstanzer Althistorische Vorträge und Forschungen 32. Konstanz.

Haavio-Mannila, Elina and Kontula, Osmo. 1993. "Seksuaaliset vähemmistöt" [Sexual Minorities]. In Elina Haavio-Mannila and Osmo Kontula, eds., *Suomalainen seksi. Tietoa suomalaisten sukupuolielämän muutoksesta* [Sex in Finland: On the Change of the Sex Life of the Finnish People]. Porvoo, Helsinki and Juva, 238–68.

Hallett, Judith P. 1989. "Female Homoeroticism and the Denial of Roman Reality in Latin Literature." *Yale Journal of Criticism* 3, 209–27.

Halperin, David M. 1990. *One Hundred Years of Homosexuality and Other Essays on Greek Love*. New York and London.

Halperin, David M.; Winkler, John J.; and Zeitlin, Froma I., eds. 1990. *Before Sexuality: The Construction of Erotic Experience in the Ancient Greek World*. Princeton, New Jersey.

Hamer, D. H.; Hu, S.; Magnuson, V. L.; Hu, N.; and Pattatucci, A. M. L. 1993. "A Linkage between DNA Markers on the X Chromosome and Male Sexual Orientation." *Science* 261, 321–27.

Harrington, D. J. 1985. "Pseudo-Philo." In Charlesworth, ed., 1985, 297–377.

Harris, Rivkah. 1990. "Images of Women in the Gilgamesh Epic." In Abusch et al., eds., 1990, 219–30.

Hays, Richard B. 1986. "Relations Natural and Unnatural: A Response to John Boswell's Exegesis of Romans 1." *Journal of Religious Ethics* 14, 184–215.

———. 1994. "Awaiting the Redemption of Our Bodies: The Witness of Scripture concerning Homosexuality." In Siker, ed., 1994, 3–17.

Heino, Harri; Salonen, Kari; and Rusama, Jaakko. 1997. *Response to Recession: The Evangelical Lutheran Church of Finland in the Years 1992–1995*. Publication no. 47 of the Research Institute of the Evangelical Lutheran Church of Finland. Tampere.

Heinämaa, Sara. 1996. "Woman—Nature, Product, Style? Rethinking the Foundations of Feminist Philosophy of Science." In L. H. Nelson and J. Nelson, eds., *Feminism, Science, and the Philosophy of Science*. Dordrecht, 289–308.

Held, George F. 1983. "Parallels between *The Gilgamesh Epic* and Plato's *Symposium*." *Journal of Near Eastern Studies* 42, 133–41.

Henderson, Jeffrey. 1975. *The Maculate Muse: Obscene Language in Attic Comedy*. New Haven and London.

Herodotus. *Herodotus. Vol. I. Books I and II*. Trans. A. D. Godley. LCL (1920).

Herter, Hans. 1954. "Priapos." *Pauly–Wissowa* 22, 1914–1942.

_____. 1960. "Die Soziologie der antiken Prostitution im Lichte des heidnischen und christlichen Schrifttums." *Jahrbuch für Antike und Christentum* 3, 70–111.

Herzer, Manfred. 1985. "Kertbeny and the Nameless Love." *Journal of Homosexuality* 12, 1–26.

Hirschfeld, Magnus. 1991 (1910). *Transvestites: The Erotic Drive to Cross-Dress.* Trans. M. A. Lombardi-Nash. Buffalo, New York.

Hoffner, Harry A., Jr. 1973. "Incest, Sodomy and Bestiality in the Ancient Near East." In Hoffner, ed., 1973, 81–90.

Hoffner, Harry A., Jr., ed. 1973. *Orient and Occident: Essays Presented to Cyrus H. Gordon.* Alter Orient und Altes Testament 22. Kevelaer and Neukirchen-Vluyn.

Hoheisel, Karl. 1992. "Homosexualität." *Reallexikon für Antike und Christentum* 122/123 [16], 289–364.

Homer. *The Iliad. Vol. I–II.* Trans. A. T. Murray. LCL (1924–1925).

_____. *The Odyssey. Vol. I–II.* Trans. A. T. Murray. LCL (1919).

Horner, Tom. 1978. *Jonathan Loved David: Homosexuality in Biblical Times.* Philadelphia.

Howell, Peter. 1980. *A Commentary on Book One of the Epigrams of Martial.* London.

Huehnergard, John. 1987. *Ugaritic Vocabulary in Syllabic Transcription.* Harvard Semitic Studies 32. Atlanta, Georgia.

Humbert, Paul. 1960. "Le substantiv *tô'ēbâ* et le verbe *t'b* dans l'Ancien Testament." *Zeitschrift für die alttestamentliche Wissenschaft* 72, 217–37.

Hunger, Hermann. 1992. *Astrological Reports to Assyrian Kings.* State Archives of Assyria 8. Helsinki.

Isaac, E. 1983. "1 (Ethiopic Apocalypse of) Enoch: A New Translation and Introduction." In Charlesworth, ed., 1983, 5–89.

Jacobsen, Thorkild. 1987. *The Harps that Once . . . Sumerian Poetry in Translation.* New Haven and London.

Jastrow, Marcus. 1903. *Dictionary of the Targumim, the Talmud Babli and Yerushalmi, and the Midrashic Literature.* Vols 1 and 2. London and New York.

Jones, Stanton L. and Workman, Don E. 1994. "Homosexuality: The Behavioral Sciences and the Church." In Siker, ed., 1994, 93–115.

Josephus. *Jewish Antiquities, Books I–IV.* Trans. H. St. J. Thackeray. LCL (1930).

_____. *Jewish Antiquities, Books V–VIII.* Trans. H. St. J. Thackeray. LCL (1934).

_____. *Jewish Antiquities, Books XV–XVII.* Trans. Ralph Marcus. LCL (1963).

_____. *The Life. Against Apion.* Trans. H. St. J. Thackeray. LCL (1926).

_____. *The Jewish War, Books IV–VII.* Trans. H. St. J. Thackeray. LCL (1928).

Jung, Patricia Beattie and Smith, Ralph F. 1993. *Heterosexism: An Ethical Challenge.* New York.

Junge, Friedrich. 1995. "Die Erzählung vom Streit der Götter Horus und Seth um die Herrschaft." *Texte aus der Umwelt des Alten Testaments* III/5, 930–50.

Juvenal. *Juvenal, The Satires.* Trans. E. Courtney. Instrumentum Litterarum 1. Rome 1984.

Kasvamaan yhdessä: Piispojen puheenvuoro perhe- ja seksuaalietiikan kysymyksistä [Growing Together: An Address of the Bishops on Family and Sexual Ethics]. 1984. Helsinki.

Kee, H. C. 1983. "Testaments of the Twelve Patriarchs: A New Translation and Introduction." In Charlesworth, ed., 1983, 775–828.

Keuls, Eva C. 1985. *The Reign of Phallus: Sexual Politics in Ancient Athens.* New York.

Kilmer, Anne Draffkorn. 1972. "The Mesopotamian Concept of Overpopulation and Its Solution as Reflected in Mythology." *Orientalia* NS 41, 160–77.

_____. 1982. "A Note on an Overlooked Word-Play in the Akkadian Gilgamesh." In G. van Driel et al., ed., *Zikir Šumim: Assyriological Studies Presented to F. R. Kraus on the Occasion of his Seventieth Birthday*. Leiden, 128–32.

King, M. & McDonald, E. 1992. "Homosexuals Who Are Twins: A Study of 46 Probands." *British Journal of Psychiatry* 160, 407–9.

Kinsey, A. C.; Pomeroy, W. B.; and Martin, C. E. 1948. *Sexual Behavior in the Human Male*. Philadelphia.

Kinsey, A. C.; Pomeroy, W. B.; Martin, C. E.; and Gebhard, P. H. 1953. *Sexual Behavior in the Human Female*. Philadelphia.

Koch-Harnack, Gundel. 1983. *Knabenliebe und Tiergeschenke: Ihre Bedeutung im päderastischen Erziehungssystem Athens*. Berlin.

Köcher, Franz & Oppenheim, A. L. 1957/58. "The Old Babylonian Omen Text VAT 7525." *Archiv für Orientforschung* 18, 62–77.

Koskenniemi, Erkki. 1994. "Myötätuuleen: Huomioita Martti Nissisen artikkelista" [Downwind: Remarks on the article of Martti Nissinen]. *Teologinen Aikakauskirja* 99, 80–84.

Kramer, Samuel Noah. 1951. "'Inanna's Descent to the Nether World' Continued and Revised." *Journal of Cuneiform Studies* 5, 1–17.

Kroll, Wilhelm. 1988. "Römische Erotik." In Siems, ed., 1988, 70–117 (= *Zeitschrift für Sexualwissenschaft und Sexualpolitik* 17, 1930, 145–78).

Kuss, Otto. 1963². *Der Römerbrief 1*. Regensburg.

Lambert, Wilfried G. 1960. *Babylonian Wisdom Literature*. Oxford.

_____. 1975. "The Problem of the Love Lyrics." In H. Goedicke and J. J. M. Roberts, eds., *Unity and Diversity: Essays in the History, Literature, and Religion of the Ancient Near East*. Baltimore and London, 98–135.

_____. 1992. "Prostitution." In Haas, ed., 1992, 127–58.

Landsberger, B. and Gurney, O. R. 1957/58. "igi.duḫa = *tāmartu*, Short Version." *Archiv für Orientforschung* 18, 81–86.

Lane, Eugene N. 1996. "The Name of Cybele's Priests the 'Galloi.'" In Lane, ed., 1996, 117–33.

Lane, Eugene N., ed. 1996. *Cybele, Attis and Related Cults: Essays in Memory of M. J. Vermaseren*. Religions in the Graeco–Roman World 131. Leiden et al.

Lee, Guy. 1990. *The Poems of Catullus*. Oxford.

Leichty, Erle. 1970. *The Omen Series Šumma izbu*. Texts from Cuneiform Sources 4. Locust Valley, New York.

Leick, Gwendolyn. 1991. *A Dictionary of Ancient Near Eastern Mythology*. London and New York.

_____. 1994. *Sex and Eroticism in Mesopotamian Literature*. London and New York.

Lerner, Gerda. 1986. "The Origin of Prostitution in Ancient Mesopotamia." *Signs* 11, 236–54.

LeVay, Simon. 1991. "A Difference in the Hypothalamic Structure between Heterosexual and Homosexual Men." *Science* 253, 1034–37.

Levin, Christoph. 1993. *Der Jahwist*. Forschungen zur Religion und Literatur des Alten und Neuen Testaments 157. Göttingen.

Liddell, Henry George and Scott, Robert. 1940⁹. *A Greek-English Lexicon*. Rev. 1977. Oxford.

Lilja, Saara. 1983. *Homosexuality in Republican and Augustan Rome*. Commentationes Humanarum Litterarum 74 1983. Helsinki.

_____. 1990. *Antiikkia ja myyttejä* [Antiquities and Myths]. Porvoo, Helsinki, and Juva.

Limet, H. 1971. "Le poème épique 'Inanna et Ebiḫ' Une version des lignes 123 à 182." *Orientalia* 40, 11–28.

Livingstone, Alasdair. 1989. *Court Poetry and Literary Miscellanea.* State Archives of Assyria 3. Helsinki.

Loader, J. A. 1990. *A Tale of Two Cities: Sodom and Gomorrah in the Old Testament, Early Jewish and Early Christian Traditions.* Contributions to Biblical Exegesis and Theology 1. Kampen.

Locher, Clemens. 1986. *Die Ehre einer Frau in Israel: Exegetische und rechtsvergleichende Studien zum Deuteronomium 22,13–21.* Orbis Biblicus et Orientalis 70. Freiburg, Switzerland, and Göttingen.

Long, Thomas G. 1996. "Living with the Bible." In Seow, ed., 1996, 64–73.

Longus. *Daphnis and Chloe.* Trans. George Thornley, rev. J. M. Edmonds. LCL (1916).

Looser, Gabriel. 1980. *Homosexualität—menschlich–christlich–moralisch: Das Problem sittlich verantworteter Homotropie als Anfrage an die normative Ethik.* Europäische Hochschulschriften 23/143. Bern, Franfurt a.M., and Las Vegas.

López, Aurora; Martínez Cándida; and Pociña, Andrés, eds. 1990. *La mujer en el mundo mediterráneo antiguo.* Granada.

Lucian. *Lucian. Vol. VII.* Trans. M. D. MacLeod. LCL (1961).

Malick, David E. 1993. "The Condemnation of Homosexuality in 1 Corinthians 6:9." *Bibliotheca Sacra* 150, 479–92.

Marjanen, Antti. 1996. *The Woman Jesus Loved: Mary Magdalene in the Nag Hammadi Library and Related Documents.* Nag Hammadi and Manichaean Studies 40. Leiden et al.

Marmor, Judd, ed. 1980. *Homosexual Behavior: A Modern Reappraisal.* New York.

Marrou, Henrì Irénée. 1965[6]. *Histoire de l'education dans l'antiquité.* Paris.

Martial. *Epigrams in Two Volumes.* Trans. Walter C. A. Ker. LCL (1920).

Martin, Dale B. 1996. "*Arsenokoitês* and *Malakos:* Meanings and Consequences." In Brawley, ed., 1996, 117–36.

Masters, W. H. and Johnson, V. E. 1979. *Homosexuality in Perspective.* Boston.

Maul, Stefan M. 1992. "*kurgarrû* und *assinnu* und ihr Stand in der babylonischen Gesellschaft." In Haas, ed., 1992, 159–72.

Mauser, Ulrich W. 1996a. "Creation and Human Sexuality in the New Testament." In Brawley, ed., 1996, 3–15.

_____. 1996b. "Creation, Sexuality, and Homosexuality in the New Testament." In Seow, ed., 1996, 39–49.

Mayer-Bahlburg, H. F. L. 1977. "Sex Hormones and Male Homosexuality in Comparative Perspective." *Archives of Sexual Behavior* 6, 297–325.

_____. 1979. "Sex Hormones and Female Homosexuality: A Critical Examination." *Archives of Sexual Behavior* 8, 101–10.

McClain-Taylor, Mark. 1996. "But Isn't 'It' a Sin?" In Seow, ed., 1996, 74–85.

McNeill, John J. 1976. *The Church and the Homosexual.* New York.

Meier, G. 1938. "Eunuch." *Reallexikon der Assyriologie* 2, 485–86.

Melcher, Sarah J. 1996. "The Holiness Code and Human Sexuality." In Brawley, ed., 1996, 87–102.

Melton, J. Gordon. 1991. *The Churches Speak on Homosexuality: Official Statements from Religious Bodies and Ecumenical Organizations.* Detroit.

Miller, Patrick D. 1996. "What the Scriptures Principally Teach." In Seow, ed., 1996, 53–63.

Moberly, E. 1983. *Psychogenesis: The Early Development of Gender Identity.* London.

Moloney, Francis J. 1979 "Matthew 19:3–12 and Celibacy: A Redactional and Form Critical Study." *Journal for the Study of the New Testament* 2, 42–60.

Money, John. 1980. "Genetic and Chromosomal Aspects of Homosexual Etiology." In Marmor, ed., 1980, 59–74.

———. 1987. "Sin, Sickness, or Status? Homosexual Gender Identity and Psychoneuroendocrinology." *American Psychologist* 42, 384–99.

Morgan, David. 1992. *Discovering Men*. London.

Mossé, Claude. 1990a. "Courtisanes et/ou femmes mariées." In López, Martínez, and Pociña, eds., 1990, 27–34.

———. 1990b. "Les femmes dans les utopies platoniciennes et le modèle spartiate." In López, Martínez, and Pociña, eds., 1990, 73–82.

Moxnes, Halvor. 1988. "Honor, Shame, and the Outside World in Paul's Letter to the Romans." In Jacob Neusner et al., eds., *The Social World of Formative Christianity and Judaism: Essays in Tribute to Howard Clark Kee*. Philadelphia, 207–18.

Nanda, Serena. 1990. *Neither Man nor Woman: The Hijras of India*. Belmont, California.

Nelson, James B. 1994. "Sources for Body Theology: Homosexuality as a Test Case." In Siker, ed., 1994, 76–90.

Neumann, J. and Parpola, Simo. 1987. "Climactic Change and the Eleventh—Tenth-Century Eclipse of Assyria and Babylonia." *Journal of Near Eastern Studies* 46, 161–82.

Neusner, Jacob. 1988. *The Mishnah: A New Translation*. New Haven and London.

Niditch, Susan. 1982. "The 'Sodomite' Theme in Judges 19–20: Family, Community, and Social Disintegration." *Catholic Biblical Quarterly* 44, 365–73.

Nissinen, Martti. 1991. *Prophetie, Redaktion und Fortschreibung im Hoseabuch: Studien zum Werdegang eines Prophetenbuches im Lichte von Hos 4 und 11*. Alter Orient und Altes Testament 231. Kevelaer and Neukirchen-Vluyn.

———. 1993. "Die Relevanz der neuassyrischen Prophetie für die alttestamentliche Forschung." In Dietrich and Loretz, eds., 1993, 217–58.

———. 1994. *Homoerotiikka Raamatun maailmassa*. [Homoeroticism in the Biblical World] Helsinki.

———. 1998. "Love Lyrics of Nabû and Tašmetu: An Assyrian Song of Songs?" In Dietrich and Kottsieper, eds., 1998, 585–634.

Nock, Arthur Darby. 1988. "Eunuchs in Ancient Religion." In Siems, ed., 1988, 58–69 (= *Archiv für Religionswissenschaft* 23, 25–33).

Nötscher, F. 1930. "Die Omen-Serie Šumma âlu ina mêlê šakin (CT 38–40) (Fortsetzung)." *Orientalia* 51–54. Rome.

Olyan, Saul. 1994. "'And with a Male You Shall Not Lie the Lying Down of a Woman': On the Meaning and Significance of Leviticus 18:22 and 20:13." *Journal of the History of Sexuality* 5, 179–206.

Olyan, Saul M. and Nussbaum, Martha C., eds. 1998. *Sexual Orientation and Human Rights in American Religious Discourse*. New York and Oxford.

Oppenheim, A. Leo. 1950. "Mesopotamian Mythology III." *Orientalia* 19, 129–58.

———. 1956. *The Interpretation of Dreams in the Ancient Near East: With a Treatise on an Assyrian Dream-Book*. Philadelphia.

———. 1969. "New Fragments of the Assyrian Dream-Book." *Iraq* 31, 153–65.

Otto, Eckart. 1991. *Körperverletzungen in den Keilschriftrechten und im Alten Testament: Studien zum Rechtstransfer im Alten Testament*. Alter Orient und Altes Testament 226. Kevelaer and Neukirchen-Vluyn.

———. 1993. "Das Eherecht im mittelassyrischen Kodex und im Deuteronomium." In Dietrich and Loretz, eds., 1993, 259–81.

Ovid: see Bömer 1977.

Pachis, Panayotis. 1996. "'*Gallaion Kybelēs ololygma*' (*Anthol. Palat.* VI, 173). L'élément orgiastique dans le culte de Cybèle." In Lane, ed., 1996, 193–222.

Page, Denys. 1955. *Sappho and Alcaeus: An Introduction to the Study of Ancient Lesbian Poetry.* Oxford.

Parker, W. H. 1988. *Priapea: Poems for a Phallic God.* Croom Helm Classical Studies. London and Sydney.

Parpola, Simo. 1993. "The Assyrian Tree of Life: Tracing the Origins of Jewish Monotheism and Greek Philosophy." *Journal of Near Eastern Studies* 52, 161–208.

———. 1997a. *The Standard Babylonian Epic of Gilgamesh: Cuneiform Text, Transliteration, Glossary, Indices and Sign List.* State Archives of Assyria Cuneiform Texts 1. Helsinki.

———. 1997b. *Assyrian Prophecies.* State Archives of Assyria 9. Helsinki.

Parpola, Simo and Watanabe, Kazuko. 1988. *Neo-Assyrian Treaties and Loyalty Oaths.* State Archives of Assyria 2. Helsinki.

Patzer, Harald. 1982. *Die griechische Knabenliebe.* Sitzungsberichte der wissenschaftlichen Gesellschaft an der Johann Wolfgang Goethe -Universität Frankfurt am Main 19.1. Wiesbaden.

Paulsen, Henning. 1992. *Der zweite Petrusbrief und der Judasbrief.* Kritisch-exegetischer Kommentar über das Neue Testament XII/2. Göttingen.

Petersen, William L. 1986. "Can *arsenokoitai* Be Translated by 'Homosexuals'? (1 Cor. 6:9, 1 Tim. 1:10)." *Vigiliae Christianae* 40, 187–91.

Petuchowski, Jakob J. 1982. "Die 'Bräuche der Völker.'" *Judaica* 38, 141–49.

Philo. *Philo. Vol. I–X.* Trans. F. H. Colson et al. LCL (1929–1962).

———. *Philo. Suppl. Vol. I–II.* Trans. Ralph Marcus. LCL (1953–1962).

Phipps, Willian E. 1996. *The Sexuality of Jesus.* Cleveland, Ohio.

Plato. *Symposium.* Trans. Alexander Nehamas and Paul Woodruff. Indianapolis and Cambridge (1989).

———. *Phaedrus.* Trans. C. J. Rowe.Warminster (1986).

———. *Laws in Two Volumes.* Trans. R. G. Bury. LCL (1961).

———. *Laches. Protagoras. Meno. Euthydemus.* Trans. W. R. M. Lamb. LCL (1924).

———. *Charmides. Alcibiades I and II. Hipparchus. The Lovers. Theages. Minos. Epinomis.* Trans. W. R. M. Lamb. LCL (1927).

Plutarch. *Plutarch's Lives. Vol. I: Theseus and Romulus, Lycurgus and Numa, Solon and Publicola.* Trans. Bernadotte Perrin. LCL (1914).

———. *Plutarch's Lives. Vol. V: Agesilaus and Pompey. Pelopidas and Marcellus.* Trans. Bernadotte Perrin. LCL (1917).

———. *Plutarch's Moralia. Vol. III: 172A–263E.* Trans. Frank Cole Babbitt. LCL (1931).

———. *Plutarch's Moralia. Vol. IX: 697C–771E.* Trans. Edwin L. Minar, F. H. Sandbach, and W. C. Helmbold. LCL (1961).

———. *Plutarch's Moralia. Vol. XIII Part II: 1033A–1086E.* Trans. Harold Cherniss. LCL (1976).

Pomeroy, Sarah B. 1975. *Goddesses, Whores, Wives and Slaves: Women in Classical Antiquity.* New York.

———. 1994. *Xenophon Oeconomicus: A Social and Historical Commentary with a New English Translation.* Oxford.

Pope, Marvin H. 1976. "Homosexuality." *Interpreter's Dictionary of the Bible, Supplementary Volume,* 415–17.

Priapea: see Parker 1988.

Price, S. R. F. 1990. "The Future of Dreams: From Freud to Artemidoros." In Halperin, Winkler, and Zeitlin, eds., 1990, 365–87.

Pronk, Pim. 1993. *Against Nature? Types of Moral Argumentation regarding Homosexuality.* Trans. John Vriend. Grand Rapids, Michigan.

Pseudo-Lucian. *Lucian. Vol. VIII.* Trans. M. D. MacLeod. LCL (1967).

Räisänen, Heikki. 1972. *The Idea of Divine Hardening: A Comparative Study of the Notion of Divine Hardening, Leading Astray and Inciting to Evil in the Bible and the Qur'ān.* Publications of the Finnish Exegetical Society 25. Helsinki.

_____. 1975. "Homoseksualismi ja raamattukysymys" [Homosexuality and the Problem of Biblical Interpretation]. *Teologinen Aikakauskirja* 80, 261–84.

Ratzinger, Joseph Cardinal. 1994. "Letter to the Bishops of the Catholic Church on the Pastoral Care of Homosexual Persons (1986)." In Siker, ed., 1994, 39–47.

Rayor, Diane. 1991. *Sappho's Lyre: Archaic Lyric and Women Poets of Ancient Greece.* Berkeley, Los Angeles, and Oxford.

Reinsberg, Carola. 1989. *Ehe, Hetärentum und Knabenliebe im antiken Griechenland.* Beck's Archäologische Bibliothek. Munich.

Reisman, Daniel. 1973. "Iddin-Dagan's Sacred Marriage Hymn." *Journal of Cuneiform Studies* 25, 185–202.

Renger, Johannes. 1969. "Untersuchungen zum Priestertum der altbabylonischen Zeit 2." *Zeitschrift für Assyriologie* 59, 104–230.

_____. 1972/75. "Heilige Hochzeit: A. Philologisch." *Reallexikon der Assyriologie* 4, 251–59.

Richlin, Amy. 1983. *The Garden of Priapus: Sexuality and Aggression in Roman Humor.* New Haven and London.

_____. 1993. "Not before Homosexuality: The Materiality of the *Cinaedus* and the Roman Law against Love between Men." *Journal of the History of Sexuality* 3, 523–73.

Rogers, Susan M. and Turner, Charles F. 1991. "Male-Male Sexual Contact in the U.S.A.: Findings of Five Sample Surveys, 1970–1990." *Journal of Sex Research* 28, 491–519.

Römer, Willem H. Ph. 1965. *Sumerische 'Königshymnen' der Isin-Zeit.* Leiden.

_____. 1993. "Mythen und Epen in sumerischer Sprache." *Texte aus der Umwelt des Alten Testaments* III/3, 351–506.

Roscoe, Will. 1996. "Priests of the Goddess: Gender Transgression in Ancient Religion." *History of Religions* 35, 195–230.

Roth, Martha T. 1995. *Law Collections from Mesopotamia and Asia Minor.* SBL Writings from the Ancient World Series 6. Atlanta, Georgia.

Sandbach, F. H. 1975. *The Stoics.* London.

Sanders, G. M. 1972. "Gallos." *Reallexikon für Antike und Christentum* 8, 984–1034.

Sandmel, Samuel. 1979. *Philo of Alexandria: An Introduction.* New York and Oxford.

San Nicolò, M. 1938. "Entmannung." *Reallexikon der Assyriologie* 2, 402–3.

Sappho. *Greek Lyric. Vol. I. Sappho, Alcaeus.* Trans. David A. Campbell. LCL (1982). (See also Page 1955, Rayor 1991.)

Satlow, Michael L. 1994a. "'They Abused Him Like a Woman': Homoeroticism, Gender Blurring, and the Rabbis in Late Antiquity." *Journal of the History of Sexuality* 5,1–25.

_____. 1994b. "'Wasted Seed': The History of a Rabbinic Idea." *Hebrew Union College Annual* 65, 137–75.

Schauenburg, Konrad. 1975. "*Eurymedōn eimī*": *Mitteilungen des Deutschen Archäologischen Instituts (Athenische Abteilung)* 90, 97–121.

Schmithals, Walter. 1988. *Der Römerbrief: Ein Kommentar.* Gütersloh.

Schroer, Silvia and Staubli, Thomas. 1996. "Saul, David und Jonathan—eine Dreiecksgeschichte?" *Bibel und Kirche* 51, 15–22.

Schweizer, Eduard. 1981³. *Das Evangelium nach Matthäus.* Das Neue Testament Deutsch 2. Göttingen

Scroggs, Robin. 1983. *The New Testament and Homosexuality: Contextual Background for Contemporary Debate.* Philadelphia.

Seebaß, Horst. 1973. *"bôš." Theologisches Wörterbuch zum Alten Testament* 1, 568–80.

Seksuaalirikokset 1993. Rikoslakiprojektin ehdotus [Sexual Crimes: A Proposal of the Criminal Law Project]. 1993. Oikeusministeriön lainvalmisteluosaston julkaisu 8/1993. Helsinki.

Seneca. *Seventeen Letters.* Trans. C. D. N. Costa. Warminster (1988).

Seneca the Elder. *Vol. I. Controversiae, Books 1–6.* Trans. Michael Winterbottom. LCL (1974).

Seow, Choon-Leong. 1996a. "Textual Orientation." In Brawley, ed., 1996, 17–34.

———. 1996b. "A Heterotextual Perspective." In Seow, ed., 1996, 14–27.

Seow, Choon-Leong, ed. 1996. *Homosexuality and Christian Community.* Louisville, Kentucky.

Sergent, Bernard. 1986. *La homosexualidad en la mitología griega.* Trans. A. Clavería Ibáñez. Arte del Zahorí 2. Barcelona.

Shutt, R. J. H. 1985. "Letter of Aristeas." In Charlesworth, ed., 1985, 7–34.

Siems, Andreas Karsten, ed. 1988. *Sexualität und Erotik in der Antike.* Wege der Forschung 605. Darmstadt.

Sievers, Kai and Stålström, Olli, eds. 1984. *Rakkauden monet kasvot: Homoseksuaalisesta rakkaudesta, ihmisoikeuksista ja vapautumisesta* [The Multiple Faces of Love: On Homosexual Love, Human Rights, and Liberation]. Espoo.

Siker, Jeffrey S., ed. 1994. *Homosexuality in the Church: Both Sides of the Debate.* Louisville, Kentucky.

Sjöberg, Åke W. 1975. "in.nin šà.gur₄.ra. A Hymn to the Goddess Inanna by the en-Priestess Enḫeduanna." *Zeitschrift für Assyriologie* 65, 161–253.

Smend, Rudolf. 1984³. *Die Entstehung des Alten Testaments.* Theologische Wissenschaft 1. Stuttgart et al.

Smith, Morton. 1973. *Clement of Alexandria and a Secret Gospel of Mark.* Cambridge, Mass.

Socarides, Charles W. 1978. *Homosexuality.* New York.

Stålström, Olli. 1997. *Homoseksuaalisuuden sairausleiman loppu* [The Sickness Label of Homosexuality as a Historical and Social Construction]. Helsinki.

Stenbäck, Asser. 1993. *Mitä homoseksuaalisuus on?* [What Is Homosexuality?]. Trans. Matti Aaltonen. Helsinki.

Stoller, R. & Herdt, G. 1985. "Theories of Origin of Male Homosexuality: A Crosscultural Look." *Archives of General Psychiatry* 42, 399–404.

Stone, Ken. 1995. "Gender and Homosexuality in Judges 19: Subject—Honor, Object—Shame?" *Journal for the Study of the Old Testament* 67, 87–107.

Strecker, Georg. 1982. "Homosexualität in biblischer Sicht." *Kerygma und Dogma* 28, 127–41.

Strömsholm, Gustav. 1997. *De homosexuella som kyrklig spelbricka: En analys av aktörerna, aktionerna och debatten i Finland år 1993* [The Homosexuals as Pawns in an Ecclesiastical Game: An Analysis of Actors, Actions and the Debate in the Church of Finland in 1993]. Åbo.

Suetonius. *Suetonius, Vol. I.* Trans. J. C. Rolfe. LCL (1913).

———. *Suetonius, Vol. II.* Trans. J. C. Rolfe. LCL (1914).

Swaab, D. and Hofman, M. 1990. "An Enlarged Suprachiasmatic Nucleus in Homosexual Men." *Brain Research* 537, 141–48.

Swidler, Arlene, ed. 1993. *Homosexuality and World Religions.* Valley Forge, Penn.

Taaffe, Lauren K. 1993. *Aristophanes and Women.* London and New York.

Tatchell, Peter. 1990. *Out in Europe: A Guide to Lesbian and Gay Rights in 30 European Countries.* London.

Taylor, Rabun. 1997. "Two Pathic Subcultures in Ancient Rome." *Journal of the History of Sexuality* 7, 319–71.

Terrien, Samuel. 1985. *Till the Heart Sings: A Biblical Theology of Manhood and Womanhood*. Philadelphia.

Thucydides. *History of the Peloponnesian War, Books I and II*. Trans. Charles Forster Smith. LCL (1919).

Tourney, G. 1980. "Hormones and Homosexuality." In Marmor, ed., 1980, 1–58.

Trible, Phyllis. 1978. *God and the Rhetoric of Sexuality*. Philadelphia.

———. 1984. *Texts of Terror: Literary-Feminist Readings of Biblical Narratives*. Philadelphia.

Tropper, Josef. 1986. "'Beschwörung' des Enkidu? Anmerkungen zur Interpretation von GEN 240–43//Gilg. XII, 79–84." *Die Welt des Orients* 17, 19–24.

Ungnad, Arthur. 1944, "Besprechungskunst und Astrologie in Babylonien." *Archiv für Orientforschung* 14, 251–84.

Uro, Risto. 1987. *Sheep among the Wolves: A Study on the Mission Instructions of Q*. Annales Academiae Scientiarum Fennicae B Diss 47. Helsinki.

Valerius Maximus. *Valère Maxime: Actions et Paroles Mémorables*. Trans. Pierre Constant. Paris (1935).

van den Aardweg, G. J. M. 1986. *On the Origins and Treatment of Homosexuality*. New York.

van der Horst, P. W. 1985. "Pseudo-Phocylides." In Charlesworth, ed., 1985, 565–582.

van der Toorn, Karel. 1989. "Female Prostitution in Payment of Vows in Ancient Israel." *Journal of Biblical Literature* 108, 193–205.

———. 1994. *From Her Cradle to Her Grave: The Role of Religion in the Life of the Israelite and the Babylonian Woman*. Trans. Sara J. Denning-Bolle. The Biblical Seminar 23. Sheffield.

van Tilborg, Sjef. 1993. *Imaginative Love in John*. Biblical Interpretation Series 2. Leiden et al.

Vanggaard, Thorkil. 1971. *Phallos: Symbol und Kult in Europa*. Trans. Herbert Drube. Munich.

Veijola, Timo. 1975. *Die ewige Dynastie: David und die Entstehung seiner Dynastie nach der deuteronomistischen Darstellung*. Annales Academiae Scientiarum Fennicae B 193. Helsinki.

———. 1977. *Das Königtum in der Beurteilung der deuteronomistischen Historiographie: Eine redationsgeschichtliche Untersuchung*. Annales Academiae Scientiarum Fennicae B 198. Helsinki.

Verstraete, Beert C. 1980. "Slavery and the Social Dynamics of Male Homosexual Relations in Ancient Rome." *Journal of Homosexuality* 5, 227–36.

Virolleaud, Ch. 1908/12. *L'Astrologie Chaldéenne: Le livre intitulé* "enuma (Anu) iluBêl." Paris.

von Schuler, Einar. 1982. "Hethitische Rechtsbücher." *Texte aus der Umwelt des Alten Testaments* I/1, 96–125.

von Soden, Wolfram. 1970. "Zur Stellung des 'Geweihten' (*qdš*) in Ugarit." *Ugarit-Forschungen* 2, 329–30.

Wacker, Marie-Theres. 1992. "Kosmisches Sakrament oder Verpfändung des Körpers? 'Kultprostitution' im biblischen Israel und in hinduistischen Indien: Religionsgeschichtliche Überlegungen im Interesse feministischer Theologie." *Biblische Notizen* 61, 51–75.

Waetjen, Herman C. 1996. "Same-Sex Sexual Relations in Antiquity and Sexuality and Sexual Identity in Contemporary American Society." In Brawley, ed., 1996, 103–16.

Watanabe, Kazuko. 1992. "Nabû-uṣalla, Statthalter Sargons II. in Tam(a)nūna." *Baghdader Mitteilungen* 23, 357–69.

_____. 1993. "Ein neuassyrisches Siegel des Mīnu-Aḫti-Ana-Ištari." *Baghdader Mitteilungen* 24, 289–308.

Wehr, Hans and Cowan, J. Milton. 1976³. *A Dictionary of Modern Written Arabic*. Ithaca, New York.

Weidner, Ernst F. 1935/36. "Aus den Tagen eines assyrischen Schattenkönigs." *Archiv für Orientforschung* 10, 1–48.

Wender, Dorothea. 1984. "Plato: Misogynist, Paedophile, and Feminist." In J. Peradotto and J. P. Sullivan, eds., *Women in the Ancient World: The Arethusa Papers*. Albany, 213–28 (= *Arethusa* 6, 75–90).

Westendorf, Wolfhart. 1977. "Homosexualität." *Lexikon der Ägyptologie* 2, 1272–74.

Westenholz, Joan Goodnick. 1989. "Tamar, *qĕdēšâ, qadištu*, and Sacred Prostitution in Mesopotamia." *Harvard Theological Review* 82, 245–65.

Whitaker, Richard E. 1996. "Creation and Human Sexuality." In Seow, ed., 1996, 3–13.

White, Nicholas P. 1978. "Two Notes on Stoic Terminology." *American Journal of Philosophy* 99, 111–15.

Wilhelm, Gernot. 1990. "Marginalien zu Herodot: Klio 199." In Abusch et al., eds., 1990, 505–24.

Wilkinson, L. P. 1978. *Classical Attitudes to Modern Issues*. London.

Wilson, John A. 1969. "Egyptian Myths, Tales, and Mortuary Texts." In J. Pritchard, ed., *Ancient Near Eastern Texts Relating to the Old Testament*. 2d ed., Princeton, New Jersey, 3–36.

Winkler, John J. 1990. *The Constraints of Desire: The Anthropology of Sex and Gender in Ancient Greece*. New York and London.

Wintermute, O. S. 1985. "Jubilees: A New Translation and Introduction." In Charlesworth, ed., 1985, 35–142.

Wischmeier, Oda. 1996. "*physis* und *ktisis* bei Paulus: Die Rede von Schöpfung und Natur." *Zeitschrift für Theologie und Kirche* 93, 352–75.

Wright, David F. 1984. "Homosexuals or Prostitutes? The Meaning of *arsenokoitai* (1 Cor. 6:9, 1 Tim. 1:10)." *Vigiliae Christianae* 38, 125–53.

_____. 1989. "Homosexuality: The Relevance of the Bible." *The Evangelical Quarterly* 61, 291–300.

Würthwein, Ernst. 1984. *Die Bücher der Könige: 1. Kön. 17 – 2. Kön. 25*. Das Alte Testament Deutsch 11,2. Göttingen.

_____. 1985². *Die Bücher der Könige: 1. Könige 1–16*. Das Alte Testament Deutsch 11,1. Göttingen.

Xenophon. *Hellenica, Books VI & VII; Anabasis, Books I–III*. Trans. Carleton L. Brownson. LCL (1921).

_____. *Symposium and Apology*. Trans. O. J. Todd. LCL (1961).

_____. *Memorabilia and Oeconomicus*. Trans. E. C. Marchant. LCL (1965).

Yamauchi, Edwin M. 1973. "Cultic Prostitution: A Case Study in Cultural Diffusion." In Hoffner, ed., 1973, 213–22.

INDEX OF ANCIENT DOCUMENTS

INDEX OF ANCIENT AUTHORS

INDEX OF MODERN AUTHORS